Lengthening the Arm of the Law

Enhancing Police Resources in the Twenty-First Century

Julie Ayling
The Australian National University

Peter Grabosky
The Australian National University

Clifford Shearing
University of Cape Town

CAMBRIDGE
UNIVERSITY PRESS

CAMBRIDGE UNIVERSITY PRESS
Cambridge, New York, Melbourne, Madrid, Cape Town, Singapore, São Paulo, Delhi

Cambridge University Press
32 Avenue of the Americas, New York, NY 10013-2473, USA

www.cambridge.org
Information on this title: www.cambridge.org/9780521732598

First published 2009

Printed in the United States of America

A catalog record for this publication is available from the British Library.

Library of Congress Cataloging in Publication Data
Ayling, Julie, 1957–
    Lengthening the arm of the law : enhancing police resources in the 21st Century /
    Julie Ayling, Peter Grabosky, Clifford Shearing. – 1st published 2008.
       p.   cm. – (Cambridge studies in criminology)
    Includes bibliographical references and index.
    ISBN 978-0-521-49351-2 (hardback) – ISBN 978-0-521-73259-8 (pbk.)
    1. Police administration.   2. Police – Finance.   3. Police – Equipment and
    supplies.   I. Grabosky, Peter N., 1945–   II. Shearing,
    Clifford D., 1942–   III. Title.   IV. Series.
    HV7935.A95 2008
    363.2068'7–dc22   2008011640

ISBN 978-0-521-49351-2 hardback
ISBN 978-0-521-73259-8 paperback

LENGTHENING THE ARM OF THE LAW

Relentless fiscal pressures faced by the public police over the last few decades have meant that police organisations have had to find new ways to obtain and harness the resources needed to achieve their goals. Through entering into relationships of coercion, commercial exchange, and gift with a wide variety of external institutions and individuals operating in both public and private capacities, police organisations have risen to this challenge. Indeed, police organisations are increasingly operating within a business paradigm. But what are the benefits of these relationships and the nature of the risks that might accompany reliance upon them? This book examines these modes of exchange between police and 'outsiders' and explores how far these relationships can be taken before certain fundamental values – equity in the distribution of policing, cost-effectiveness in the delivery of police services, and the legitimacy of the police institution itself – are placed in jeopardy.

Julie Ayling is a Research Associate in the Regulatory Institutions Network at The Australian National University and Associate Investigator in the Australian Research Council Centre of Excellence in Policing and Security. She previously worked as a senior lawyer in a number of Australian government departments and authorities.

Peter Grabosky is Professor in the Regulatory Institutions Network at The Australian National University and Deputy Director of the Australian Research Council Centre of Excellence in Policing and Security. He is the 2006 winner of the Sellin-Glueck Award of the American Society of Criminology. He is author, most recently, of *Electronic Crime* (2007) and *Cyber Criminals on Trial* (with Russell G. Smith and Gregor Urbas; Cambridge University Press, 2004), which won the Outstanding Book Award of the American Society of Criminology's Division of International Criminology.

Clifford Shearing is Professor of Law at the University of Cape Town, South Africa, and a Visiting Fellow in the Regulatory Institutions Network at The Australian National University. He has held positions at the University of Toronto, The Australian National University, and the University of the Western Cape. He is author, most recently, of *Imagining Security* (with Jennifer Wood; 2007) and *Governing Security* (with Les Johnston; 2003).

CAMBRIDGE STUDIES IN CRIMINOLOGY

Editors

Alfred Blumstein *H. John Heinz School of Public Policy and Management, Carnegie Mellon University*

David Farrington, *Institute of Criminology, University of Cambridge*

Recent books in the series:

Contents

Foreword

I was delighted to be asked to write a foreword to this book. It is one of those really thought-provoking and original books about policing that come along all too infrequently, but when they do, they cause you to reflect hard about developments that have become, almost surreptitiously, a part of the wallpaper. The central focus of this book is money, the demand to account for it, the lack of it, and the way that police forces have sought to fill the gap between demand and supply by privatising, reducing core functions, seeking sponsorship, and entering partnerships. I recognise all of these dimensions.

My own career started at the beginning of the 1980s when a rapid expansion of British policing numbers was swiftly followed by a growing interest from the British Treasury in finding ways to hold policing to account for expenditure. Initially, this was through accounting for numbers of police officers. Over the next two decades, it evolved into full-blown managerialism, with a series of attempts to link budgets with performance data. The accompanying scope for chiefs to square the circle between inputs and demand by raising income, securing sponsorship, and entering into partnerships has changed the relationship between the police and the citizen in many, often subtle, ways.

This book explores not only the financial developments but the consequences of each development. There have been a number of studies of police reform that have looked at the impact of corruption and crisis; very few, like this book, have looked behind the headlines and explored the ways in which resources and accounting for them have affected policing. As someone who has been the 'accounting

officer' for multimillion-pound budgets for policing, I am particularly
pleased to see this, because my own experience has shown that one of
the most important parts of a modern chief officer's role is securing and
managing the resources necessary for the organisation. Furthermore,
the most intense democratic scrutiny has been reserved for my budget
proposals rather than my operational decisions.

This book pushes us toward a critical and overdue debate about
'value-added' policing. Through the last twenty years, public
demand for policing and of policing in the Western world has
risen inexorably. Political leaders have promised more and more
security and pushed policing to achieve stretching performance
targets. However, there comes a point, particularly with pressures
ranging from neighbourhood policing to counter-terrorism, when
choices have to be made. The balance between policing local
communities and managing risk is at the heart of the dilemmas that
police leaders face, with limited ability to identify the objective
standards that might help make the best choices. Given the complex
resource mechanisms discussed in this book and the wider pressures
on public spending, the time has come for an open, informed public
debate about the trade-offs between resource, policing, and risk.

Peter Neyroud
Chief Constable and Chief Executive
National Policing Improvement Agency, UK

Acknowledgments

This book is the culmination of a three-year project conducted with the financial support of the Australian Research Council (DP0450247). We are grateful to our respective universities, The Australian National University (ANU) and the University of Cape Town, for their financial, administrative, and material assistance over that period. In particular, we would like to thank the Regulatory Institutions Network at the ANU, where most of the research for this book was done, for providing both support and intellectual sustenance in spadefuls.

Many individuals and organisations provided us with information and access to documents without which this book would have been the poorer. In particular, we are grateful to a number of Australian police organisations; Victoria Police, New South Wales Police Force, and the Australian Federal Police, and the officers within them, were generous in sharing their time, their knowledge, and their thoughts on where policing is heading for those organisations. Other individuals with special insight into police organisations also helped inform our study – many thanks are offered to Peter Neyroud, Liu Jianhong, Toshie Tanaka, Li Xiancui, Chris Devery, Tony Warren, Peter Fleming, Mark Burgess, Clive Harfield, Hamish McCardle, Jim Dunlap, Adrian Whiddett, John McFarlane, and Simone Steendyk. We thank Lucy Strang, Caroline Dubs, and Melanie Poole for their outstanding research that informed a number of chapters of the book. In addition, we are grateful for the assistance of Julie Berg in South Africa and George Blades, Yiran Liu, Matej Malicek, and Henry Makeham in Canberra whose research gave us a more global perspective. We are especially indebted to our colleagues, present and past, at the

Regulatory Institutions Network and in the wider ANU for their unfailing generosity in making time to comment on earlier versions of the chapters and to point us in new directions for information, in particular Peter Drahos, Jen Wood, Lyn Hinds, Monique Marks, Jenny Fleming, Juani O'Reilly, Simon Bronitt, Nicholas Seddon, and Nina Leijon. We also thank Jessica Robertson for her cheerful administrative assistance. Colleagues from other Australian and overseas universities also provided thoughtful comments on certain chapters or key points within them, including Janet Ransley, Lorraine Mazerolle, John Hudzik, Cindy Davids, Adam Crawford, and Fusun Sokullu-Akinci.

Lastly, we would like to thank our families for their patience and support.

The authors and publisher are grateful to the following publishers for permission to reproduce material for which they hold the copyright:

  Transaction Publishers – parts of Chapters 1, 6, and 8 draw from "Toward a Theory of Public/Private Interaction in Policing", published in Joan McCord (ed.) (2004) *Beyond Empiricism: Institutions and Intentions in the Study of Crime*. New Brunswick, NJ: Transaction Publishers;

  Blackwell Publishing – an initial version of Chapter 3 was published as "Policing by Command: Enhancing Law Enforcement Capacity Through Coercion" in *Law and Policy* (2006) 28(4): 420–443;

  Emerald Group Publishing – an earlier version of Chapter 4 Part 1 appeared as "When Police Go Shopping" in *Policing: An International Journal of Police Strategies and Management* (2006) 29(4): 665–690;

  Sage Publications – Chapter 5 Part 1 was first published in an earlier form as "Taking Care of Business: Police as Commercial Security Vendors" in *Criminology and Criminal Justice* (2008) 8(1): 27–50;

  Taylor and Francis Group – an earlier version of Chapter 6 Part 1 appeared as "Private Sponsorship of Public Policing" in *Police Practice and Research: An International Journal* (2007) 8(1): 5–16;

  Mahesh K. Nalla – who gave permission as editor-in-chief of the *International Journal of Comparative and Applied Criminal Justice* in which an earlier version of Chapter 6 Part 2 first appeared as "Force Multiplier: People as a Policing Resource" (2007) 31(1): 73–100;

  Elsevier – Chapter 7 was first published as "Ambiguous Exchanges and the Police" in the *International Journal of the Sociology of Law* (2006) 35(1): 18–28.

LENGTHENING THE ARM OF THE LAW

CHAPTER ONE

INTRODUCTION

Many of us would find it difficult to imagine a police car with commercial advertising on its sides. The practice would strike some as preposterous, an affront to the dignity of the police service. At the end of 2006, we asked a senior Australian police officer if this could ever happen in her country. "Never say never" was her reply.

This book is about the dramatic transformation in police management that is occurring at the beginning of the twenty first century. The change is astonishing. In some jurisdictions, to commence an investigation, or to introduce a crime prevention project, requires one to present a 'business case'. A senior Singapore police officer recently mused that he was as much a businessman as a policeman, and suggested, not entirely metaphorically, that the Singapore Police might one day be listed on the Stock Exchange. He predicted a bull run.

There was a time, not that long ago, when policing in English-speaking democracies was very different from what it is today. It was done almost exclusively by career public employees, known commonly, if not universally, as 'police.' They tended to join the ranks at a relatively early age (the late teens in some places) and after a brief period of instruction and physical training at a police academy, to learn their craft on the job. Most knew that if they kept out of trouble and didn't make waves, they had a job for life, and would be able to retire on a pension after a period of service ranging from twenty to forty years. Their chief executives, usually called 'commissioners', 'chief constables' or simply 'chiefs,' enjoyed quasi-judicial independence. In most places, the organisations in which they served enjoyed ample, or at least sufficient, resources. When special needs arose, they were able to obtain supplementary appropriations from grateful and generous governments.

It was not always thus, nor is it now. The police as we know them did not exist before the creation of the London Metropolitan Police in 1829. Prior to that time, policing was done by volunteers, or by commercial organisations. In frontier settings or during periods of significant civil unrest, the military too played a role. This "mixed economy" of policing (absent significant military involvement) enjoyed a renaissance after World War II, and became very noticeable by about 1980. The growth of the private security sector has continued unabated since it first began to attract attention a quarter-century ago.

This booming market in private security was, and remains, indicative of an increasing public demand for more security services and the state's inability and/or unwillingness to allocate taxpayers' funds for their provision (Garland 2002; Zedner 2003). Regardless of objective security needs, many citizens, communities and institutions are prepared to spend their own money on services previously delivered by government. They speak with their cheque-books. At the same time, the abundant resources to which police had become accustomed have begun to dry up. Police agencies themselves are being called upon to be more resourceful – to achieve more with less. This book is about the way in which public police agencies have sought to meet this challenge.

THE POSTWAR TRANSFORMATION

At the end of the 1960s, when social scientists began to turn their attention to policing as an institution worthy of analysis, the challenges facing police were different from those prevailing in years past.

The baby boomers born at the end of World War II came of age beginning in 1960, and, as is typical of males between the ages of fifteen and twenty-five, started to generate work for police. The long boom and increasing material abundance in Western industrial societies were accompanied by a profusion of consumer goods that were easily stolen and resold.

Resources were less of a problem in those days, as governments were fairly generous with police. The challenges faced by police in the

1970s had less to do with financial and material resources and more to do with legitimacy. Traditional institutions of authority were being called into question in settings as diverse as China and France. In the United States, the civil rights movement intensified, and the racism and abusive practices of many police officers began to attract increasing attention and condemnation. Confrontations between police and antiwar demonstrators during the Vietnam War years severely strained the legitimacy of police in the eyes of many young people. The use of illicit drugs increased as well, creating yet another axis of conflict between police and youth.

In the shadow of these events, developments were in train that would contribute to dramatic changes in policing. Economists and ideologues were hard at work. Once marginal economic thinkers such as Hayek and Friedman began to attract the attention of influential conservative politicians. Those with instinctive aversions to 'big government' were captivated with ideas that the state should withdraw from many of its traditional roles and leave them for market forces to deliver.

And so began the revolution in public administration that was summarized by the term "managerialism" (Freiberg 2005). Its more extreme advocates suggested that government agencies should shed everything other than their core business. Greater cost efficiency would become the paramount value for those remaining functions that were to be performed by public employees, and the processes to achieve this were to mimic those of business. Government agencies were urged to recover the costs of their services wherever possible. Citizens were to be regarded, and sometimes referred to, as "customers."

At first, it was thought that public law enforcement agencies might be spared the scrutiny being directed at other public sector institutions. Margaret Thatcher is quoted as having said "Never, ever, have you heard me say we will economise on law and order" (quoted in Leishman et al. 1995: 26). But this was not the case. It became apparent that an increase in police resources did not translate automatically into a reduction in crime rates. Although conservative governments had been traditionally solicitous of police and inclined to bestow generous powers and resources on them, they did not excuse police from the imperatives of managerialism. The Thatcher government in the United Kingdom was one of the first anywhere to demand value for money in policing.

The relentless fiscal pressures faced by police could not be ignored. So it was not long before police too became subject to fiscal discipline, corporate planning, and the full panoply of business thinking. Despite the brave new world of managerialism, the path to greater efficiency and effectiveness in policing had some familiar landmarks. Achieving more with less meant reliance on some time-honoured strategies. These "old friends" as well as some less familiar means of resource enhancement newly adopted for the purpose are the subject of this book.

The revolution that has characterised policing in western industrial societies over the past quarter of a century has received a great deal of attention. Perhaps the best overview to date is provided by Bayley and Shearing (2001), who refer to the 'multilateralisation' of policing. By this they mean the proliferation of organisational forms relating to who authorises policing and who actually performs the police function.

This proliferation may be explained by a combination of factors. On the one hand, there is unprecedented demand on traditional public police organisations. The challenge is compounded by the traditional insularity and inflexibility of police organisations, some of which have been slow to adapt to their changing environment (Davids and Hancock 1998).

At the same time, what we have come to know for the past three decades as the 'fiscal crisis of the state' (O'Connor 1973) means that governments are disinclined to spend taxpayers' monies unless impelled by political survival. Indeed, across a number of policy domains, governments have been encouraging their publics to assume greater responsibility for their affairs. In Australia, retirement income and health insurance are two domains in which governments of both sides of politics have consciously sought to shift the burden back to the private individual. It is no longer novel to suggest that criminal justice is immune to this trend. The apposite if awkward term 'responsibilisation' has been used in the context of crime prevention (Garland 1996; O'Malley and Palmer 1996). Thus one sees increasing investment in residential alarm systems, motor vehicle engine immobilisers, and a burgeoning private security industry.

EXCHANGE RELATIONSHIPS AND THE POLICE

Police have long prided themselves on their competency and self-sufficiency, but they rarely operate in a vacuum. They interact with a wide variety of external institutions and individuals operating in private commercial and nonprofit capacities, and with other public sector bodies. These interactions are themselves diverse. One way of classifying them would envisage a continuum of engagement ranging from the most coercive to the least coercive. But it would help to simplify this. The eminent historian Natalie Zemon Davis (2000) refers to three basic relational modes of exchange: *coercion*, *sale* and *gift*.

Let us look first at *coercion*. Elsewhere, one of us has used the term conscription to refer to the process by which the state commands commercial organisations to engage in certain actions in furtherance of law enforcement (Grabosky 1995). Perhaps the most prominent of these are cash transaction reporting requirements, where banks and other defined entities are required by law to report transactions over a particular threshold, or those of a suspicious nature regardless of their amount, to law enforcement authorities. Similar requirements are imposed on specified professionals in the case of suspected child abuse and neglect, and on second hand goods dealers and pawn-brokers. We have already begun to see the conscription of Internet Service Providers in some jurisdictions in certain circumstances.

Next, we can see the *commercial exchange* of goods and services. This is nothing new to public police organisations, which, since their establishment in the nineteenth century, have purchased commodities from pencils, to means of transport, to weaponry. What *is* new is the growing tendency on the part of police organisations to purchase services that might otherwise have been provided from their own ranks. By way of illustration, the first person whom one encounters upon entering the headquarters of the Australian Federal Police in Canberra is a private security guard. Of course, the new challenges facing public police organisations may require specialised expertise which may not always reside within police ranks: skills relating to information technology, for example. And circumstances may arise where outside assistance may be required for a short period. For instance, the New South Wales Police engaged specialised expertise relating to the prevention of credit card fraud during the Sydney 2000 Olympics.

And police also have products to sell. Most commonly, we see them charging for their services in what are commonly referred to as 'user-pays' or 'fee-for-service' policing. They may also charge for the use of their logo, or for providing technical advice to film and television producers. They may sell police-related products.

The third mode of exchange is the donation or *gift*. By this we mean private sponsorship of public policing. It can entail the giving of cash grants, or the provision of complimentary goods and services to the police organisation, usually in return for acknowledgment or recognition. Voluntary assistance to police is included. Gift giving to police is more familiar in the United States and South Africa, relatively uncommon in Australia, and unheard of, if not prohibited by law, in many other places. But if current trends continue, it may well take on greater importance in more jurisdictions around the world.

In discussing these various strategies of resource enhancement, this book addresses a number of questions of fundamental importance in contemporary policing. The first relates to how successfully police use these exchange relationships to enhance their resource base in an era of chronic and enduring fiscal restraint. Do these relationships serve their intended purpose? The second relates to the nature of risks that might accompany reliance upon these relationships. Specifically, how far can these exchanges be taken before certain fundamental values, such as equity in the distribution of policing, cost-effectiveness in the delivery of police services, and legitimacy of the police institution, are placed in jeopardy?

FUNDAMENTAL VALUES

The three fundamental values that underpin our analysis are equity, cost-effectiveness, and legitimacy. The three are not unrelated. By *equity* we mean a basic equality in the delivery of policing services, commensurate with the objective needs of the citizen-customer. The issue is more complicated than it may at first blush appear, since citizens can vary substantially in terms of both their objective needs and their subjective judgment. Some people are extreme risk takers.

Others have an aversion to authority. These people may prefer that police pay less attention to them. Some residents of Australian indigenous communities, despite experiencing crime rates much, much, higher than the national average, complain that they are over-policed. By contrast, other citizens are risk averse, or their life circumstances are such that their objective likelihood of criminal victimization is relatively low. Nevertheless, these people still may place great value on the reassurance provided by a visible police presence in their neighbourhood. Some citizens may feel a taxpayer's sense of entitlement to immediate police attendance in response to a call for service for a relatively trivial matter. One of the great challenges facing police today is to distribute their finite resources in a manner that attends to objective needs and balances this with attention to subjective needs.

Such management of finite resources requires a certain degree of attention to *cost-effectiveness* or the extent to which the police organisation achieves its goals and at what price. Another way of putting this is 'value-for-money'. Of course, public expectations of police are diverse, and in some cases, inconsistent. Moreover, the public may favour inefficient outcomes: a generally visible police presence may be preferred by residents in a relatively crime-free neighbourhood, but the most productive allocation of finite police resources might involve targeting crime hot spots elsewhere.

We embrace Sunshine and Tyler's (2003: 514) definition of *legitimacy* as "a property of an authority or institution that leads people to feel that that authority or institution is entitled to be deferred to and obeyed." The legitimacy of police is manifest in a variety of forms, including the citizen's willingness to comply with the law, report crimes or provide information about suspicious behaviour. Legitimacy may be instinctive, but it may not be immutable. Perceptions that police are disrespectful, or are favouring one constituency over another, or are squandering their limited resources on wasteful or unnecessary activities can erode general perceptions of legitimacy. If police are perceived to be neglecting some citizens while delivering gold-plated service to others, legitimacy may suffer.

One can see that the three core values are inextricably interrelated, and are enormously relevant to the three modes of exchange that are the subject of this book. We will see in Chapter 3 that coercive measures may enhance efficiency in policing, but may be administered in a discriminatory manner that serves to erode the legitimacy of the police institution. Chapter 5 will show that user-pays or fee-for-service policing may be an important strategy to control excess consumption of policing services. One would nevertheless like to be reassured that this would free police resources to attend to the needs of those constituents who may not be able to afford policing services on a quasi-commercial basis. And when police organisations are the beneficiaries of private largesse, does this create the impression that donors are entitled to a better degree of service than ordinary taxpayers?

One can see from this brief introduction that managing exchange relationships in a manner that delivers equity and value for money, while preserving the legitimacy of the police organisation, is a formidable challenge. A proper balance of these fundamental values should result in effective service provision.

PURPOSE OF THE BOOK

The purpose of this book is not to discuss what an ideal institutional configuration or 'system' of protection should look like. Rather it is, first, to explore the means of resource enhancement now being employed by police and, second, to begin to develop a framework for analysing the balance of advantage in those circumstances where there is a mix of public and private interests. The basic questions are *who pays* and *who benefits*. At its most basic, one can think of three interests that might be served by some combination of police–private interface: the interest of the private actor, that of the police, and that of the general public. Our concern is to discourage circumstances in which the first two of these interests benefit at the expense of the third. For instance, as we will see in Chapter 5, some police agencies may engage in fee-for-service or cost recovery activities. In some circumstances, this is done in a strictly regulated and highly accountable manner. At the other extreme, however, revenue enhancement can be less formal, and take the form of organisational corruption or extortion. Where cost recovery or outright profiteering becomes the goal of police work, it occurs at the expense of the public interest and the legitimacy of the law enforcement agency itself.

There are circumstances in which the public police organisation, a private actor or institution and the general public might all benefit from a given configuration of exchange relationships. When the promoter of a concert is required to engage police on a fee-for-service basis, the event may be safer, and ultimately more profitable. The police recover some of the costs of their deployment. Concertgoers may be more secure, and the local economy may benefit as a result. We might call this a win-win-win or 'trifecta'. Whatever the mode of exchange, this should be our goal.

We are also concerned to develop a theory that will explain the interrelationship of various modes of engagement between police and external institutions. Do the three types of exchange relations occur together, or do they vary inversely with one another? In other words, is a police organisation that is reliant on cost recovery less likely to use coercive methods? Is one that actively solicits contributions and sponsorship less likely to charge for its services? Or is the behaviour of exchange relationships idiosyncratic?

PLAN OF THE BOOK

This introductory chapter has outlined the basic dimensions of exchange involving police organisations, and the fundamental values that should guide the conduct of public police agencies in the modern era. Chapter 2 briefly surveys resource flows within police agencies, in particular the principles that guide decision-making about resource acquisition and allocation and how those principles interact.

Subsequent chapters address each of the basic forms of exchange that can enhance resources, but also threaten these fundamental values. Chapter 3 discusses coercion, and reviews the many ways in which police may command information or cooperation from members of the public. It also discusses how public law enforcement agencies may commandeer or confiscate property.

Chapters 4 and 5 discuss police as buyers and sellers, respectively, of goods and services. Readers may be surprised at the degree of commercialism that characterizes contemporary public policing. Arguably unique to the contemporary era is the degree to which police engage in merchandising. When J. Edgar Hoover transformed the U.S. Federal Bureau of Investigation into an iconic organisation, it was political, not financial, capital that he sought to generate. In the fullness of time, other law enforcement agencies realized that their brand was worth something, and began to assert their brand ownership.

The final mode of exchange, the subject of Chapter 6, is that of gift. One does not immediately think of police as recipients of private largesse. But they receive many gifts in cash and in kind from individuals and from businesses. There are many benefits that can accrue from accepting such gifts, not least of which is an enhanced ability to meet demand for policing services. But there can also be risks in relying too much on the munificence of others.

Chapter 7 addresses an issue long apparent to observers of exchange relationships: basic relationships of exchange rarely exist in their pure form. Relations are often hybrid in nature. Davis's (2000) typology of coercion, sale, and gift, while conceptually distinct, may not be so clearly visible in the real world. Indeed, Davis herself concedes that the three forms of exchange may overlap or interact in certain circumstances. Chapter 7 looks at various combinations of exchange relationships – coercion/commerce; gift/commerce; coercion/gift – and concludes that the line separating them is often blurred.

The concluding chapter, Chapter 8, summarizes the thrust of the preceding chapters, in the process reaffirming the principles that should underlie exchange relationships in contemporary policing. We consider some of the implications that can be drawn from the evidence we have placed before the reader about the nature of public policing today. Some thought is also given to theories that might explain how the three modes of public/private exchange interrelate in practice.

A half-century ago, one had a pretty good idea of what the future of policing might look like. This is proving to be wrong. We are not bold enough to suggest where policing will be fifty years hence, but we can offer some indications, and some suggestions about how to negotiate the uncharted terrain that lies ahead.

CHAPTER TWO

OBTAINING AND ALLOCATING POLICE RESOURCES

INTRODUCTION

It will probably come as no surprise that public police budgets are not a common subject in the academic literature about policing. With a few exceptions, most policing scholars prefer to deal with policing objectives, methodologies and outcomes rather than come to grips with the more technical and undoubtedly drier subject of the financial underpinnings of police work. For many of us, budgets and accounts, with their long columns of figures and specialist language, are mystifying entities that we would prefer to remain the exclusive domain of accountants.

Police, however, have no choice but to grapple on a daily basis with issues concerning acquisition and allocation of resources. Not only must police get the job done, but they must be seen to be doing so in a way that is both efficient (not wasteful of resources) and effective (achieving desired outcomes). Political imperatives, such as the translation of private sector mentalities and methods into public sector activities over the last three or so decades, have driven changes in the way in which police strategize and implement resource decisions. Budgets for public policing are by all accounts getting tighter. Competition for security work is increasing, in the form of private security providers and volunteer organisations, while public demand for visible accessible public policing continues to grow. Police are facing the singular challenge of being required to function within a business paradigm while still trying to provide a 'public service' which delivers 'justice' and does so equitably and coherently. They must do so in a context of political volatility, criminal justice policy faddism and rapid technological change that introduces new complexities and uncertainties into the policing environment (Manning 2003: 164–170). How police perform in the light of all these demands may indeed dictate whether they stay 'in business' and what that business looks like in the future. In any study of how public law enforcement might be enhanced in the twenty-first century, laying the groundwork with an examination of current police resourcing practices is therefore crucial.

Not that we propose that this chapter be some sort of financial management demystification exercise. Others are far better qualified than we are to tackle that Goliath. John Hudzik has done just that for both Australian policing agencies (1988) and various United States criminal justice organisations (e.g., Hudzik et al 1981). Most other writers in this area have explored the relationship between the quantitative and qualitative aspects of police work in various respects; for example, Grabosky (1988), Smith (1989), Collier (2001a and 2001b) and Loveday (2005). Bordua and Haurek (1970) considered the connections between police budgets and effective law enforcement generally, particularly as reflected in crime rates, and several scholars have considered the link between budgets and proactive law enforcement (Hernandez 1981; Bumgarner and Sjoquist 1998).

This chapter focuses not on the minutiae of budgets and financial accounts but on the overall picture of resource flows in public policing agencies at the level of principles. As academics our understanding of police budgeting, and of police financial management and reporting processes, is necessarily limited. Nevertheless, it is clear that some major issues, or what Braithwaite and Drahos (2000) might call 'contests of principles', arise as the resources flow into police agencies and out again. This chapter attempts to draw out the principles that shape resourcing decisions and the interactions between them. Identifying those interactions goes some way, we believe, to enhancing our understanding of the development of police agencies, at least those in Western industrialised nations, over the last half century. In that time these agencies have evolved from almost wholly tax-based and state-controlled organisations towards a much more entrepreneurial and partnership-oriented model. This process of change reflects a broader social trend to public sector revenue stream diversification, which in turn is itself part of the neoliberal reform agenda of privatisation and increased public sector fiscal efficiency and accountability, referred to earlier, that has taken a strong hold in those states (Davids and Hancock 1998).

The first part of this chapter considers why the issue of policing resource flows should be addressed. It asks the question 'are police budgets getting tighter?' and notes that the answer lies not merely in the quantity of a police organisation's resources but also in the expectations for their use. The sources of police resources and the processes involved in obtaining them are briefly outlined. In the second part of the chapter we identify and examine a number of principles underpinning police resourcing decisions: whole-of-government, effectiveness, transparency, accountability, managerialism, marketization, risk management, centralization and devolution. These constructs constitute principles in that they are "abstract prescriptions that guide conduct" (Braithwaite and Drahos 2000: 9). Being non-specific, they have relevance to a variety of circumstances while still propelling action in a particular direction. As principles, they function to pattern the creation and application of specific rules. In any decision about acquiring and allocating resourcing for policing, these principles will be given weight in various measures. The third part of the chapter discusses how these principles relate to each other. The complementarities and tensions between them affect both the content and direction of resourcing decision making. The chapter concludes by exploring further the practical value for police of understanding these principles and the ways in which they interact.

RESOURCING OF POLICING – THE ISSUE

Before moving on to consider the principles that govern resource flows within police organisations, let us consider why resourcing of policing is worthy of discussion.

Resourcing of policing has become a very real issue in recent decades. There is no dearth of commentators saying that police

TABLE 2.1. *Australian policing recurrent expenditures (in AUD)*

Expenditure Year	Total recurrent expenditure on police services (TRE) (billion $)[*]	TRE less revenue from own sources (billion $)	TRE per person ($)	Police staff salaries as a percentage of TRE (%)
1996–1997	3.66	–	200	78
1997–1998	3.75	–	202	80
1998–1999	4.12	–	217	76
1999–2000	4.36	–	228	77
2000–2001	4.60	–	236	77
2001–2002	4.80	4.6	244	77
2002–2003	5.25	4.8	264	77
2003–2004	5.55	5.2[**]	276	75

[*] The figures are rounded by the AIC.
[**] This figure includes a deduction for payroll tax.
Figures drawn from "Australian Crime: Facts and Figures", 1998–2005, Australian Institute of Criminology, at http://www.aic.gov.au/publications/facts/ (accessed 20 November 2006).

budgets are getting 'tighter' (for examples, see Johnson 2003; Police Forum for Income Generation 2003/2005). But do police have less money in their budgets each year?

As an example, take Australian policing across all States and Territories. It can be seen in Table 2.1 that in absolute dollar amounts the total recurrent expenditure on police services (TRE) has in fact increased. In the period of eight years from 1996 to 2004, TRE rose some two billion dollars. Even as measured in relation to population growth (i.e., TRE per person), TRE increased approximately 38 percent in the same period. TRE of course includes not only the government-provided element of police income but also other income. However, TRE less revenue from 'own sources' (only measured for the last three financial years of the period) has also increased (column 2). This trend, for the government-provided element of funding (tax funding and grants) to increase, has continued to this day (Productivity Commission 2006: 5.3).

But is this absolute increase an increase in real terms? Can police organisations do more with their budgets each year, or are budgets

TABLE 2.2. *Real increase in Australian police total recurrent expenditures 1997–2004 (in AUD)*

Year	Australian Consumer Price Index (CPI) (weighted average of 8 capital cities)[*]	Constant TRE (billion $) i.e. ($1997×CPI year of interest)/CPI 1997	Actual TRE (billion $)	Real increase (billion $)
1997	120.2	–	3.66	–
1998	121.0	3.68	3.75	0.07
1999	122.3	3.72	4.12	0.30
2000	126.2	3.84	4.36	0.52
2001	133.8	4.07	4.60	0.53
2002	137.6	4.19	4.80	0.71
2003	141.3	4.30	5.25	0.95
2004	144.8	4.41	5.55	1.14

Note: [*] Base of each index: 1989–90 = 100.0.

TABLE 2.3. *Real increase in Australian police recurrent expenditures per person 1997–2004 (in AUD)*

Year	Australian Consumer Price Index (weighted average of 8 capital cities)[*]	Constant TRE per person ($)	Actual TRE per person ($)	Real increase($)
1997	120.2	–	200	–
1998	121.0	201	202	1
1999	122.3	203	217	14
2000	126.2	210	228	18
2001	133.8	223	236	13
2002	137.6	229	244	15
2003	141.3	235	264	29
2004	144.8	241	276	35

Note: [*] Base of each index: 1989–90 = 100.0.

effectively buying less? To answer this question properly involves a correlation with inflation rates. Tables 2.2 and 2.3 reveal that the increase is, in fact, a real one, mirroring Hudzik's (1988) findings for the period 1978–1987.

However, even though the increase is real when measured in relation to CPI,[1] it may not reflect a real increase in resources. For one
thing, costs associated with compliance with new regulatory requirements, such as those relating to the collection, collation and reporting
of data, may eat into the increase to such an extent that it is rendered
illusory. One only has to consider the raft of innovations in the
policing domain that has taken place in the United Kingdom over the
last two decades (see McLaughlin et al. 2001; Hale et al. 2005; Maguire
and John 2006) to appreciate this potentiality. Other regulatory
regimes, such as those related to occupational health and safety and
equal opportunity, are also costly for police organizations.

External forces relating to changing societal conditions may also
affect how much a dollar will buy in terms of security and public safety.
Bordua and Haurek's 1970 study of local police expenditures in the
United States between 1902 and 1960, when there were dramatic
increases in police budgets, showed this clearly. That study controlled
for increases in population, urbanisation and motor vehicles as well as
for inflation.

Furthermore, tighter budgets are not just about how much each
dollar will buy but about how much each dollar is expected to buy. To
properly dissect the issue would require one to take into account some
measure of expectations about what the police should be doing with
their funds, something that is not easily calculated and furthermore is
ever changing. The fact that, as can be seen in Table 2.1, revenue
from 'own sources' is also increasing, may suggest that Australian
police are responding to a perception that there is a need to expand
their sources of income to properly perform their function. The
government-provided element of the budget may simply not be
considered sufficient to cover all the tasks they are now expected to
perform. Moreover, measures introduced to improve efficiency, such

---

[1] The CPI, or Consumer Price Index, measures the change in prices over time paid
by households for goods and services for consumption purposes (rather than
investment purposes). It is calculated on the cost of purchasing a fixed basket of
consumer goods and services of constant quality and similar characteristics that are
considered to be representative of households' expenditure during a specified
period. The CPI operates as an indicator of inflation. The Retail Price Index, or
RPI, is the CPI equivalent in the United Kingdom.

as the introduction of new technologies, may in fact create pressures to do more and do it more quickly.

In Australia, revenue from other sources is slowly assuming greater significance. Anecdotal evidence supports this.[2] Other countries are more advanced down this road. In the United Kingdom, where police authorities have been forced to consider raising taxation levels of local communities to supplement their government appropriation (often by much more than has proved politically acceptable[3]), it has been recognised that police need to generate extra income to operate. In 2003 the U.K Police Forum for Income Generation (PolFIG) produced a guide to income generation for police organisations, covering strategies such as bidding for external funding (including funding from European bodies and charitable trusts and foundations), registering a charity or foundation, obtaining sponsorship, donations and loans, and charging for services, supplies and products. Similar trends are seen in North America, where these kinds of strategies have been longer employed and with some success. Despite this, many smaller police departments in the United States are closing completely for lack of funds, with the towns they service contracting for services from larger police agencies in adjacent municipalities or counties (American Police Beat [nda]; Vaznis 2004).

The increasing importance of outside sources of revenue to police agencies points to the fact that, despite real increases in actual dollar amounts of budgets in many jurisdictions, budgets *are* getting tighter. This can only be explained in terms of other pressures on police such as the need to balance ever-increasing demands from both governments and the public for "equitable, responsive and client-focused services" (Victoria Police Business Plan 2006/07) with the requirements of a managerialist philosophy that emphasizes value-for-money and fiscal accountability (Vickers and Kouzmin 2001). The tightening of police budgets clearly has implications for

[2]   The authors spoke to a number of Australian police organisations in 2006–07 and this was a constant theme.

[3]   See, for example, "Police funding", response of North Wales Police to expected £350 million funding shortfall, 20 October 2004, available at http://www.epolitix.com/briefings/article-detail/newsarticle/police-funding (accessed 2 July 2008).

the police response, both in relation to dealing with law and order, and in respect of the way in which police organisations are managed. It affects police priorities and how low-priority tasks are dealt with.

The problem of how to equitably and efficiently ration services is not, of course, unique to police; other public sector areas, particularly welfare and public health, also struggle with how to deal with fiscal constraints. Cost containment in these areas, as in policing, can only be taken so far. 'Priority-setting' has gained currency, particularly in health care, as the best means of allocating resources (Saltman and Figueras 1997: chapter 3), while at the same time avoiding negative connotations of 'rationing' as decision making that may discriminate against particular groups on the basis of 'deservingness' (Handler and Hasenfeld 1991; Healy and McKee 2004; van Oorschot 2005).

Police, too, engage in priority-setting, both informally, in the exercise of individual discretion, and at an institutional level. The Australian Federal Police (AFP), for example, operate a Case Categorization and Prioritization Model (CCPM) for resource allocation decisions (including response times). Systems like this enable police to diminish their level of provision of some services or even withdraw services altogether. Police may also choose to contain costs by employing lower-paid civilians to undertake tasks. The introduction of Police Community Support Officers in the United Kingdom, for instance, was to some extent a response to requirements for economy that were part of ongoing public sector managerialist reforms (Crawford and Lister 2004). Charging for services that were previously provided at no cost (such as events policing) may also be adopted to bridge the gap between resources and demand and deter unnecessary or excessive consumption of police services.

Tighter budgets push police towards financial 'solutions', such as increasing commercialization, that may carry risks and result in consequences for efficiency, equity and police legitimacy. Increased pressures on a police organization's budget have repercussions at all levels within the organization.

THE BIG PICTURE – RESOURCE FLOWS

In order to comprehend the big picture of public police agency resource flows, we will initially briefly explore the end points of these flows: where the resources come from and where they go.

Sources of Income

The main sources of revenue for the public police are taxation, grants, donations, sales and forfeiture.

Taxation. The tax base of a country or jurisdiction is still the biggest source of incoming funds for public policing. In Australia, for instance, where each State and Territory has its own police force, by far the largest proportion of money for policing comes from State and Territory budgets (Productivity Commission 2006: 5.2). In the United Kingdom (U.K.), the majority of funding for the budgets of the 43 police forces comes from central government (the Home Office) by way of an appropriation (the Police Grant made under s.46 of the Police Act 1996) determined in accordance with a funding formula. There is also a Revenue Support Grant allocated by the Deputy Prime Minister and distributed according to the formula.

Taxes to fund policing can also be collected at a more local level. The second largest proportion of funding for U.K. policing comes from the levying of a precept on the payers of council tax. The level of the precept is set each year by the Police Authority for each particular area,[4] so the rates vary between areas. Nondomestic Rates (NDR), a tax on properties other than flats and houses, also provides a goodly proportion of funds for policing. The level of NDR is set by central government and distributed to local and police authorities in proportion to residential populations.

In the United States, there are well over seventeen thousand law enforcement agencies, at federal, state and local levels. The local level includes county, metropolitan, city and town police

---

[4] In the Greater London Metropolitan District the precept is set not by the Metropolitan Police Authority but by the Greater London Assembly, having regard to the recommendations of the Mayor of London. See http://www.mpa.gov.uk/about/publications/factsheets/mpa-budget.htm (accessed 2 July 2008).

departments. Also included in this figure are special purpose police
organisations, having functionally or geographically specific remits
(for example, transport, university or parks police). Taxation by the
governmental authority at the relevant level forms the main basis of
police funding. Sometimes voters are asked to approve increases in
taxes, such as sales tax or property tax, to fund additional policing
resources.[5] Revenue-sharing (the distribution of a proportion of
taxation revenues down to lower levels of government – for example,
from state to local level) is also a source of funds for law enforcement
purposes.

Grants. Bidding for grant monies is a common way for police to
obtain resources. In the U.K. for instance, police can bid for grants
offered by various agencies of central government including
nondepartmental government bodies (or quangos), by the European
Community, by regional bodies and by charitable trusts and foundations (Police Forum for Income Generation 2003/2005). In the
United States, there are similar grants available from government
agencies, private companies and charitable organisations. Many are
specific to a particular type of policing strategy (for example, grants
under the 'COPS' and 'Weed and Seed' programs) or to the provision
of particular equipment, such as accelerant-detecting canines, auto-
mated external defibrillators and utility vehicles. Some funds are
granted to enable police to conduct training on particularly troubling
issues such as youth gangs and violence or drug awareness.

Partnerships with other government agencies or with community
organisations are often a prerequisite to obtaining a grant, or may at
least improve the chances of obtaining one. Partnerships also open

---

[5] In Springfield, Oregon, citizens voted in 2006 in favour of ballot
Measure 20–112 which imposes a five-year levy on taxpayers to fund
additional police officer positions as well as positions in the municipal court
and funds for the city jail. See http://www.registerguard.com/news/2006/10/21/
d1.cr.springjail.1021.p1.php?section=cityregion and http://www.ci.springfield.or.
us/CMO/Elections2006/2006ElectionInfo.htm (accessed 11 January 2007). A
similar ballot held in Las Vegas, Nevada, in 2004 which aimed to increase sales tax
to fund extra police positions was also approved; see http://www.lasvegassun.com/
sunbin/stories/text/2004/oct/14/517666757.html and http://www.reviewjournal.
com/lvrj_home/2005/May-28-Sat-2005/news/26618935.html (accessed 11 January
2007).

up to police new sources of funding that they might otherwise be unable to access.

On the downside, many grants are noncontinuing but carry expectations that the grantee will continue the program begun under the grant using funds raised elsewhere. The uncertainties generated by this approach may hamper the development of long-term strategies and divert resources that should be used in accomplishing the work of the grant into the sourcing of additional funds.

Donations. Another source of income for police is donations (including sponsorship) (see Chapter 6). In 2005 in Dallas, Texas, four brothers gave the police department U.S. $15 million from their father's estate to buy equipment and pay for consultants, maintenance and other programs (Dow Jones 2005). Although cash is a not infrequent medium of donation, amounts of this magnitude are unusual. Donations of equipment, office space and livestock (usually horses) are also widespread (for U.S. examples, see Coe and Wiesel 2001: 724). Additionally, people will often donate their time and energy to assisting police, thus freeing up police resources for other expenditures. It is also becoming more acceptable for police to approach private sector entities with a view to negotiating sponsorship deals for police activities. In many jurisdictions direct solicitation of individuals for donations is forbidden to police but indirect appeals (for instance, through intermediaries such as police foundations) may occur.

Sales of goods and services. Fee-for-service policing is found to varying extents in most industrialised Western nations, although there are still some jurisdictions where charging for police services is not generally practised (see Chapter 5, Part 1). Amongst other things, charges may be levied for activities like traffic control services, guards and escorts, and forensic services; for the provision of police patrol services; or for long-term complete policing packages under contract. It is, for example, a common practice for smaller cities and municipalities in the United States to contract with the county sheriff's office or with other municipal police departments for law enforcement services. Police also sell goods, merchandise such as clothing, stationery, and toys; surplus livestock (for example, dogs); and lost and found property for which they have been unable to trace an owner (see Chapter 5, Part 2). Occasionally police will sell fixed assets such as buildings.

Forfeiture. As we note in Chapter 3, police are often given legislative power to require the forfeiture of a person's assets on the basis of a suspicion that the asset has a connection with a crime, whether or not a conviction of the owner of the asset is secured. In many U.S. jurisdictions, police forces are able to keep or sell confiscated property, such as cash and vehicles, to fund their own law enforcement activities (Saltonstall and Rising 1999). A scheme for the repatriation of recovered criminal assets (cash) or sums from the sale of recovered noncash criminal assets to the police forces which were instrumental in seizing those assets was introduced in the United Kingdom in 2004/05 (New Zealand Police 2006: 16). Here, however, as in a number of other jurisdictions, police are not able to keep the seized assets themselves.

Items of Expenditure

For what kinds of activities and items are police given funding? Expenditure occurs both on police work and to keep the police organisation itself running. In most cases police work could not be done without the support of the smoothly idling engine of a police department. The costs involved in general police work will usually amount mainly to costs that could be said to be administrative (salaries, travel, equipment etc.), so there is an overlap here. The Metropolitan Police Service of London divides its 'service expenditure' into four classes – Reducing Crime, Investigating Crime, Promoting Public Safety, and Assistance to the Public (MPA Statement of Accounts 2004–2005: 18). These classes encompass a range of activities, among them patrols, investigations, traffic control, and crime prevention activities. In addition, police organisations generally conduct specific policing programs, for example, community policing, terrorism exercises, and so on. Expenditure on the officers, both sworn and unsworn, that carry out these activities and programs constitutes the biggest item of expenditure. This includes money for recruitment, education and training, salaries, overtime, allowances, travel costs, workers' compensation and pensions. Equipment is also expensive, including items like vehicles, communications and IT hardware and software, clothing (including protective apparel), weapons, stationery, office equipment and livestock. Other supplies and services, including cleaning, kitchenware, publicity, rent, insurance costs, capital maintenance and works, consultancies and other outsourcing costs (including contract management), research activities and interest on borrowings, make up the bulk of the remaining expenditure.

THREE STAGES OF FINANCIAL RESOURCING OF POLICE ORGANISATIONS

Looking more closely at the flows of resources between the end points, it is helpful to see this as a three-stage process. These three stages constitute a financial cycle.

The first stage is *acquisition*, or obtaining the resources. The acquisition of resources involves a great deal of work for police organisations as they make the case for a particular grant of government funds or make decisions about where and how to obtain resources from third parties. Political, economic and pragmatic factors all play a part in state decisions about the extent of funding of police organisations. Even though most of the budget in any given year is unchanged from the previous year, police organisations still need to be sensitive to these factors when lobbying for funding for change at the margins.

The second stage is that of *allocation* itself. This involves complex and sometimes protracted decision-making within the police organisation about the amounts of newly acquired financial resources to grant to each part of the organisation and for what purpose they should be granted, and the kind of methodologies that should govern those decisions. Decisions about whether to reallocate existing resources (those few that are flexible) also need to be made. One of the most important ways for police to demonstrate effective and efficient use of resources is by allocating resources toward higher priority tasks. Difficult issues are bound to arise when making these decisions, for instance, in relation to how much innovation is appropriate and how to manage associated risks.

Expenditure is the third stage: taking those resources and using them. Even a simple expenditure, say, on salaries of staff undertaking a particular task, may involve decisions about how many staff are needed and what their roles should be. Even more complex are outsourcing decisions. Choosing the best item to buy or the most appropriate provider of services may be a difficult decision (see Chapter 4 Part 1). A final step is accounting for and reporting on expenditure, a part of the process crucial to obtaining further resources in the future. Thus the third stage feeds back into the first stage to complete the cycle.

PRINCIPLES

Braithwaite and Drahos in their influential work *Global Business Regulation* (2000) argue that principles stand behind the 'thicket of rules' in any regulatory regime and understanding them, and the contests between them, is key to understanding how that regime operates and the directions in which it is developing. Principles, they say, inform the creation and application of rules, in that decision makers weight one principle or set of principles over another in order to incorporate into their regulatory system "changes that are consistent with their general values, goals and desires" (Braithwaite and Drahos 2000: 19). The weighting of principles sets the direction for action and enables the generation of detailed rules of conduct to further that action.

Although Braithwaite and Drahos are examining business regimes and how they are globalizing, in our view this kind of analysis, identifying principles that actors in the system employ, is useful in considering the regulatory system governing police resourcing decisions. Police organisations are, after all, increasingly operating as businesses, as one senior police officer recently made clear when he stated that "I am a businessman as much as a policeman".[6]

---

[6] Senior Assistant Commissioner Ang Hak Seng of the Singapore Police delivering a paper at the symposium *Securing the future: Networked policing in New Zealand*, held 22 November 2006 in Wellington, New Zealand.

What principles underlie decision making about policing resource flows? The principles outlined in the following paragraphs all have direct implications for resource management by police.

Whole-of-Government

The principle of whole-of-government is concerned with the political and legal environment in which a police organisation operates. Clearly, this context has implications for police resourcing decisions.

Whole-of-government approaches to public policy-making have become increasingly popular in the Western world over the last few decades. The idea is that an holistic approach should be adopted, avoiding the 'silo' mentality of previous decades and thereby achieving better coherence across government, a lack of inconsistencies between policies, and a better use of scarce resources. An increase in police productivity due to increased resources, for example, might have the consequence that downstream courts and correctional institutions become clogged and badly in need of more resources themselves. Whole-of-government approaches were designed to address such problems.[7] Pollitt (2003: 35), discussing the U.K. version of the idea known as 'joined-up government', says it "denotes the aspiration to achieve horizontally and vertically co-ordinated thinking and action". In the United Kingdom, the concept of joined-up government goes beyond policy creation within government circles to encompass policy implementation, particularly suggesting that access to services for citizens should be 'seamless'. It may in some cases go even further, to include 'joined-up governance': circumstances where public sector bodies coordinate with private sector bodies to deal with a problem (Pollitt 2003: 38). In the United States, this is known as 'networked government' or 'government by network' (Goldsmith and Eggers 2004).

What does a whole-of-government approach mean for police resourcing decisions in those jurisdictions where it has been adopted?

---

[7] The Law Enforcement Assistance Administration (LEAA) that existed in the United States from 1968 to 1982 provides an example. The LEAA had as its aim the institutionalisation of comprehensive planning and coordination among criminal justice agencies at all levels of government. See Hudzik (1994) for a full account of the birth, evolution, benefits and problems of the LEAA.

For police, it means that they now need to be cognizant of a much wider spectrum of rules and policies about what they can and cannot do. For instance, in the procurement area, whole-of-government policies and rules may constrain choice in relation to acquisition of, among other things, vehicles, stationery, computers and even utilities providers. Such policies might require government purchasers to maximise opportunities for local and regional suppliers to sell to government, or they may hinder police in taking advantage of commercial opportunities.

At a policy level, the whole-of-government principle is beginning to be adopted in police work itself. There is a move for police to not only be better connected with other parts of the criminal justice system but also to engage with other public sector service organisations, community and business groups to formulate and implement strategies to deliver integrated crime prevention programs.

Integrated is the key word here. There is a difference between a whole-of-government approach and simply entering into discrete public-private partnerships. Homel (2004: 5) suggests that it may sometimes be better to avoid whole-of-government approaches and travel the less ambitious path of partnerships and inter-agency arrangements. He points out that a whole-of-government approach, such as was used in the now defunct U.K. Crime Reduction Programme, is organisationally complex, requiring a significant management and coordination effort. In order to effectively implement such an approach, police need skills of diplomacy, the ability to, in the words of Hood and Lodge (2006: 96), "work effectively in a context where rules are precarious and direct orders cannot formally be given by one person or unit to another ... the ability to understand and work across different 'worlds' within and beyond government".

Whether whole-of-government thinking is used just in agency purchasing and other administrative decisions, or in the design of police work itself, by necessity it feeds back into the budgeting process. Budgets must incorporate this thinking when considering what and how to purchase (allocate and expend), and when anticipating the shape of future cooperative arrangements between police, public agencies and private or community groups. Instead of the police asking themselves "what can *we* do and how can we do it best? ", they need to have a good appreciation of both existing security problems and the other actors who they can enlist or by whom they can be enlisted to address those problems (Shearing 2006). In formulating budgets, they need to think about the ways that working together in cooperative arrangements with others will impact on their need for resources. In some cases it may reduce the call on police resources; in others, it may increase it. There may even be a case for entering into joint budgeting arrangements with other agencies for some programs.

Effectiveness

Effectiveness is a, perhaps *the*, basic principle of police resourcing decisions. "What do we need to throw at this problem or situation to get the job done?" is always the primary question police ask them-selves when allocating resources. Effectiveness is so fundamental that it is easy to overlook as a principle driving resourcing decisions. To be effective is the *raison d' être* of any police organisation; a lack of effectiveness may be judged more harshly by the man or woman in the street than is a wasteful use of resources or a lack of transparency or accountability in their use.

Transparency

Transparency of decision making has not historically been the police's strength. However, a recent focus upon the local and immediate, seen in the rise of community policing and, more lately, of reassurance policing, indicates an increasing concern with iden-tifying what the public wants from the police and acting upon that knowledge. Other government agencies, individuals and business and community groups are now being referred to as 'stakeholders' in the policing enterprise or particular aspects of it. There is no big step between having a stake in an endeavour and caring about the deci-sions that are at its heart, including those apropos resourcing. Shareholders in any private company expect to be privy to its major decisions and even to make some decisions themselves.

Transparency of decision making goes hand-in-hand with consul-tation with stakeholders. One cannot properly consult without put-ting the options on the table – making all possible decisions and their rationales transparent. Consultation between police and 'stake-holders' about security issues, although by no means ubiquitous, is becoming more common. Sir Ian Blair, the Metropolitan Police Commissioner, in his 2005 Dimbleby Lecture talked about 'embedding the citizen' in everything the police do and of moving "from policing by consent ... which is passive, to policing by direct collaboration, which is active."

When people can see inside police decision-making and have an input into debate about the proper role of police or particular aspects of service provision, this clearly has the capacity to influence policing resource flows at all stages of the financial cycle – the objectives for which funding is sought, the sources from whom it is sought, the allocation of funds obtained and the what and how of expenditure. And the influence of 'outsiders' on resource flows is also sometimes direct. Police Authorities in the United Kingdom consist not of police officers but of councillors from the relevant Local Authority, magistrates and independent members, who are responsible for developing the annual policing plan for the area, including setting police priorities and targets, as well as fixing the level of the council tax precept to pay for this policing. Furthermore, consultation by the Police Authority with people in the Authority's area is mandatory when developing the plan (Police Act 1996 ss.7(3), 8(2) and 96(1)).

Transparency as a principle that guides decision-making with respect to resource flows is increasing in strength.

Accountability
Related to transparency but not reliant upon its existence is police accountability. The need for accountability, or "informing and explaining" (Mulgan and Uhr 2000), now pervades all aspects of public policing. Accountability is important because for the police to be effective they need to be viewed as legitimate and worthy of trust, and accountability promotes this view (Jones 2003: 606; Patten 1999: 25). Accountability in policing has grown to some extent out of its adoption as a principle of general public sector reform, but also the principle has been given 'policing flesh' by inquiries into police corruption and the establishment of new institutions designed to deal with it (such as the Independent Commission Against Corruption

[New South Wales] and the Crime and Misconduct Commission [Queensland]) (Fleming and Lafferty 2000).

But accountability is not only a tool to deal with instances of police misbehaviour. Police must also account for the quality of the service they provide in terms of effectiveness (Ransley et al. 2007: 145). So accountability requirements also influence decisions about what activities to seek funding for and how monies are ultimately spent. Police, at the end of the day, need to explain and defend what they do with the funds they obtain, through annual reports and audited financial statements, and often more publicly in response to media questions or before public sector oversight bodies such as audit offices, commissions of inquiry, ombudsmen and parliamentary committees. As Wood and Shearing (2007) point out, police are subject to both legal and political accountability mechanisms. As a result, police are ever mindful of this need to report and justify their actions.

Accountability has affected the look and feel of budgets too. Budgeting for most public sector bodies in Australia moved in the 1980s from traditional line-item or 'control' budgeting, where the budget consisted of lists of items of revenue and expenditure and the current year's allocation was the starting point for planning the next year's request, to program budgeting, where the budget justifies expected expenditures according to the functions for which the funds are to be used, grouping outputs into identifiable programs. Program budgeting requires connections to be made between work to be done and organisational objectives, and allows for more thought to be given to innovation than did traditional budgeting (Hudzik 1988: 32–37). This has been taken further with a recent emphasis on outcomes rather than the means of producing them (outcomes-based budgeting).

To articulate these outcomes publicly, police organisations publish general strategic documents, ranging from annual reports to business plans. Victoria Police, for example, in its Strategic Plan 2003–2008 *The Way Ahead* (Victoria Police 2003: 8), states that the organisation "will aim to reduce the crime rate by 5% over the life of the plan; reduce the road toll and incidence of road trauma in accordance with Arrive Alive! 2002–2007; increase levels of community perceptions of safety over 2003–2008; and increase levels of customer satisfaction over

2003–2008". It backs up these outcome aspirations with a Business Plan that details service delivery targets for the financial year as well as the strategies to deliver them, placing these objectives within the context of the Victorian Government's policies on "Growing Victoria Together" and "A Fairer Victoria" (Victoria Police 2006: 9).

These changes to budget forms over time have not only required major adjustments to capacities within police organisations themselves, but they have also altered the processes of budget negotiation between police and government, requiring police to justify what they are doing or want to do at a fundamental purposive level, to be clear on benefits and risks and on synergies between their actions and other public sector activities, and to see appropriate connections between police objectives and overall governmental policy directions. At the other end of the resource flow process, too, police performance needs to be justified by reference to outcomes.[8] A failure to report and properly justify the use of resources will lead to allegations of misuse and have undesirable repercussions both for police and government. With desired and actual outcomes being laid out on the table by police organisations, accountability as a principle used in resourcing decisions has never been stronger.

Managerialism
Managerialism concerns the adoption of the philosophies and techniques of managing a commercial business for the running of police organisations.[9] Managerialism has certainly led to some

[8] Accountability metrics are far more complex than can be discussed here. How performance is measured in a sense defines the purpose of the work, and may be dependent upon what type and range of data are available. Accountability may be measured by various types of audit, including a resources audit (have funds been spent as they were supposed to be?), an activities audit (was work carried out as it was supposed to be?) and a goals audit (was something of value achieved? Did that something meet specified goals?). We are grateful to Professor John Hudzik for sharing his expertise on this subject.
[9] For discussions of the rise of managerialism or the "new public management", and its impact on the police service, in the United Kingdom, see Jones 1993; Leishman et al. 1995; Cope et al. 1997; McLaughlin et al. 2001; Jones and Newburn 2002; Butterfield et al. 2004; Maguire and John 2006; in Australia, see Davids and Hancock 1998; Fleming and Lafferty 2000; Vickers and Kouzmin 2001; Hoque et al. 2004; Freiberg 2005.

improvements in management, including increased transparency and accountability as discussed above. It is also of direct relevance to police resourcing decisions.

Performance management (measuring effectiveness). At first, an emphasis on results rather than procedures begot an obsession with performance measurement, to be achieved by assessing police performance against predetermined performance indicators. While the aim of performance measurement is to measure how well police are doing their job (effectiveness), the way performance indicators are framed can result in instead measuring efficiency or impact.

Research soon showed that crime rates and clear-up rates were inefficient ways of measuring the effectiveness of police (Finnimore 1982; Robinson 1989: 22; Hale et al. 2005: 2–3). There are many variables that go into a change in the crime rate, not just policing (Leggett 2002: 60). Furthermore, a significant proportion of police resources is devoted to activities unrelated to preventing crime and enforcing the law (Grabosky 1988: 1; Robinson 1989: 22; Leggett 2002: 61), crime rates and clear-up rates are unreliably recorded and open to manipulation (Robinson 1989: 23; Leggett 2002: 64) and reliance on such performance indicators prevents the development of culturally and regionally appropriate policing methods (Freiberg 2005: 22). Other research has shown that there is no necessary inverse relationship between budgets and crime rates (Collier 2001b: 36; Robinson 1989: 23; Hudzik 1988: 18–19; Grabosky 1988: 4) – pouring more resources into policing will not necessarily bring down crime. Moreover, the performance culture that insists on measuring how well police are doing their jobs by reference to quantitative targets sometimes provides a perverse incentive to meet those targets through qualitative behaviour that flies in the face of police commitment to equitable and humane provision of services (Collier 2001b; BBC News 2007). Concentrating on ends can distort means (Freiberg 2005: 34). Nevertheless, performance indicators are still a major form of performance management in many jurisdictions. As an example, the 2006–2007 Purchase Agreement between the Australian Capital Territory (ACT) and the Australian Federal Police (AFP) that governs the provision of policing services in the ACT specifies that the AFP will strive to meet certain indicators (laid down in the form of percentages, absolute figures, or comparisons with the Australian average), including targets relating to crime rates and clear-up rates.[10]

That is not to say that performance management has been all bad. The initial focus on quantitative performance measures in many jurisdictions, having been informed by research, has been somewhat tempered now so that more qualitative measures are starting to be used, such as consumer satisfaction with police. For example, in Australia, an annual National Survey of Community Satisfaction with Policing (NSCSP) is carried out by a private research firm contracted by the Australasian Centre for Policing Research. It explores community perceptions of police in terms of services provided and personal experiences of police contact. Data from the NSCSP is used in various ways, including in individual police departments' Annual Reports and in the Productivity Commission's Report on Government Services published each year. Qualitative indicators such as surveys, of course, have their own problems. Leggett (2002: 80) suggests that surveys of public satisfaction need to be closely targeted to persons who have had recent experience with the police, to negate as far as possible the effects of culturally transmitted negative views of the police.

Efficiency. A major aspect of adopting private sector techniques into public services like policing is a concern with economic efficiency, or the production of maximum outputs with the minimum resource input. With such a goal in mind, the U.K. Audit Commission in its 1993 report *Helping with Enquiries: Tackling Crime Effectively* exhorted police organizations to make better use of proactive strategies and techniques. Following this report, the United Kingdom went on to roll out its National Intelligence Model that, according to Maguire and John (2006:83), "offers a framework of business processes for the

---

[10] The AFP police the ACT as "ACT Policing". The purchase agreement is available at http://www.jcs.act.gov.au/eLibrary/act_community_policing/2006–7%20Purchase %20Agreement%20-%20Final.pdf (accessed 2 July 2008). Examples of the indicators include 55% of offences against the person cleared and a maximum of 9300 offences against property reported.

management of policing priorities of all kinds", thus enabling the most rational use of resources.

With the emphasis firmly on value-for-money, police in the United Kingdom and elsewhere have been forced to start thinking like private sector business managers – not only about efficiency, but also about effectiveness and productivity, fiscal accountability and sustainability. Thinking more clearly about how to obtain and use resources efficiently will almost always benefit the public, although the public may not always appreciate efficiency measures (for example, the closing of police stations). But whether a business model is the best vehicle for that thinking is another question. Some have questioned whether the *quality* of justice – in terms of values like equity, consistency, fairness and affordability – is incorporated into, or sufficiently well served when operating within, a business paradigm (Freiberg 2005; Crawford and Lister 2006).

Marketization

Because of the need for fiscal austerity that is part of the managerialist philosophy, police organisations have increasingly become involved in reshaping the boundaries of their role in a bid to supplement government-provided resources. Although innovation has not traditionally been a forte of the police (Robinson 1989: 26), marketization of policing has been one growing avenue police have adopted to harness resources. This has involved, for example, full or partial withdrawal of public police resources from some activities, leaving the 'market' to provide. An example is police responses to security alarms – in many places, this is no longer the domain of police, but of private security companies; in others, police require licences for alarms before they will attend calls. The level of outsourcing of police services is also increasing, private sector companies being contracted by the police to provide services that the police themselves previously provided, such as parking enforcement or the provision of prisoner custody and transportation. Additionally, marketization is revealed in activities that police now do, activities that involve elements of commerce, which they did not previously undertake. Police in many jurisdictions are entering the marketplace by selling their own

services, by selling goods, or by entering into sponsorship arrangements with private, often corporate, institutions and individuals.

Marketization can have the effect of reshaping public expectations
of what the police do. As Bourne (1989: 122) notes, "where public
police resources come 'with a price attached' the potential users of
police services re-examine their requirements accordingly."

Police are under pressure to be efficient, effective and productive
(Grabosky 1988). With each budget cycle, the peripheries of the
police role are reassessed to ensure that, firstly, resources are not
being used unwisely, inefficiently or in such a way that core responsibilities are under-resourced, and secondly, that all possible
resources available to police are garnered in a manner consistent with
government objectives for the police. Those objectives, or at least
their emphases, will inevitably vary from cycle to cycle, as community
concerns and government priorities alter the political accent on what
is important for public safety and order (Maguire and John 2006: 69).
This continuous reassessment of where the boundaries of public
policing lie, of what police are really about, exerts its own peculiar
pressures on police, one of which is a concern with the risks that
pushing the boundaries brings.

Risk Management
The police are always concerned about minimizing their exposure to
risk. At its heart, this is at least as much about ensuring their own
legitimacy and hence the survival of public policing as an institution
as it is about being fiscally responsible. Manning suggests that in fact
management of risk plays a central role in policing – police attempt to
control contingencies, those external to and those inhering in the
organization, in order to give an "illusion of control" (2003: 34, 40–
41, 53, 238). Ericson and Haggerty (1997: 3) see this role as collaborative: "policing consists of the public police coordinating their
activities with policing agents in all other institutions to provide a
society-wide basis for risk management (governance) and security
(guarantees against loss)."

Every innovative 'solution' to a crime problem or to a resourcing
problem will carry with it some risk or possible unintended consequence. Recognizing this, command levels within police organizations

are increasingly adopting the language and practice of risk management.[11] Thames Valley Police in the United Kingdom define risk
management as "a planned and systematic approach to the identification, evaluation and management of risks in order to achieve continuous improvement. It includes the appraisal of options for
managing and controlling such risks, and the implementation of cost-
effective mitigation" (Thames Valley Police [nda]). Note that risk
management is not primarily about getting rid of risks altogether, but
rather about reducing vulnerabilities to acceptable levels in the light of
the benefits accruing from an activity. Many police organisations in
contemporary industrialised nations have at least introduced risk
management policies, sought to minimize financial risk through
insurance and introduced training courses for their staff in risk management. Victoria Police in Australia may go one step further – it is
considering the introduction of a "Business Analysis Framework" which
essentially would be a system for assessing whether a proposed innovation (in particular, commercialization opportunities) should be
pursued. It would involve evaluation of the proposal against a set of
'filters' based on corporate objectives and strategies, costs, benefits and
risk levels. The espoused purpose of this system is "to assist Victoria
Police to plan and make decisions about the most efficient and effective
options/models to deploy available resources, in pursuit of its stated
objectives."[12]

Built into any decision, then, about how police will obtain, allocate
and expend resources is some consideration of the costs, risks and
consequences involved in that course of action. Such cost-benefit
assessments may be made at various times within the fiscal cycle and
at various levels within police organisations.

Centralization

One aspect of managerialism is the belief that it is the job of management to manage, and because managers have specialist skills, this

---

[11] However, Archbold (2005) reports that risk management is as yet used in very few
of the largest U.S. law enforcement agencies despite steadily increasing costs
associated with liability payouts over the past few decades.
[12] This information is based on personal communication and documentation
provided to the authors by Victoria Police in December 2005 and April 2006.

is not a job that can be delegated down the line. Management is there to keep tight control over the reins of an organisation. This belief, in some jurisdictions, is reflected in the centralization of decisions about policing priorities, that is, about the situations and problems that call for an expenditure of police resources.

In England and Wales, for instance, although there are forty-three police forces, policing matters are becoming increasingly determined from the 'centre' (Loveday 2005; Hale et al. 2005). Legislation provides that that the Home Secretary must, in his annual National Policing Plan, determine strategic policing priorities for all forces maintained for police areas in England and Wales for a period of three years (Police Reform Act 2002 s.1), and that he must determine objectives for the policing of the areas of all police authorities (Police Act 1996 s.37).[13] It is required that these national priorities and objectives influence the setting of priorities and objectives in Police Authority's Local Policing Plans and three-year strategy plans (Police Reform Act 2002 s.92). Police performance on national targets is also assessed by national bodies such as the Police Standards Unit (PSU) and Her Majesty's Inspectorate of Constabulary (HMIC). The National Intelligence Model, designed by the Association of Chief Police Officers, has also been "a further pressure for local forces to conform to demands and structures which are generated externally to them" (Loveday 2005: 276).[14] According to Hale et al. (2005), the inevitable outcome of all this centralization will be the development of a national policing model.

In contrast, in the United States with its police agencies numbering in the tens of thousands, the degree of centralization is much less. Setting police priorities and making resourcing decisions is essentially a local matter for law enforcement agencies. The availability of grants from national bodies such as the Department of Justice

[13] Loveday (2005: 275) notes that the central interventionist tendencies of the Home Office (which has enforced observance of these objectives by punishing bad performance by local police commanders) has been supplemented by the influence wielded by the Treasury and the Prime Minister's Delivery Unit in policing decisions.

[14] For further information on the National Intelligence Model initiative, see http://www.acpo.police.uk/asp/policies/Data/nim2005.pdf (accessed 2 July 2008).

provides an incentive to follow particular paths (such as community policing, problem oriented policing, etc.) or engage in particular activities (such as providing drug education for school students) but national priorities are not mandated as they are in the England and Wales. National programs and commitments are also advanced through nationally coordinated networking of federal, state and local law enforcement agencies and training of their officers;[15] other approaches are spread by a modelling mechanism. Legislation enables the Department of Justice to sue state and local governments in federal court to correct a "pattern or practice" of police misconduct, but this is generally used for cases generated by civilian complaints about racial discrimination or excessive use of force, rather than as a way to intervene in how police spend their funds.

Australian police forces are large but few in number. Policing priorities are set at the highest levels in each force. Cooperation between two or more State and Territory police organisations does occur to tackle particular problems. However, there are no mandated national strategic priorities, although the Australasian Police Ministers' Council (comprised of the Ministers responsible for police from the Australian Government, each of the States and Territories and New Zealand) periodically issues a document entitled "Directions in Australasian Policing" (the latest being for 2005–2008) which sets out a national policing strategy, the purpose of which is "to present a shared vision and a framework for cooperation and partnerships" (Australasian Police Ministers' Council 2005). As in the United Kingdom and the United States, national issues tend to be dealt with by State and Territory police as they arise in their jurisdictions as well as through the creation under federal legislation of national institutions with specific functions.

Devolution
In a number of countries, while priorities are mandated or at least proclaimed at the highest levels (government and/or police

---

[15] For examples of national priorities advanced in this way, see the Department of Justice Web site at http://www.usdoj.gov/whatwedo/whatwedo_fsc.html (accessed 2 July 2008).

organisation management), financial management has been
devolved to lower levels in the organisation. Westerberg and Forssell
(2005) have traced such a development in the Swedish police organisation where budget allocation in accordance with centrally stated
objectives was devolved to Police Authorities. However they note that
increased devolution has led to a degree of re-regulation in terms of
reporting systems.

Devolution of responsibility for budgeting also began in the
United Kingdom with the introduction of the Police and Magistrates' Courts Act 1994 (PMCA) and the Financial Management
Code of Practice (FMCP) in 1995. Police authorities were encouraged to delegate financial management to Chief Constables and
further devolution down the line to local police commanders (who
head basic command units or BCUs[16]) was recommended (Collier
2001a: 473). In the police force which Collier studied, after initial
resistance, devolution was seen as a way to shift resources to
initiatives that would satisfy both the communities being served
and performance targets. However, four years later, Loveday
(2005: 277) reports that most budget responsibilities are effectively exercised at force management level rather than at BCU
level, basically because greater degrees of devolution could
interfere with the common line on a range of policing issues
that force managements believe should be adopted by all BCU
commanders.

In New York, it was recognized many years ago that precinct
commanders were best placed to make most operational decisions,
including those related to allocation of resources. The introduction of
COMPSTAT in the mid-1990s tied this devolution of responsibility
to an expectation of compliance with rigorous performance standards, with associated sanctions for underperformance.[17] Other law
enforcement agencies in the US have adopted and adapted the

---

[16]   Each of the forty-three forces in England and Wales is divided into a number of
       BCUs based on region. Cumbria Police force, for example, is divided into three
       BCUs covering North, West and South Cumbria. BCUs carry out frontline
       policing.
[17]   For more information on COMPSTAT, see Shane 2004.

New York Police Department's COMPSTAT system (Moore and Braga 2003).

Financial management within Australian police forces has traditionally been a top-down affair (Hudzik 1988: 48–49). Recently, however, the story has begun to change. In one large Australian police department, as part of a general strategy known as "Local Priority Policing" (LPP), the management of police resources is devolved to the appropriate local level where the resources are to be deployed.[18] However, because budgets are tight and management is held accountable, local commanders must often still make a persuasive business case in order to obtain funds to finance any new initiatives they think worth pursuing (for example, in the field of crime prevention).

INTERACTIONS BETWEEN PRINCIPLES

The principles discussed earlier – whole-of-government, effectiveness, transparency, accountability, managerialism, marketization, risk management, centralization and devolution – do not work together like bullocks in harness, pulling always in the same direction. In fact, there are clear interactions and sometimes tensions between them which affect both the content and directions of resourcing decision making. Figure 2.1 depicts these interactions in abstract form, as three modes of interaction that coexist: contest mode, mutual support mode and oppositional mode. In a contest mode of interaction, an increase in strength of one principle tends to bring about a decrease in strength of a second ($\uparrow \sim \downarrow$). In mutual support mode, an increase in strength of one principle is likely to go hand-in-hand with an increase in strength of a second ($\uparrow \sim \uparrow$). And in oppositional mode, two principles by their very nature pull in opposite directions, requiring a balance between them to be reached ($\leftrightarrow$). Some examples of each of these modes of interaction between principles are discussed here.

---

[18] For more information on LPP, see http://www.police.vic.gov.au/content. asp?document_id=286 (accessed 18 December 2006).

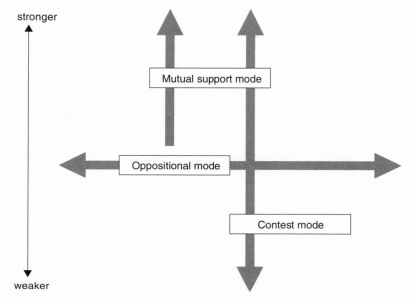

Figure 2.1 Interactions between Principles

Contest Mode ↑∼ ↓

Whole-of-government and managerialism (performance manage-
ment). A focus on an individual police department's achievements
in terms of specific quantitative targets does not sit well with a philosophy that police need to work with other agencies and individuals
both within and outside government to produce effective police
work. Pollitt (2003: 42) suggests that in a contest between these
principles, it is whole-of-government that is likely to "remain on the
margins". The measurement of an individual organisation's performance against targets specific to that organisation is considerably
simpler than determining cross-cutting indicators for a group of
organisations and measuring one's performance against them in the
light of the performance of one's partners and as some proportion of
the total result.

Some police organisations, however, deal with reconciling performance management and whole-of-government principles by
designating performance indicators as mere 'targets'. The ACT-
AFP Purchase Agreement for 2006–2007 goes further in declaring

that the targets there specified "encompass the jurisdiction of a great many public and private institutions and individuals who contribute to the overall results and standings. Success in these targets is not the sole domain or responsibility of ACT Policing". It would be interesting to discover whether allowances are actually made for the actions of these others when the performance of the AFP in the ACT is being judged and the following year's targets set.

Whole-of-government and effectiveness. Whole-of-government app-roaches may impede not only the measurement of a police organi-sation's effectiveness but also that effectiveness itself. According to Freiberg (2005: 34), whole-of-government approaches "can ultimately inhibit productive action through over bureaucratisation, internecine squabbling, lack of leadership and ownership of pro-blems, poor funding and fund management, and too much cen-tralised or top-down control". Whether police can achieve desired results in the context of a whole-of-government approach boils down to the management of that approach. If properly coordinated, with a strong leadership structure, effective action should be the product. However, human nature being what it is, especially in the light of the varying cultures of the different agencies (including police) that can be enlisted for crime prevention activities, Freiberg may have a point.

Whole-of-government and accountability. It stands to reason that an approach to a policing problem that involves different agencies (whether only governmental or also involving nongovernmental bodies) will have the effect of blurring lines of accountability (Pollitt 2003: 42–43). Furthermore, policing approaches focused on pur-suing not only quantitative targets but also qualitative ones may increase the likelihood that wrong or at least arguable resourcing decisions will be made, and as a result, whole-of-government approaches may provide police (and their partners) more to be accountable for.

Police may resist entering into whole-of-government arrange-ments if to do so threatens to increase either the reporting workload or the potential for police oversight bodies to make negative findings. Unwillingness to cooperate with other organisations may decrease the effectiveness of police in dealing with particular problems. However, the tensions between accountability and whole-of-government approaches may be reconciled at least to some extent through good and specific agreements (Homel 2004: 5: 681) and a flexible management approach (Eggers and Goldsmith 2003: 32; Homel 2004: 5).

Transparency and effectiveness/efficiency. Oiling the squeaky wheel, or responding to the concerns of the most vocal community members, will not necessarily result in the most efficient or most equitable outcomes. Opening up police resourcing decisions to scrutiny and participation by community groups and individuals clearly has the potential to result in undue influence on those decisions by those who wish to push particular agendas, and may jeopardise police efforts to best serve the public interest as a whole. Again, the extent of conflict between the principles of transparency and those of efficiency and effectiveness may come down to a matter of process and design. Transparency will best serve the public when the public concerns and suggestions identified are truly representative, perhaps through the use of mechanisms that encompass more rather than fewer sources (for instance, well-designed surveys rather than police consultation with self-nominated groups or individuals).

Accountability and effectiveness. As stated earlier, accountability requirements pervade all aspects of public policing, particularly those to do with resource allocation. One of the aims of increasing accountability through mechanisms such as audit is to increase police effectiveness. Meeting reporting requirements, however, does involve a lot of work collecting, collating and analysing data. In the end, this data may or may not be used. This work itself uses resources, resources that might otherwise have been directed into achieving performance targets related to law enforcement and crime prevention. Freiberg (2005: 34) puts it this way: "Instead of focusing on delivering a good outcome for end users, energy is diverted to constructing the right measures and ensuring that the targets are *seen to be* met, rather than being met. The danger is that these processes encourage meaningless reporting which bears no relationship either to transparency or quality". However desirable accountability is in itself, the bureaucratic machinery associated with accountability may sometimes act to impede police effectiveness (Anechiarico and Jacobs 1996).

Marketization and accountability. Insofar as marketization results in a sharing of responsibility for the provision of policing services to the public, there may be an associated decrease in account-ability by the police for actions taken by other providers. In the context of purchasing decisions, for example, questions about the locus of liability and responsibility for remedial action in relation to the poor performance of contractors may arise. However, Mulgan and Uhr (2000: 12) argue that the public will not readily accept devolution of accountability for error in public adminis-tration away from the state to other agencies or to contractors. One explanation they give (2000: 11) is that the rights of custo-mers of a private sector body may be limited to 'exit rights' (the right to seek another provider) rather than encompassing 'voice rights' (the right to demand explanation and seek remedies, including improvements in overall policies) which are more prevalent in the public sector.

Where the police themselves enter the marketplace and provide services in direct competition with private service providers, it may be more difficult to hold police accountable for inefficient use of resources if the initial decision to enter the marketplace was sound and losses occurred only because of the vicissitudes of the market. Commercialization of policing may well reduce accountability for resource use unless commercialization is closely tied to the achievement of the specified normative commitments of the political system in addition to efficiency.

Mutual Support Mode ↑∼ ↑
Marketization and risk management. Clearly, as the marketization of policing (in whatever form that takes) proceeds, so too does the

need increase for risk management procedures to be put in place. Risk management is itself a costly business, being labour intensive. Setting in place such procedures will inevitable require resource allocation itself, but may be essential to effectiveness. Furthermore, although financial risk may partially be shifted to the private sector where public-private partnerships or commercial arrangements are entered into, political risk is always close at hand. As one police employee said to us, "No matter what one thinks, one can't outsource risk".

Devolution and accountability. Devolution of financial management responsibilities almost always leads to increased accountability of the person to whom the responsibilities have devolved. In the case of COMPSTAT, for instance, New York Police Department top executives are able to scrutinize each precinct commander's performance through the use of 'Commander profile reports', which are updated on a weekly basis, and take action if there is cause for concern. Accountability in this case is accountability to one's own police organisation. As one Chief Constable of a U.K. police organisation puts it (quoted in Collier 2001a: 479), "[i]f you get the loot you may get the boot – this is the other side of devolvement".

Whether increased internal accountability has, as a corollary, increased accountability of police organisations to the public is another question. There is evidence that in some places this may be so. Some police organisations invite the media and others to attend the weekly COMPSTAT meetings (Janetta 2006). In addition, a proportion of the mountains of data generated through the COMPSTAT process is passed to the Mayor of New York by the Police Commissioner, and some of that, in turn, is provided to the public through inclusion in the Mayor's Management Report (MMR). These reports provide useful information about performance against a range of indicators as well as a table of agency resources (expenditures, revenues, personnel, overtime and capital commitments). However, they do not put these two things together and account for the use of resources on specific functions. The MMRs are more about effectiveness than about value for money and give little insight to the public on resourcing decision making.

Oppositional Mode ↔

Centralization and devolution. The tension between centralization and devolution is really a question of who does the "steering", who does the "rowing" (Osborne and Gaebler 1992) and where lies the difference between steering and rowing in terms of the division of labour. Many arrangements on the continuum between centralization and devolution are possible. In the earlier discussion, we saw that some kind of reconciliation of these principles has been achieved in a number of jurisdictions with the setting of general policing priorities and sometimes strategies being largely centralized, and the administration of budgets (the allocation of funds amongst local priorities) being devolved to different extents down the line. Hudzik (1988: 53) makes clear that while the state remains central to policing there will always be some forms of top management authority over financial matters, given that it provides the funnel through which taxation funds are channelled from government treasuries. He outlines a number of tasks that arguably cannot be devolved: budget submissions to government, the enforcement of budgeting procedures and accounting standards, the setting of auditing and purchasing procedures, and priority and strategy setting.[19] There is unlikely to be a situation of total devolution, and current trends indicate that it is unlikely there will be a return to total centralization either.

Managerialism (efficiency) and effectiveness. Grabosky (1988: 2) has pointed out that efficiency and effectiveness are not inextricably linked. A policing action may be inefficient but effective, or it may be efficient but ineffective, or it may be neither, or both. However, a tendency to focus on either efficiency (for example, on cutting costs in times of fiscal austerity) or effectiveness (for instance, on achieving politically obligatory reductions in crime rates) can undercut achievement of the other (Hudzik 1988: 44). Finding the right balance between the principles can be difficult. It may well require a

---

[19] Note that some of these tasks, such as the setting of auditing and purchasing procedures, in the intervening years since Hudzik wrote about police budgets in Australia, have become tasks not of the upper echelons of the police organisation but of other government agencies in whole-of-government contexts.

superior skill set, or at least specific training, to be able to act like a
police officer and think like an accountant (Hudzik 1988: 50).

CONCLUSION

Resource acquisition, allocation and expenditure are activities police
must undertake daily. Tighter budgets may not necessarily mean less
money from governments but they do reflect increasing expectations
of police efficiency and effectiveness emanating from both the community and the police's political masters. Police are faced with a real
challenge in trying to satisfy and manage these expectations with the
resources available to them. In many places, police have felt the need
to supplement state appropriations with resources derived from
grants, donations, sponsorship arrangements and commercial
activities. A clearer understanding of the financial foundations of
police organisations and the way resourcing decisions are made
assists in discerning the challenges faced by police, and the current
and future contours of police organisations.

Despite the importance of this issue, policing scholars have so far had
little to say on the subject. This chapter's contribution lies in extracting
a number of principles that shape police resourcing decisions–whole-
of-government, effectiveness, transparency, accountability, managerialism (performance management and efficiency), marketization,
risk management, centralization and devolution – and reflecting on
various interactions between them. The chapter has considered mainly
the police organisations of Western industrialised states, but many of its
observations will have at least some points of concurrence with the
experience of police in other states.

When faced with decisions as to how to obtain sufficient resources
to meet a particular expectation, or what amount and kind of existing
resources to throw at a problem, police face difficult choices. Whether
consciously or not, police give principles weight in various measures.
The interaction between principles translates into practical meaning
at this level. For instance, should police listen to concerns of a vocal
part of their community and put more officers on patrol to deter
juveniles drinking in public places, or should they put their resources
into dealing with more hidden but more serious issues, such as the

high rate of domestic violence in the poorer areas of their locale? (Should the transparency principle carry more weight here than effectiveness?) Should police outsource the provision of services to a private contractor and perhaps increase their efficiency by so doing, or will the effect of this be that citizens unhappy about the contractor's service have no recourse? (Are marketization and efficiency more important than accountability in these circumstances?) How can police effectiveness be measured for the purpose of reporting on how well performance indicators have been met when other agencies involved in formal crime prevention partnerships are not pulling their weight or are working to a different set of indicators? (Might not effectiveness and accountability suffer if we adopt this whole-of-government approach?)

Other examples could be given, but the point is that being aware of possible contests and synergies between these principles should better enable the police to weight them appropriately when making resourcing decisions. There may be lessons too for top management levels. Police at lower ranks might need help or training in balancing effectiveness and efficiency concerns, or in dealing with risk management issues when forays into the marketplace are being considered. Priorities and strategies set at the highest levels might need to incorporate provisions to address the resourcing problems they will induce. Performance indicators may need to be framed in a way that recognises the pluralised nature of policing today. Careful consideration needs to be given to the getting right the level of both community participation in policing and police participation in commercial activities, having regard to the need for an even-handed provision of services and the importance of maintaining legitimacy.

CHAPTER THREE

COERCION

INTRODUCTION

The use by the state of coercive measures to ensure that its citizens assist it in law enforcement has a long history. What was to become the monopoly of the state over legitimate physical violence (Weber 1919 [1974]: 311) was exercised in medieval England by its individual citizens. Every man had a responsibility to secure his own neighbourhood through the obligation to join in 'the hue and cry' and to keep in his house a stash of arms for the specific purpose of maintaining the peace. Judgment against an apprehended criminal was carried out not by a formal court system but by citizens themselves, and was summary, swift and usually brutal. Under Edward I's 1275 Statute of Westminster, whole villages could be fined if they failed to bring the perpetrator of a criminal act to justice (Blue 1992: 1480–81). With the advent of organised police forces in the nineteenth century, the obligation of citizens to ensure enforcement of the law through personal action gradually diminished. The police, as agents of the state, became the wielders of the capacity to use physical force and this capacity remains at the core of the public police role today (Bittner 1970). Although the obligation to legally inflict violence on one's neighbour at the state's behest largely disappeared with the 'hue and cry', the state still frequently obliges citizens to assist it in enforcing the law. In the common law world, for instance, laws punishing misprision of felony date back centuries and in some jurisdictions still exist today (for example, under U.S. law: 18USC 4). This chapter does not examine the already well-documented issue of the appropriate use of physical force and of threat of force (mental and physical coercion) by the public police. We consider instead the means by which the state today commands co-production in law enforcement. We use the term 'co-production' to refer in general to activities undertaken by private actors that complement those of state institutions. (Grabosky 2004). Where the state commands co-production (as opposed to it being provided voluntarily or as the result of a commercial arrangement), it reinforces its commands with legal sanctions for noncompliance, much as was done by Edward I. These enforceable commands constitute forms of economic and moral coercion by the state. Some of them have historical ante-cedents, but many are new tools in the law enforcement kit and involve creative interactions with both the targets of law enforcement and third parties. Their continuing development indicates that the state recognizes that, in many areas of policing, it cannot 'do it alone' (Garland 1996).

Under what circumstances should the state command an individual or private institution to assist in law enforcement? What costs does this entail, and by whom should they be borne? These are not trivial questions, as they address the fundamental relationship of the state to its citizens. Coercion of the type in which we are interested here may be regarded as a legitimate exercise of the rational-legal authority of the state (Weber 1919 [1974]: 312). But the relationship of state and citizen is, of course, not one-sided. Unlike the exercise of physical force, coercion through command gives citizens choices about the extent of their cooperation. Submission by citizens "is in reality determined to a very great extent not only by motives of fear and hope ... but also by interests of the most diverse kinds" (Weber 1919 [1974]: 312). Imposing sanctions for non-compliance influences those motives and interests through reducing the expected value to the target of not complying (Braithwaite and Drahos 2000: 25).

This chapter reviews some of the many ways in which the state commands its citizens to assist in law enforcement. We discuss the benefits of these coercive requirements for both the state and the targets of coercion, and some of the interests which influence com-pliance. The chapter identifies some of the costs and unintended consequences that such coercive measures may entail. It is suggested that the state might benefit from analysing the costs and benefits of using coercive measures in any specific instance. The chapter concludes by proposing some general principles for decision makers to consider when assessing the appropriateness of coercion to enhance law enforcement.

COERCION – MANDATORY REPORTING AND MANDATORY ACTION

In this chapter, we distinguish between coercion in the form of mandatory *action* and coercion in the form of mandatory *reporting*. An example of mandatory action is where a third party is required by law to undertake certain concrete measures in furtherance of law enforcement. For example, an Internet Service Provider (ISP) may be required by law to retain traffic data (details on the origin and destination of e-mail messages) for a specified period so that it might be accessible to police engaged in a criminal investigation, or to provide system passwords or encryption keys.

By contrast, mandatory reporting entails the requirement that a third party provide information on specified routine or anomalous activities to a law enforcement agency or other regulatory body. This would include, for example, laws that require ISPs who become aware of child pornography on their system to report this to the authorities.

Reporting is, of course, a form of action in itself so in this respect the distinction between action and reporting is somewhat arbitrary. Arbitrary or not, it is useful. Its usefulness lies not so much in the characterization of the activity required of the target of the command but in assisting us to explore the benefits and pitfalls that might ensue from the coercive measure.

Both mandatory action and mandatory reporting as discussed herein are part of what Mazerolle and Ransley (2005) call "third party policing". They use this term to refer to the coercion or the encouragement of third parties to take certain actions in furtherance of law enforcement. However, our focus here is purely on coercion, not encouragement, persuasion, or inducement. Moreover, we are

	FIRST PARTY	THIRD PARTY
ACTION	• Mandatory self-regulation • Required record keeping e.g. environmental records • Required private interface e.g. required to be audited or to have liability insurance • Bail or probation conditions e.g. requiring compliance with a curfew or electronic monitoring, or regular reporting to a police station • Driver not to leave scene of an accident (1st *or* 3rd party) • Anti -loitering or "move-on" powers • Civil and criminal forfeiture • Criminal restitution • Drug testing of prisoners and parolees	• Duty to rescue • Withholding of taxes by employers • Garnishing of wages by employers in satisfaction of a court order • Requirements that ISPs archive traffic data • Requirements that telecommunications carriers assist with interception • Record keeping by 2nd hand goods dealers • Checking of travel documents by airlines • Requirements that carriers use due diligence to prevent importation of illicit drugs • Emergency powers: commandeering of infrastructure (transport, media etc.) • Special taxation to fund law enforcement e.g. fees on vehicle registration • Requirements that proprietors of licensed premises practice Responsible Service of Alcohol

REPORTING	• Corporate disclosure
	  o Financial
	  o Environmental
	  o OHS
	  o EEO
	• Compulsory processes e.g.
	  o Requirements to attend and answer self-incriminating questions if asked by a Royal Commission
	  o Requirement to provide encryption key
		• Mandatory reporting e.g.
		  o Child/elder abuse
		  o Statutory rape
		  o Medical error
		  o Child pornography discovered on computer
		  o Illegal immigrants applying for certain U.S. welfare programs
		  o Suspicious financial transactions
		  o Violent medically ill patients
		  o Precursor chemicals
		• Informants (when coerced)

Figure 3.1

concerned not only with coercion of third parties but also with coercion of 'first parties' – the direct targets of policing.

The matrix at Figure 3.1 illustrates these various forms of coercion. The examples included in Figure 3.1 are drawn from various jurisdictions including the United States, the United Kingdom, Australia, Japan, Turkey and South Africa. The figure is not intended to be comprehensive or exhaustive.

MANDATORY REPORTING

Perhaps the classic example of coercion today is the mandatory reporting of financial transactions over a certain threshold of value, or of an apparently suspicious nature. Designed to discourage the concealment of ill-gotten gains, or the concealment of legitimate income from taxation authorities, cash transaction reporting requirements are a fact of life in most if not all advanced capitalist states (Reuter and Truman 2004). And they are becoming even more widespread. In China in 2007, banks were for the first time required to report on suspicious transactions. The new laws were based upon standards promulgated by the intergovernmental body, the Financial Action Task Force on Money Laundering (FATF).

Coercion is by no means limited to reporting of suspected or potential criminal activity, however. Often there is a requirement to report about compliance with existing laws and regulations. For instance, corporations may be required to report on their environmental and accounting practices and financial status, with provision for significant penalties in cases of detected nondisclosure. Detailed corporate reporting about financial issues is required in Australia by both Commonwealth laws (such as the Corporations Act 2001) and the Australian Stock Exchange listing rules. In addition, the Corporations Act 2001 (s. 299(1)(f)) requires corporations to include details on their performance in relation to any significant Commonwealth or State environmental regulation in the director's report. State laws like the Queensland Environmental Protection Act 1994 also require reporting on a variety of matters such as operation of livestock dips, storage of pesticides and so on.

Mandatory reporting is not, however, limited to financial transactions and corporate disclosures. Jurisdictions in various places have introduced mandatory reporting of suspected child abuse (for example, s. 159 Children and Young People Act 1999 [Australian Capital Territory]), spouse abuse (for example, Kentucky's Adult Protection Act KRS 209) and elder abuse (provided for in all U.S. states but not in Australia). Usually these requirements are directed at professionals in a position of care or responsibility towards the subject person; for instance, school teachers, health workers, counsellors, even police officers themselves. Clergy members too may be required to report incidents of child abuse, even when such information is obtained through a confidential communication (Pudelski 2004: 713). In the U.S. states of New Hampshire and West Virginia, for example, clergy are listed as mandated reporters and penitent-clergy privilege is denied in the case of child abuse or neglect. There are similar provisions in the child abuse reporting laws of North Carolina, Rhode Island and Texas (National Information Clearinghouse 2004).

In some U.S. jurisdictions, such as South Dakota, computer technicians who in the course of their work come across downloaded child pornography are mandated to inform authorities. An example is found in South Dakota's Senate Bill 184 s. 25, signed into law in 2002. That Act also obliges employees of Internet Service Providers and of film and photograph print processing businesses to report child pornography encountered in the course of their employment (ss. 23 and 24).

Hospitals in some Australian and U.S. states are required to report to medical boards and similar regulatory bodies about 'adverse' and 'sentinel' events resulting from medical errors.[1] A doctor treating another health professional may be obliged to report to the relevant regulatory body where they believe their patient's health is likely to impair his or her ability to practise and put the public at risk (for instance, s. 37 of Victoria's Medical Practice Act 1994). Physicians treating elderly patients are obliged to report to the relevant authority those who appear unfit to operate a motor vehicle (Kane 2002).

In the United States, state government workers who administer certain federal welfare programs must report to federal immigration officials the details of immigrants known to be illegally in the United States who are attempting to access those programs (Smith 1995; National Immigration Law Centre 2000).

---

[1] Adverse events are "any untoward medical occurrence in a patient or clinical investigation subject administered a pharmaceutical product and which does not necessarily have a causal relationship with this treatment" (Keech et al 2004); sentinel events are "events in which death or serious harm to a patient occurs" (Australian Council for Safety and Quality in Health Care 2004).

There is also a worldwide system of chemical controls involving, amongst other things, mandatory reporting in many countries of import and export of precursor chemicals (that is, chemicals commonly used in the production of illicit drugs). Parties to the United Nations Convention Against Illicit Traffic in Narcotic Drugs and Psychotropic Substances 1988, 28 ILM 493 (1989) are obliged to develop a system to monitor international trade in substances covered by the Convention so as to facilitate identification of suspicious transactions (Art. 12.9).[2] Similar reporting requirements are being implemented in many jurisdictions in relation to chemicals that can be used in the manufacture of explosives. In Australia, for example, all States and Territories agreed in 2004 to introduce, as a counter-terrorism measure, a licensing scheme for 'security sensitive ammonium nitrate' or SSAN, a product that is used as an agricultural fertiliser but becomes an explosive when combined with fuel oil. The scheme includes a requirement that licensees report any loss or theft of SSAN (Council of Australian Governments 2004).

Somewhat different to other forms of mandatory reporting, and perhaps more draconian, is the requirement that persons who are the target of an investigation themselves provide information to state authorities. The power to compel testimony or the disclosure of information where it may be self-incriminating is precluded in the United States by the Fifth Amendment to the U.S. Constitution, but exists elsewhere in the common law world, most notably in the context of royal commissions or other judicial inquiries. Common in both the United Kingdom and Australia, judicial commissions provide a mechanism for conducting criminal investigations independently of the police and the executive. Legislation is required to confer these coercive powers upon such bodies (see, for example, s. 30 Australian Crime Commission Act 2002).[3]

---

[2] In the United States, the Controlled Substances Act requires that importers and exporters be registered with the Drug Enforcement Administration (DEA) and that records be kept of all quantities of controlled substances manufactured, purchased, and sold. These records serve to trace the flow of any drug from initial importation to final distribution and so to pinpoint any diversion of a precursor for manufacture of illicit drugs (Drug Enforcement Administration 2005: 6).

[3] Under the Australian Crime Commission Act 2002 (Cth) a witness appearing at an examination may not refuse or fail to answer a question or refuse or fail to produce

Arguments for Mandating Reporting

Most mandatory reporting schemes are designed to shed light on significant social problems. These include, for instance, exploitation of the vulnerable (children, the elderly, consumers, investors etc), drug trafficking, money laundering, environmental degradation through irresponsible or illegal activity, illegal immigration, public health problems and so forth. Once the problem is exposed, appropriate action to deal with it can be taken. Very often mandatory reporting replaces an existing system of voluntary reporting that has been deemed inadequate to address the problem in question. For cultural or professional reasons, persons in a position to report have felt unable or unwilling to do so. The further step of making reporting mandatory can often elicit fierce public debate. Seligman (1983), for instance, charts a history of controversy over corporate disclosure requirements in the United States.

In many cases of mandatory reporting, the very fact of its existence can act as a deterrent to the commission of an offence. A corporation which must report on its pollutant emission levels or storage practices for toxic chemicals may think twice about breaching related laws and regulations. Moreover, disguising illegal accounting practices is made much more difficult when transparency and accountability principles enshrined in legislation require a company to disclose financial information to its shareholders and the world at large (Seligman 1983: 45). Mandatory reporting by companies therefore serves wider social objectives such as consumer protection from fraud. It is clear that voluntary reporting by companies of their financial and environmental performance would not yield the same kinds of benefits for either individual investors or the public generally, as there will always be a tendency to be selective about the information revealed (Walsh 2002: 392).

Where law enforcement against a company *is* necessary, it may be facilitated because of the public availability of information about its practices. Both the cost of and time spent in prosecuting a corporation

---

a document required to be produced under summons (subs. 30(2)). Contravention of this provision is an offence punishable by a fine or imprisonment (subs. 30(6)).

for criminal practices may be reduced. A company's track record as a 'good corporate citizen', illustrated through its disclosure practices, may also assist the company to survive through the dark times of prosecution.

When professionals are conscripted to report on their clients or patients or colleagues, as in the case of spouse, child or elder abuse or medical error reporting, a difficult decision has been made for them – should I, or should I not, report this? Provided the guidelines are clear about the circumstances in which reporting should occur, professionals may be 'let off the hook' about their role in the matter. This might ensure that trust between client and institution, or between patient and health professional, is not disrupted by an arbitrary whim of the latter. It can also address the problem of a well-meaning but misguided professional who wrongly decides that he or she is best placed to deal with the client's or patient's problems.

Mandatory reporting may also generate statistics in areas where they are sorely needed. Mandatory reporting of child abuse, for instance, may provide both law enforcement and welfare authorities with a much more comprehensive understanding of the breadth of the problem and its social and geographic distribution. Patient safety is clearly enhanced by a system of mandatory reporting that enables the sharing of information between hospitals about what can and does go wrong. This information is unlikely to come to light through a close examination of medical negligence cases because a high percentage of these are settled out of court and are subject to confidentiality agreements (Hunter 2001: 59).

Legislation that requires the target of an investigation to provide information that may incriminate him or herself can be, of course, a boon to law enforcement. Some deference to the target's rights is generally given in that the direct use of a commission witness's compelled evidence in a subsequent criminal trial of that witness is prohibited. However, derivative evidence (evidence obtained by following up on the compelled testimony) is often admissible and the use of compelled evidence in noncriminal proceedings, such as disciplinary hearings, will frequently be permitted.

Costs, Risks and Adverse Unintended Consequences

The risk that well-intended public policies may have undesirable unintended consequences has long been recognized (Merton 1936; Selznick 1949; Gusfield 1969; Sieber 1981; Marx 1981; Boudon 1982; Grabosky 1995). Where professionals are required by law to report on their clients, there is a substantial risk that professional-client relations, traditionally based on an atmosphere of trust and confidentiality, may be significantly impacted (Schultz 1990; Blaskett and Taylor 2003). The profession or institution itself may be harmed, or there may be a chilling effect on prospective clients' inclinations to access the professional services in question. Under circumstances requiring disclosure or notification, the professional, previously more or less a servant of the client, becomes to some degree an agent of the state. Once the client's champion, the professional may become more of an adversary.[4] Whether big money or merely high emotions are involved, this change of status may even put those who report at risk of retribution or retaliation from unhappy clients (Dearne 2004; Blaskett and Taylor 2003: 7, 25–6).

Mandatory reporting by medical professionals is a blunt instrument. It may be against the wishes of the patient. For example, a pregnant teenager under the legal age of consent may be reluctant to seek pre-natal care if there is a risk that, as a result of compelled disclosure by medical professionals, she may be subject to investigation or the prospective father to criminal sanctions (Tunzi 2002). In some jurisdictions, that risk is high: Oliveri (2000: 497) reports that in the United States close to 50 percent of prosecutors say they always or almost always file charges when statutory rape cases are referred to them by law enforcement and that in some states, such as California, the percentage is even higher. This is despite the fact that most

---

[4] In many U.S. states, Prescription Drug Monitoring Programs (PDMPs) require disclosure of prescription practices by medical professionals in order to monitor prescription drug diversion. It has been reported that, because of the scrutiny associated with PDMPs, practitioners may fear that legal action will be taken against them regarding their prescribing practices, and that this is likely to result in widespread under-treatment of pain, with consequent severe health consequences for patients: National Center on Addiction and Substance Abuse at Columbia University 2005: 86–87.

teenage girls are reluctant to see their older boyfriends prosecuted (Oliveri 2000: 484).

That reporting may intrude into the privacy of clients is an issue for professionals in many contexts (Woolford 1997: 616; Blaskett and Taylor 2003: 26; Dearne 2004). So making reporting mandatory can put professionals in difficult positions, often trying to judge whether the risks of noncompliance are worth taking. Clergy may find the decision virtually impossible. Secular law may require a clergy member to report information about suspected child abuse obtained in the confessional, but the Catholic Church's Code of Canon law (Can.983 §1; Can.1388 §1) makes it a crime punishable by excommunication for priests to divulge information passed to them in this context.

Where victim and alleged offender are in an ongoing relationship (as in many cases of spouse or elder abuse, for instance), the mobilization of law through mandatory reporting may make restoration of that relationship extremely difficult. Blaskett and Taylor, in their 2003 study of mandatory reporting of suspected child abuse in Victoria, Australia, found that the concern of some professionals to safeguard links with and within the family provided a disincentive to report the suspected abuse. They would take into account the type of abuse and supposed severity of abuse when considering whether to comply with mandatory reporting requirements.

Mandatory reporting may also entail significant additional costs to law enforcement, welfare and medical systems, overwhelming existing capacity. Mandatory reporting may lead to a sharp increase in reported cases. In New South Wales, for example, the number of child protection notifications increased by 82 percent between 1999 and 2002 (Australian Bureau of Statistics 2003). Fear of the sanctions that can be imposed for nonreporting may result in some degree of over-reporting.

Increases in reporting will tax the capacity of the system to deal with them. Where resources *can* be found to follow up on reports, this may be at the expense of resources for prevention and support. Moreover, sheer numbers may make it more difficult to differentiate the more serious cases from those that may be unfounded or relatively trivial. This may in turn result either in potentially tragic inaction or in unwarranted interventions.

For cash dealers such as banks and insurance companies that are required to make reports about their clients, reporting may involve significant compliance costs (Levi 1996: 4). These may include costs in relation to training for workers, development of new information databases and implementation of risk-based procedures. Such costs are likely to be passed on to clients in the form of higher fees or premiums. A 2006 proposal to extend the reach of the Australian *Financial Transactions Reports Act 1988* to accountants, real estate agents and betting agencies was criticized for the negative impact it would have on business efficiency (Dearne 2004).

In the case of corporate disclosures, the costs of compliance may exceed the market value of the information disclosed, to the detriment of shareholders (Blair 1992: 188; Walsh 2002: 391). Mandating corporate disclosure may also have the unintended effect of creating a false sense of security amongst investors who do not then see a need for independent enquiries into the company's financial stability. This can have dire consequences, as the Enron scandal in the United States and the collapse of HIH Insurance in Australia illustrate.

Such broader societal costs as these may also become clear when the legality of mandatory reporting requirements is challenged. Telephone and Internet companies in the United States are required, under the U.S. Patriot Act of 2001, to provide customer records to the Federal Bureau of Investigation (FBI) in response to secret demands, called national security letters (NSLs). The letters also contained gag orders forbidding the companies from telling their customers, or anyone else, about the record disclosures. Some 143,000 NSLs were issued between 2003 and 2005. Whilst they understand the need to assist police with investigations, many companies see secret violations of their customers' privacy as bad for business. The Federal District Court for the Southern District of New York, in a case brought by the American Civil Liberties Union on behalf of an ISP, recently (September 2007) ruled that the provision of the Patriot Act authorizing these letters was unconstitutional, violating the separation of powers and First Amendment free speech guarantees (Eggen 2007; Liptak 2007). As we write, this decision has been appealed by the U.S. government (Armas 2007).

In some jurisdictions, mandatory reporting may complicate the task of other agencies of government. Consider, for example, the mandatory reporting of undocumented immigrants by state authorities. In federal systems such as the United States, to require state police agencies to check documentation of suspected illegal immigrants, or otherwise to assist in the enforcement of federal immigration laws, may seriously jeopardize police-community relations in some ethnic communities. Laws of this nature were passed in Arizona in 2004 (Proposition 200 approved November 2004 and incorporated in the Arizona Taxpayer and Citizen Protection Act).

As far as the provision of self-incriminating information is concerned, the imposition of a requirement to do so might be regarded as the antithesis of one of the basic principles of Western law, that a person is considered innocent until proven guilty and the burden of so proving is on the prosecution. Such compulsory processes might be accused of leaning too far toward the state in that precarious balance between human rights and the power of the state (*Murphy v. Waterfront Comm'n of New York Harbor* 378 U.S. 52, 54 (1964); *Environmental Protection Authority v. Caltex Refining Co Pty Ltd* (1993) 178 CLR 477). However, bills of rights are no panacea, as any scholar of the Fifth Amendment will agree.[5] A safeguarding of rights might just as well be achieved by ensuring that the procedures through which compulsory powers are exercised are equitable and transparent. Special judicial oversight may be appropriate.

MANDATORY ACTION

Coercion is not limited to the making of reports. There are also many other types of action mandated by law and regulation. So it is that the state may conscript third parties to help enforce the law of the land. In advanced industrial societies, it is commonplace to require employers to withhold a proportion of their employees' wages and pay it directly

---

[5] The self-incrimination clause of the Fifth Amendment has been described as "an unsolved riddle of vast proportions, a Gordian Knot", and its jurisprudence as "in a jumbled transitional phase", as "a quagmire" and as having "a great many doctrinal corners and crevices, [making] exposition difficult" (Amar, 1997: Chapter 2).

to taxation authorities (for example, the United States Internal Revenue Code 26 USCS § 3402). Some jurisdictions require citizens to come to the assistance of police when requested (for example, s.44 Fiji Police Act and s.28 Tasmania Criminal Code Act 1924, Schedule 1). Many, if not most, jurisdictions require persons involved in a motor vehicle accident to remain at the scene. Further examples of this wider body of mandated actions are given in this section.

Instances of Mandatory Action

Good Samaritan laws. Many jurisdictions mandate bystanders to assist persons in distress. These obligations are particularly prevalent in European countries, but less widespread (although not unknown) in common law countries where criminal laws have traditionally been used for acts of commission rather than omission. Where such assistance is mandated, failure to render it may result in criminal liability punishable by fines or imprisonment. In France, for instance, a failure to assist is punishable by imprisonment for up to five years and a 75,000 Euros fine (Article 223–6 of the French Penal Code). The duty may be general, that is, owed to anyone in need of assistance (as in Australia's Northern Territory under subs. 154(1) of the Criminal Code Act, Schedule I) or it may arise out of special connections between the bystander and the person in need. A special connection may result from a personal relationship (e.g., parent and child), a fiduciary relationship (e.g., soldier and commanding officer), a professional relationship (e.g., doctor and patient), or a contractual relationship (e.g., airline and passenger) (Feldbrugge 1966: 649), or through voluntary assumption of the responsibility of care (*R. v Taktak* (1988) 14 NSWLR 226). The duty may arise at common law or be the subject of specific legislation. International law requires assistance to those in distress at sea.[6]

Most of the legal systems which have Good Samaritan laws require that there must exist, as a trigger for the obligation to assist, an imminent or direct danger to a person of a degree that would

---

[6] Safety of Life at Sea Convention 1974 (SOLAS), 14 ILM 959 (1975), Ch. V; United Nations Convention on the Law of the Sea (UNCLOS), 21 ILM 1261 (1982), article 98.1; International Convention on Salvage 1989, IMO/LEG/Conf. 7/27.

probably lead to that person's death. Danger to the person in a position to provide assistance and sometimes danger to third persons will in most jurisdictions excuse a failure to take action (Feldbrugge 1966: 636).

Why add legal liability to moral culpability for a failure to assist a person in danger? Preventing harm is a legitimate function of the criminal law, and bystander intervention to rescue a person in danger would surely prevent harm. The other side of the coin is that omissions can cause harm, and in many circumstances the criminal law treats an omission as severely as a commission. The classical example is parental neglect resulting in a child's starving to death. The argument goes as follows: no moral distinction between commissions and omissions that cause harm can be made and therefore no legal distinction should be made either (Silver 1985; Bagby 2000).

Necessity can present an even stronger case – the police cannot be at every crime scene or supervising every potentially lethal activity and so must rely on ordinary members of the public to take appropriate action to prevent harm occurring. Framing this duty as a legal one ensures that the public knows of this expectation. It may also deter antisocial behaviour (callous disregard of a person in need of assistance) (Bagby 2000: 583) and even shape societal norms (Silver 1985: 429).

Third-party liability systems. In addition to direct command backed up by penal sanctions, the state may structure its legal system to provide coercive instruments for mandatory reporting as a means of providing assistance in cases of need. Mental health professionals who are reasonably confident that one of their clients may engage in serious violent behaviour risk civil action by anyone who suffers damage as a result of the professional's failure to act on that knowledge: *Tarasoff v. Regents of University of California* 17 Cal. 3d 425, 551 P.2d 334, 131 Cal. Rptr. 14 (Cal. 1976); *Estates of Morgan v. Fairfield Family Counseling Ctr.* 77 Ohio St.3d 284 (1997).[7]

---

[7]　*Tarasoff* has not been uniformly followed in the United States and the situation is less than clear in other common law jurisdictions such as Australia; see McSherry 2004: 4–6.

As well as requiring people to act on its behalf to assist others, the state may also co-opt third parties to enforce laws for it. Private institutions supplement public policing efforts either through the disclosure of information gathered in the course of their activities (mandatory reporting) or through direct action against wrongdoers' conduct (Gilboy 1998: 136). Businesses and other entities that are in the position of 'gatekeepers' or intermediaries between legal and illegal environments (Kraakman 1986) are especially well placed to undertake an enforcement role that involves taking action to prevent crime (Gilboy 1998: 141). Sanctions for noncompliance with mandated enforcement duties can include not only traditional criminal penalties (such as fines) but also penalties more tailored to the particular activity carried on by the private entity, such as loss of licence, a cessation of government use of the business, or even confiscation of goods illegally produced by the business (Gilboy 1998: 142).

Examples of third-party responsibility for law enforcement abound in many different contexts and cultures. It is common in many industrialized economies for employers to be required to garnish an employee's wage in satisfaction of court orders for child support or other debt payments. Telecommunications carriers may be required to assist the state in telecommunications interception (for example, s. 317 of Australia's Telecommunications Act 1997). Airlines have an obligation to enforce immigration laws by checking the validity of travellers' documentation. In the United States, commercial carriers are required to use due diligence to prevent the use of their conveyance for the importation of illegal drugs. In some jurisdictions in Australia, occupiers of certain public premises (shopkeepers, restaurateurs and so on) have a duty to enforce nonsmoking laws, and licensed venues such as hotels and restaurants are obliged to implement Responsible Service of Alcohol practices, such as not serving intoxicated patrons, in order to prevent alcohol-related harm. In Liverpool, England, proprietors of licensed premises must also ensure that glass containers do not leave their premises, in order to reduce assaults with glass objects (Scott and Goldstein 2005: 9).

Mazerolle and Ransley (2005) observe how in the Australian State of Queensland, parents may be fined for the truancy of their children. Elsewhere in Australia, the New South Wales Children (Protection and Parental Responsibility) Act 1997 provides for orders to compel parents to exercise a greater degree of control over their children. Similarly, the British government has taken measures to force parents to take responsibility for their children's misbehaviour, including requiring parents to sign contracts in which they agree to attend parenting programs and ensure their children go to school (Branigan 2005; Crawford 2006c: 456).

Like mandatory reporting, the use of third parties to carry out law enforcement tasks provides additional resources in areas where they are needed. It may also expand, with relatively little expense, the range of specialist expertise and equipment available to ensure compliance with the law.

Civil Forfeiture. Civil forfeiture is an example of first party mandatory action (action required of a target of law enforcement). In many jurisdictions police or prosecutors have the power to require the forfeiture of a person's assets on the basis of a suspicion that the asset has a connection with a crime, whether or not the owner of the asset has been convicted of the crime or ever will be.[8] Assets that are subject to forfeiture are of three different types:[9] pure contraband, that is, objects like drugs and firearms the possession of which constitutes a crime; proceeds of crime, that is, stolen goods or earnings from illegal activities; and "instrumentalities" or tools of crime, that is, objects used in the commission of a crime, such as a getaway car.[10] In civil forfeiture proceedings, civil standards of proof apply. So under proceeds of crime legislation in Australia, for example, a civil court can order the forfeiture of property that 'on the balance of probabilities' is proven to be 'tainted' either because it constitutes proceeds

---

[8] Criminal forfeiture, in contrast, can only follow a criminal conviction. Criminal forfeiture is an *in personam* action (against the offender); civil forfeiture is an *in rem* action (against property) and proceeds on the basis of a legal fiction that objects themselves can be guilty of wrongdoing (Worrall 2001: 173–74).

[9] This typology was set out in the dissenting judgment of Justice Stevens in *Bennis v. Michigan*, 517 US 1163 (1996).

[10] A commercial aircraft carrying passengers and cargo on a scheduled flight has been the subject of forfeiture because cannabis resin was discovered on board: see the European Court of Human Rights' decision in *Air Canada v United Kingdom* (1995) 9/1994/456/537.

of a crime or was used in connection with the commission of an offence (Lusty 2002: 348). Generally too, the onus of proof falls on the person challenging a forfeiture order to establish the lawful origins of the property (a reversal of the usual onus of proof in judicial proceedings).[11]

In Australia, civil forfeiture legislation is of relatively recent origin. Proceeds from the sale of confiscated property end up in the coffers of the Commonwealth government or of the relevant state executive. A similar situation prevails in the United Kingdom and Japan. The state may eventually return a percentage to the confiscating agency for use in their crime fighting activities. In many U.S. jurisdictions, however, police forces are able to keep or sell confiscated property to fund their own law enforcement activities. The proceeds from forfeiture are often used to buy equipment for law enforcement agencies such as vehicles, office supplies and computer systems, as well as fund investigations and education programs (see Saltonstall and Rising 1999). Worrall (2001) reports that a substantial proportion of the 770 municipal and county law enforcement agencies that responded to a 1998 survey were dependent on civil forfeiture as a *necessary* budget supplement. In South Africa, under the Prevention of Organised Crime Act, 121 of 1998, confiscated monies and assets are placed into the Criminal Asset Recovery Fund (CARA) from which law enforcement and other government departments receive grants. In 2006, R33.7 million of the R73.8 million distributed from CARA was given to the South African Police Service (South African Press Association 2006a).

Forfeiture laws are said to be an essential tool for law enforcement because they address the moral issue that crime should not pay. But they are also a practical device to diminish the capacity of criminals to engage in further illegal activities, and may have a deterrent effect by reducing the expected financial returns of such activities (Lusty 2002: 345).

[11] In the U.S., the Civil Asset Forfeiture Reform Act 2000 changed this burden of proof by requiring the government to prove by a preponderance of evidence that the property should be forfeited. However this legislation only applies to forfeiture under federal laws (subject to certain exceptions) and leaves state forfeiture laws untouched.

Adverse Unintended Consequences

One of the major problems with coercive measures is that they are often blunt instruments. Fisse and Braithwaite (1993) use the term "spillover" to refer to the impact of sanctions on helpless or innocent people, those who bear no responsibility for wrongdoing. In the modern age, it may be unrealistic to assume that every parent can exercise perfect supervision over their children. One cannot ignore the collateral damage that coercive measures may produce, as this should enter into any cost/benefit analysis of their use.

Good Samaritan laws. Not all Good Samaritans, or those less altruistic souls who render assistance because the law so requires, are competent. Those who administer first aid to an accident victim may do more harm than good. A bystander who fails to rescue a drowning man and also drowns him or herself is hardly promoting the general welfare, although the bystander does avoid moral and legal culpability for failing to assist.

Moreover, hindsight is a great thing. What may at the time be an indeterminate situation for bystanders (is it, or is it not, an emergency in which I should intervene?) may seem very clear in retrospect. Bystanders who do not act are not always 'bad samaritans'. Bobbitt (2002: 414–15) points out that the ambiguous nature of emergencies explains much about the often paralysed reaction of bystanders, who frequently in retrospect cannot themselves understand why they took no immediate action. The "hindsight effect" (that knowing the outcome of an event affects a person's judgment of the event), a phenomenon first reported by Fischhoff (1975), is part of the well-known mentality of "blaming the victim" (in this case, the bystander).

The risks for the bystander of delaying action or failing to act, risks of conscience, are multiplied when a legal duty is involved and the bystander may risk prosecution. The law may therefore have an unintended anticooperative effect in that its very existence may deter witnesses to a crime from coming forward or truthfully answering police questions (Volokh 1999).

In practical terms a duty to rescue carries with it costs to both the state and to individuals – the costs of increased criminal prosecutions and possibly of increased private civil litigation encouraged by the legislative recognition of a duty of care. The risk of increased civil liability also often carries with it an escalation in insurance premiums for business and individuals, especially those involved in volunteer work.[12] Similarly, there are powerful commercial disincentives to effecting rescues at sea (Davies 2003).

Third-party liability systems. Coercion of third parties may be costly. Where the third party is a commercial entity, the costs may be significant indeed. Requirements that Internet Service Providers retain traffic data that may be required some day for law enforcement purposes will necessitate greater investment in storage space. Onerous requirements that Internet Service Providers assist law enforcement may stifle innovation and inhibit the development of the information technology industry.

The burdens of coerced co-production are by no means confined to the IT industry. Many other commercial actors may not always be able to shift costs to the consumer. The literature on excessive regulatory burdens, abundant as it is, is no less apposite here.

Mandatory action may also influence the relationships of private entities to their clients or customers. The costs of compliance in terms of loss of customer or client support, or the costs to the intended target of the action itself, may be too large and outweigh the risks of detection. But as Gilboy points out (1998: 147–49), the perception of what is a cost and more importantly, of how a cost is valued, will vary, even for the same mandated action, depending on the business or profession involved. A small business involved in providing a fine dining experience to a sophisticated clientele may well value the costs of compliance with a law requiring it to enforce a nonsmoking ban quite differently to the way in which a large enterprise, which not only provides food but also gaming and entertainment facilities, values compliance with that same law. It has been shown that professionals required to report on suspected child abuse perceive in a variety of ways the benefits (or otherwise) to the child or the child's family of reporting, depending on the norms of the professional culture with which they identify (Zellman and Bell 1990).

[12] Amendments to the Western Australian Civil Liability Act 2002 were recently introduced to deal with this problem through an insurance relief package and clarification of negligence laws. New section 5AD protects good samaritans from civil liability provided they act in good faith and without recklessness.

There can also be social costs to mandating action by vulnerable sections of the population. Parents who are liable to fines for their child's truancy are often those who are in no position to pay or to turn around the conditions underlying their child's behaviour. Laws mandating parental control could well exacerbate rather than help alleviate social and economic disadvantage for those families.

Civil forfeiture. Civil forfeiture may also impose significant costs not only on the offenders targeted but also on third parties. Cheh (1998) observes that in some cases, the owners of property subject to confiscation may have been totally unaware of its misuse by others.

The annals of civil forfeiture provide some intriguing examples of overkill.[13] In *Calero-Toledo v Pearson Yacht Leasing* 416 U.S. 663 (1974), a pleasure yacht was confiscated because a quantity of marijuana was found on board. The lessor was neither involved in nor aware of a lessee's wrongful use of the yacht. In *Bennis v. Michigan* 517 U.S. 1163 (1996), the U.S. Supreme Court upheld the confiscation of a family car (without compensation to the wife, who held a half interest in the vehicle) that had been seized as a result of the husband's using it in the course of engaging the services of a prostitute. In fact, families are often the innocent victims of forfeiture laws.[14] In *United States v. 16328 South 43rd East Ave., Bixby, Tulsa County, Okla.*, 275 F.3d at 1286 (10th Cir. 2002), the home of a single mother was confiscated when her son was found growing marijuana on the property, despite the fact she had threatened her son with eviction over the issue, used weed killer on the plants and destroyed any marijuana seeds she had found. Similarly, parents who had notified police of their children's drug use and urged them to undergo rehabilitation had their home confiscated because they had failed to properly search the house or evict their children: *United States v. Two Parcels of Prop. Located at 19 & 25 Castle St.* 31 F.3d (2d Cir. 1994).

---

[13] An excellent discussion of police abuses of U.S. forfeiture laws in the context of the 'War on Drugs', and the warped law enforcement policies that have resulted from their implementation, is to be found in Blumenson and Nilsen 1998.

[14] For a discussion of the inequitable effects of civil asset forfeiture laws on women and children where family members are involved in drug use or trafficking, see American Civil Liberties Union et al. 2005.

Civil forfeiture provisions may also influence police priorities and so impose costs on the community at large. In their 2004 study, Baicker and Jacobson found that local governments in the United States capture a significant fraction of the seizures police make through reductions in other allocations to policing. This in turn affects police behaviour, in that police respond by seizing more, making more drug arrests per capita and focusing on offences for drug possession rather than sale.

CONCLUSION

For a very long time, the state has used coercive measures to ensure than its citizens assist it to enforce the law. Policing by command remains a fact of life in democratic societies today. There has been a broadening of the targets of coercion to include third parties, and the state has adopted new methods of harnessing the resources of citizens, such as civil forfeiture and mandatory reporting requirements. The older 'command and control' forms of physical and mental coercion have been joined by economic coercion and coercion through the criminalization of behaviour previously untouched by the law.

Coercion has always been a tool of tyrants, the fundamental instrument of totalitarian government. Its use in democratic societies should not be embraced uncritically. In the best of all possible worlds, coercion would be unnecessary. Norms and morality would suffice to ensure fair, effective and equitable law enforcement. Unfortunately, the complexity of life in advanced industrial societies does not always lend itself to spontaneous ordering, and to people doing the right thing. A degree of coercion may be essential to ensure decent and proper public security. The question is where, and how much? The readiness of citizens to comply with coercive measures will be, at least partially, a function of the legitimacy of those measures, the extent to which they are seen as part of the 'social contract'.[15]

Normative questions about how, when and where coercion might legitimately be used cannot be definitively answered by reference only to a limited range of instances such as those canvassed in this

---

[15] For an overview of social contract in political theory, see Hindess 1996.

chapter. But unravelling the benefits and costs of using coercion in particular cases, in the way that has been attempted here, may allow state legislatures and public police to see more clearly how decisions to use coercion impact not only on the targets but also on society as a whole, and to weigh and balance the interests affected. As Merton (1936) points out, there are both economic and psychological limits to forecasting the unintended outcomes of purposive social action (pp. 900–901). So in undertaking this task it would be useful for decision makers to have some general guidelines for assessing the appropriateness of coercive measures.

If one accepts that coercion is the antithesis of freedom, then one can say that it should be used only as a last resort, and never indiscriminately. One principle for the use of coercion, following Braithwaite and Pettit (1990), is that it be used only when only when it enhances overall freedom. How can this principle be advanced in specific cases?

First, perhaps, the issue of proportionality might be considered. Are the policy objectives in question of sufficient importance to justify the coercive measures employed? It is evident from some of the examples examined in this chapter that the state's coercive powers are sometimes mobilized in a manner grossly disproportionate to the policy objectives it seeks to realize. Draconian measures may be appropriate in response to serious organized crime but totally inappropriate to deal with shoplifting. They may be suitable as a way to harness the resources of citizens in order to control organized drug trafficking but not simple possession.

A second consideration might be the connection between the coercive measures in question and the target problem. Are they rationally related? Can a car rental company reasonably be expected to prevent the use of their vehicle to transport contraband?

Third, there is the question of whether the coercive measures are the least restrictive means of achieving the state's objectives. This raises two issues:

1. The likely effectiveness of the coercive measures in question – are they likely to produce the desired outcome taking into account the balance between costs of compliance and risks of noncompliance?; and

2. The availability of less intrusive, but equally effective, alternatives.

Fourth, one might consider the costs imposed by the coercive methods and whether those costs – financial, administrative, or affecting personal and professional relations – are outweighed by the benefits that such methods deliver. How these costs are distributed will also be relevant in a democratic state. Are they spread thinly and widely across society, or are they borne disproportionately by a particular group? How well equipped are they to bear these costs?

Fifth, and finally, the existence of procedural safeguards to guard against the arbitrary or capricious exercise of coercive powers may be of relevance. The public police are subject to all sorts of exacting standards in exercising their powers – take, for example, the execution of a search warrant in common law jurisdictions. There is no reason why the mobilization of other forms of state power aimed at ensuring that citizens assist the state with law enforcement should not similarly be grounded in safeguards against improper implementation. It may be appropriate to draw a line, as Justice Kirby did in the Australian High Court case of *R. v Swaffield* (1998) 192 CLR 159, between the legal and proper use of "subterfuge, ruses and tricks" by police and deceptive conduct, of a type common in totalitarian societies, which is unfair to the accused in overriding his or her legal rights. In some cases, judicial supervision or other mechanisms of accountability will be appropriate. Perhaps enabling legislation could contain a sunset clause or provision for some other mechanism for review over the longer term, as a safeguard against overzealous law enforcement and prosecution.

Even in the freest of societies, coercion may be a necessary evil. But one must guard against instinctive prescription of coercive solutions to every problem or crisis that emerges. The legitimacy of the state and the rule of law are at stake. What passes for good politics often results in bad policy.

CHAPTER FOUR

SALE – BUYING

Commanding co-production of security from third parties is only one way in which police obtain resources to effectively police their jurisdictions. We turn now to a second form, sale: the exchange of goods and services between police and others. In this chapter we examine instances of police buying in the goods and services they need, and the risks and benefits this entails. We look in Part 1 at police involvement in procurement and outsourcing, and then in Part 2 we turn to the acquisition of information by police through the offering of rewards and other inducements.

PART 1: SHOPPING

Introduction

Shopping does not immediately spring to mind as one of the important activities of the police. At first glance it seems an unconventional or even trivial pursuit. But the purchasing of goods and services is in fact taking up increasing amounts of the time and energy of today's police. The increasing complexity of public policing, and the climate of fiscal austerity (with attending pressures for greater efficiency and effectiveness) that characterises most Western nations, have seen police going 'outside' for more goods and services. This increasing reliance on purchasing has also been driven by new techniques of policing in response to fresh challenges such as terrorism. Contemporary policing is accompanied by a need for goods and services undreamt of thirty years ago. In 2004/05, the London Metropolitan Police spent £377m on supplies and services, £61m on transport and £194m on premises, an increase of £70m, £10m and £60m respectively over the three years since 2001/02.[1]

The range of decisions associated with shopping – whether to go shopping in the first place, what to buy, and from whom – are influenced by three basic considerations: *ideology*, *economics*, and *pragmatism*. The Thatcher and Reagan Revolutions heralded a broader global trend for government agencies to enter the market-place, driven by state ideologies of privatization and across-the-board adoption of new public service management models based on private sector philosophies and strategies (Hancock 1998: 119; Davids and Hancock 1998: 40–43; Verspaandonk 2001: 3; Murphy 2002: 14).

Over the past couple of decades police have been confronted with demands to do more with less, to implement state policies that emphasize efficiency in, and accountability for, resource use (Murphy 2002: 7). The 'bottom line' has become the fundamental consideration in many policing decisions, both operational and nonoperational. At times, this objective may be consistent with ideological goals, as when low costs and high efficiencies go hand in hand. At other times economic and ideological objectives may be in tension. Costs are not always lower when private sector management techniques are adopted, and sometimes police decisions based on economic considerations will lead to inequitable provision of policing services and exacerbate moves towards the creation of private security communities.

The third consideration, pragmatism, arises from the increased salience of policing and security in the intensely competitive arena of contemporary politics (Weatherburn 2004). Publicity crises arising from operational matters are bad enough; police commissioners and their ministers would prefer to avoid becoming implicated in addi-tional scandals arising from cost overruns or corruption allegations. This is particularly important, given the tremendous symbolic impor-tance as an agency of reassurance that police have in contemporary society (Innes 2004: 167; Crawford 2006b). A police service immersed in controversy is that much less reassuring.

---

[1] See Metropolitan Police Service and Metropolitan Police Authority Annual Reports for those financial years, available at http://www.mpa.gov.uk/reports/jointannual.htm (accessed 2 July 2008).

These three drivers will vary in importance, depending on context. A newly elected conservative government may well be hell-bent on privatizing whatever it can. A government under intense fiscal pressure may be inclined to achieve economies at every opportunity. A government under siege politically will do its utmost to avoid making waves.

Shopping has its risks as well as its benefits. Like consumers every-where, police may from time to time purchase inferior products, or pay more for an item than they might have. Sometimes, police shopping practices may be dictated by governments in a manner that prevents them from getting the best value for money. Requirements that police vehicles be leased rather than purchased and maintained in-house may derive from ideology rather than economics. And occasionally, shop-ping expeditions result in acquisitions that have unforeseen and undesirable consequences for the purchaser – in this case, for the wider police organisation. Just like other consumers, police may not always understand fully what they are getting when they shop.

The acquisition of goods and services by police agencies may be seen in a wider framework of exchange relationships in which police operate to enhance their capacity. They may command individuals or institutions to provide information or services (see Chapter 3). They may be the recipients of corporate sponsorship or donations from individuals (see Chapter 6) and they may provide their services on a cost recovery or fee-for-service basis (see Chapter 5). This invites a wider theoretical question of how the three basic modes of exchange – coercion, gift and sale – vary over time and across jurisdictions (see Chapter 8).

In the first part of this chapter, we explore the varieties of acqui-sition now engaged in by public police and the diverse ways in which shopping by police is conducted and regulated. Our descriptions are drawn from police departments around the world, with a particular emphasis on Australia. We hope to make a contribution towards the beginnings of what Wood and Kempa (2005) describe as "[a] com-prehensive mapping of all auspices and providers of policing, and the ways in which they harness the resources of others" (2005: 300). Police outsourcing and acquisition is a crucial, but heretofore neglected, part of this project.

We then consider the benefits and pitfalls of these exchange relationships between police and the private sector, and reflect on the
desirability of institutional and procedural safeguards, and the
implications of these arrangements for efficiency, equity and efficacy
in public policing. We will conclude with some observations on what
this might mean for police departments and the men and women who
manage them.

The Shopping List

Since the public institution of police was established in the nineteenth
century, police have been shopping. The initial basic requirements of
stationery, uniforms, weapons, furniture, buildings and modes of
transport have been supplemented as police organisations have
increased in size and complexity. Kitchen and bathroom fittings and
equipment, specialised apparel (riot gear, ballistic vests, bomb suits,
diving gear etc.), photographic equipment, musical instruments and
livestock (dogs and horses), together with associated food and equipment, must all be procured. Insurance, postal services, telephones, gas,
electricity and rent have long been factored into the budget. Police
organisations often require not only motor vehicles (cars, vans,
motorcycles) but also aircraft and marine launches. New forms of
communication (radiocommunications and other information technology, both hardware and software), new intelligence gathering tools
such as CCTV[2] and automatic numberplate recognition systems,[3] and
new ways of investigating crime involving novel forms of scientific
apparatus and computer programs, have been adopted by police.

Services like laundering, catering, cleaning, publishing and
maintenance of equipment, vehicles and buildings have been the

[2] Numbers of CCTV cameras are increasing rapidly in cities in industrialised countries.
    In Edinburgh, Scotland, for example, the number of cameras overlooking public
    spaces increased from 63 to 110 in three years, McEwen, 2005a.
[3] The City of London Police installed Automatic Number Plate Recognition (ANPR)
    equipment around the perimeter of the City in 1997 as part of its antiterrorist
    strategy. ANPR uses optical character recognition to read the registration plates on
    vehicles and cross-reference them with a database of stored numberplates in order
    to identify the owner. The City of London system has been used to facilitate wider
    policing objectives. More than twelve hundred people were arrested as a result of
    vehicle scanning in the first three years following installation, in connection with
    crimes as serious as murder and armed robbery. City of London Police 2008.

subject of 'outsourcing' for decades. The outsourcing of more recent services such as gym management, physical fitness testing, vaccination programs, pathology testing and audits of financial systems are uncontroversial. But the purchasing of services that traditionally have been provided from police ranks is also growing. Many police organisations around the world outsource recruit training, some traffic functions, audio tape transcriptions (e.g., of telephone interceptions), some forensic investigations and provision of prisoner custody and transportation services. In Scotland, a private firm is responsible for both prisoner transportation and the monitoring of electronically tagged adult and juvenile offenders (Jackson 2005).

Consultants are frequently hired to carry out engineering works, develop and evaluate policing programs, prepare budgets, plan accommodation strategies, conduct surveys of client satisfaction levels, implement organisational security and design and manage computer systems.[4] The South African Police Service has commissioned consultants to assist in the development of national policies, standards and procedures for police activities, including the creation of performance indicators and hiring criteria (Minnaar and Mistry 2004: 45). The Australian Federal Police have entrusted the security of their headquarters to a private security firm. London's Metropolitan Police has outsourced both the day-to-day operation and future development of its IT and radiocommunications networks. Similarly, the South African Police Service has outsourced its IT management to a state-owned agency. Outsourcing of cybercrime investigations has been contemplated by Australian police forces (Police Commissioners' Conference Electronic Crime Steering Committee 2001; Etter 2001: 12). Even the process of outsourcing itself is sometimes outsourced (Davids and Hancock 1998: 56).

These trends towards outsourcing functions that were previously performed by sworn police officers have not gone unnoticed, and have elicited criticism, especially in jurisdictions where police unions

---

[4] See, for example, Appendix G to the Tasmania Police Annual Report 2003–2004 listing consultancies and contracts; also see the list of Australian Federal Police Consultancy Services for 2006–2007, at http://www.afp.gov.au/about/requirements/consultancy_services.html (accessed 2 July 2008).

are active. Nevertheless, relentless pressures to control public expenditures make a reversal of these trends unlikely.

Modes of Acquisition: Finding the Right Shop and Getting the Right Deal

Procurement and outsourcing by police organisations is generally undertaken through contractual agreement between police and vendors of goods and services. Goods or services may be purchased for police use, or police may purchase services for third parties (known as "purchase-of-service contracting": DeHoog and Salamon 2002). Agreements may be multilayered, involving a number of contracts, both simultaneous and successive. Contracts can be for one-off purchases or for the purchase of items or services over time. Kelman (2002: 290–1) identifies two types of contracts for purchases that take place over time: "delivery order contracts" where the purchaser buys items from the contractor's list on an 'as needs' basis (e.g., stationery), and "task order contracts" where a master contract establishes labour rates or fixed prices for certain tasks, and specific assignments are agreed upon over the life of the contract (e.g., development of software). Contracts can require the contractor to achieve certain results ("completion contracts") or to do its best to achieve certain objectives ("best efforts contracts") (Kelman 2002: 293). Pricing and incentives may be structured in a variety of ways (Kelman 2002: 294–6).

In addition to the contract provisions, police will often have to comply with externally and internally imposed rules and guidelines on procurement. In the United Kingdom, for instance, police must have regard to European Community Directives aimed at ensuring a robust internal market in public procurement. Victoria Police are bound by Victorian Government Purchasing Board (VGPB) policies regarding procurement. In South Africa, all government departments, including the police, that enter into public-private partnerships (PPPs) are required to adhere to Treasury regulations to guide deals with the private sector and ensure that the state does not suffer financially (Schönteich 2004c). Policies and guidelines about procurement are likely to deal with more than just the process of finding suppliers and calling for quotes or tenders, often covering strategic

issues like risk management, probity, confidentiality, contract negotiation techniques and project management. In addition to rules and
guidelines issued at governmental level, police organisations sometimes promulgate their own detailed rules and guidelines. The
Queensland Police Service, for example, has published a document
entitled "General Conditions of Offering" containing detailed provisions about how the procurement process is to be conducted
(Queensland Police Service 2006).

Police organisations have a number of options in relation to the
kind of contracts they enter into for the acquisition of goods and
services. In relation to goods, for instance, a police organisation may
choose to purchase the good (and thus obtain outright ownership),
lease it (obtaining use but not ownership) or enter into a lease-purchase (also known as a hire-purchase) agreement (paying by instal-
ments so that ownership of the good is acquired only at the end of the
payment period). The decision will rest not only on the type of good
to be acquired and the uses to which it will be put, but also on the
characteristics of the organisation itself. Equipment that needs to be
replaced or upgraded often (such as some IT equipment and motor
vehicles where there is a need for up-to-date technology[5]) may be
better leased than purchased but, if leasing, an organisation also
needs to have the capacity to manage both the assets leased and the
lease agreement on an ongoing basis. Purchasing may be effective for
equipment that has a long life span, but staff may need to have
expertise in repairs and maintenance, and disposal costs may need to
be factored into the decision.[6]

Procurement and outsourcing sometimes go hand-in-hand. A lease
contract for goods may include terms securing the provision of services by the supplier of the goods, such as installation and maintenance of a computer system or other technological product.

---

[5] For example, New South Wales Police leased both mainframe and desktop
computers and its motor vehicle fleet in the 2003–2004 financial year; see New
South Wales Police Annual Report for 2003–2004, Notes at p.61.

[6] For a detailed discussion of the kinds of considerations that should influence
decisions by state agencies to purchase, lease or lease-purchase information
technologies, see Department of Information Resources 1998.

The political and legal environment in which a police organisation operates may also influence its decisions about the form
of contract for procurement of particular goods or services. In
Victoria, police vehicles are leased under a whole-of-government
contract, administered by VicFleet, part of the Department of
Treasury and Finance (VicFleet 2004). This contract covers a
number of state agencies including Victoria Police, so police discretion is limited in relation to the makes and models of vehicles
available to the organisation. Only vehicles that are substantially
manufactured in Australia can be procured, for example, and these
only from specified manufacturers. Issues like insurance, replacement parts and vehicle disposal are also dealt with at the whole-of-
government level.

What is known as eProcurement is becoming an increasingly
popular means of acquisition in policing and across government
agencies generally. This is "the use of electronic methods in every
stage of the purchasing process from identification of requirement
through to payment, and potentially to contract management" (U.K.
Office of Government Commerce 2008). This use of Internet-based
technology to identify vendors and negotiate supply of goods comes
in a variety of guises. Some police forces have begun to use electronic
reverse auctions or eAuctions, whereby vendors bid online (sometimes publicly) to supply goods such as stationery.[7] In the United
Kingdom, some forces adopted eProcurement under the auspices
of the Police Electronic Procurement System (PEPS) initiative that
aimed to make available shared core e-procurement systems and
collaborative solutions to all forces across England and Wales.[8]
There was also a government agency, or Non-Departmental
Public Body (NDPB), called the Police Information Technology

---

[7] Kent Police were the first to use e-auctions, leading a consortium of ten forces in
this practice (U.K. Office of Government Commerce 2007) and winning an award
at the U.K. Government eProcurement Awards in 2004.
[8] In 2005, six U.K. police forces (Avon and Somerset Constabulary, Devon and
Cornwall Constabulary, Dorset Police, Dyfed-Powys Police, Gloucestershire
Constabulary, Wiltshire Constabulary) signed up with a private organisation,
EGS, to pilot a system called Bluelight Marketplace which was then part of PEPS.
This system allowed them to access general national and regional framework
contracts and supplier details at a national, regional and force level, EGS 2007.

Organisation (PITO) which coordinated collective procurement arrangements for U.K. police agencies. PITO was replaced by the National Policing Improvement Agency (NPIA) in 2006. The NPIA manages procurement collaboration across all forces and is able to enforce national IT strategies (Clark 2007).

Closer to home, the New Zealand government proposed a centralized electronic solution to procurement, in this case across all government agencies. This system, called GoProcure, was trialled by police and a university but was discontinued in late 2003 when it became apparent that only a small number of agencies would benefit from using GoProcure at that time. The New Zealand Police, who had benefited greatly by moving to electronic procurement, subsequently signed a deal with a private company to provide an electronic hub for its contact with major suppliers (Mallard, 2003; Bell, 2003; and Hall, 2004). Victoria Police has also adopted its own eProcurement system with initial funding granted under the Victorian Government's EC4P Project (Victorian Auditor-General's Office 2003a).

Electronic procurement systems are designed to introduce more efficiencies into the procurement process, but they may also have other purposes. Sometimes governments are interested in 'levelling the playing field' for smaller companies competing against national or international firms and eProcurement assists in this process by reducing costs for tenderers. VGPB policies, for instance, require government purchasers to maximise opportunities for local and regional suppliers to sell to government, specifically requiring government purchasers to encourage these suppliers "to participate in electronic commerce initiatives" (Victorian Government Purchasing Board 2007). The EC4P Project was also expressly designed with small to medium enterprises and regional firms in mind as potential suppliers (Department of Treasury and Finance [nda]).

The forms and processes relating to procurement and outsourcing are complicated by such bureaucratic requirements. Inherent in them is the risk that, for the police, other priorities such as public safety and crime prevention may be forced to take second place when choices of 'the best' suppliers and products are being made.

DIY or ODI (Others Do It): Deciding Whether and What to Outsource

The decision that a product is needed and should therefore be purchased or leased is a fairly straightforward one (although implementation can be quite complex). The decision to engage a consultant for a particular short-term project may also prove to be a relatively simple exercise involving assessment of needs (having regard to what is available in-house) in the light of current budget limitations. But how do police departments make the decision to outsource a whole area of work from their portfolio on an ongoing basis, rather than choosing to retain or develop within police ranks over the longer term the skills and knowledge to undertake that work?

The growth of outsourcing in the public sector saw a distinction being made between 'core' and 'noncore' (also known as ancillary, peripheral or secondary) services. Davids and Hancock have traced the development of this distinction in relation to policing in Victoria and the United Kingdom (1998: 47–50) and have shown that it goes to the very heart of what it means to be engaged in public policing. Unfortunately for police, however, there is no shared or standard definition of 'core police function' from which to work. A 1998 Australian Centre for Policing Research study (Boni and Packer 1998) revealed different perceptions by the police and the public about the proper priorities for police.[9] It is likely that, if such a survey was to be conducted with participants from subgroups within these categories, or with participants from different countries, times or cultures, disagreements would persist over what should be the essential functions of police.

The mechanics of decisions to outsource is not something that police publicly discuss. The annual reports of most Australian police forces, for example, contain little about how these decisions are

---

[9] The study was conducted by surveying samples of the public and the police in Perth, Western Australia and Brisbane, Queensland. While each group agreed that criminal investigation should be a high priority, the surveyed public felt that police should place a higher priority on a wider range of tasks, particularly those concerning community service, while the police felt that their current attention to community service tasks (as well as prisoner servicing) was taking away needed attention from criminal investigation.

made, generally only listing consultancies and other contracts entered into over the relevant year.[10] Davids and Hancock suggest that 'divestiture of non-core business activities' is often actually an *ex post facto* justification for actions taken with other motives (i.e. for political or financial reasons) that are rarely revealed publicly (1998: 49–50). In contrast, Murphy makes the point that applying a distinction about core and peripheral services is something that police routinely do informally in operational decisions about allocation of their limited resources (Murphy 2002: 16). So it may be that a combination of rarely and commonly articulated factors leads to these outsourcing decisions (see later in this chapter). An assessment of what the police should be doing, what is 'core', and what can be left to others is probably only one of these factors, the importance of which varies with the context.

In one large police organisation that we studied, any sworn or unsworn officer is able to make a business case to management for outsourcing a service. It was suggested to us that the reason outsourcing is proposed may vary with the level of the proposing officer within the organisation. For example, occupational health and safety concerns over providing a service might prompt a lower level officer to propose outsourcing, whilst cost may play a greater part in the considerations of middle management, and political considerations may constitute the main driver at the executive level.

The outcomes of outsourcing decisions for similar services can be very different across police agencies. In the course of our research, we spoke to representatives of two large police agencies, one of which was required by government policy to discontinue its practice of buying and servicing its own motor vehicles (and selling them at a profit), and to begin leasing them instead, at greater cost. The justification was ideological, not economic; it was felt that the business of police is policing, and that an agency of government should not compete with second hand car dealers in the private sector. The other

---

[10] A partial exception is the Australian Federal Police (AFP) which, when listing its consultancies, states the reasons why a consultant was engaged in a particular case. These include a lack of available in-house resources, a need for specialised or professional skills, and a need for independent research or assessment, Australian Federal Police 2006a.

agency was required by government to get the greatest value for money in the purchase and management of its vehicle fleet, and continued its practice of buying and selling its own cars.

In whatever way the decision to outsource a significant part of police work is made, it is clear that it will have implications for staffing and the content of police work and possibly, as a result, for public perceptions of policing. But the question of what policing functions are *inherently* governmental is an interesting one, and conceptions are changing. Kettl (1993: 194) noted that the U.S. Environmental Protection Agency commissioned a private consultant to develop just such a definition. More recently, Singer (2003) reviews the surprising extent of private sector involvement in the delivery of military services.

Benefits of ODI

So what are the articulated benefits of getting others to provide goods or services for police organisations? As the Australian Federal Police (AFP) notes, it can address a shortage of particular skills or equipment within a police organisation. Kelman (2002: 307) points out that it is difficult for government agencies to employ top-quality experts in specialist areas like information technology and financial management because government pay rates are low compared to those in the private sector. Police could not be expected to have had the skills to develop, implement and maintain a high-speed wireless communications system like that developed by Fujitsu and Microsoft and recently piloted by Western Australia Police. This system involves the provision of hand-held computers to patrolling officers to enable them to conduct on-the-spot checks of databases containing information about vehicles and people, instead of having to rely on frequently overloaded radio systems (Fujitsu 2005). Similarly, the AFP turned to a large professional services firm specialising in financial audit and taxation to perform a performance audit of the AFP Protective Service revenue in the 2004–2005 financial year. Police in Oxford, Ohio, called upon the services of a psychic to help in the search for a missing person (Leingang 2004).

There may be times that police see the need for review, evaluation or facilitation of police activities to be conducted by an independent individual or body. The AFP Consultancy Services List for 2004–2005 lists several cases where consultants have been engaged for this reason, including the appointment of individuals to undertake pilot research on police participation in international peacekeeping and capacity building, and the appointment of an independent alcohol and drug organisation to provide estimates of the social cost of drugs to underpin the AFP Drug Harm Index.

Alternatively, police may have the skills in-house to provide a service but not have the resources (in terms of time and labour) to do so. The use of private security to guard police buildings is an example of this (Johnston 1992: 59). Such a strategy may also be cost effective. Police in high-crime areas of Cape Town in South Africa have chosen to use private armed response companies to protect their stations from attack and armed robbery while they carry on with basic job of policing the streets (Schönteich 2004a: 12). In Scotland police have entrusted to a private firm, Reliance, prisoner court custody and transportation duties throughout Scotland and, more recently, 'noncore' escorting duties such as inter-prison transfers and transport to prisoners' hospital appointments in some parts of the country (Scottish Prison Service 2004). Prison escort services are also outsourced in the Australian Capital Territory under the Custodial Escorts Act 1998. In South Africa, after an inquiry into the escape of several People Against Gangsterism and Drugs (Pagad) members from police holding cells in 2001 (South African Press Association 2001), the Independent Complaints Directorate recommended outsourcing the South African Police Service's prisoner transportation and court security functions in order to free up police resources for crime reduction and crime prevention work.

Cost often plays a major part in the decision to outsource a task or area of work. Because private contractors aim both to generate a profit and to attract business they have an incentive to maximise productivity, and to do so at competitive rates. They may be able to cost a project or task at a lower rate than can the police because, without the red tape of bureaucratic processes to contend with, they are able to make savings in the areas of procurement and of hiring and deploying employees (Schönteich 2004b: 17–18).

This is not to say that outsourcing always saves police organisations money. According to one commentator, outsourcing is most likely to produce savings "where the required service can be easily specified and monitored" (Mulgan 2001). The difficulties and time involved in negotiating and monitoring complex or multiple contracts relating to the outsourcing of a particular task can have consequences for the cost-efficiency of the deal. The London Metropolitan Police recently sought to consolidate its IT and telecommunications contracts into a single outsourcing tender with the aim of reducing its expenditure on the in-house management systems needed to service a number of different providers (McCue 2004). And anyway, cost may not be the sole decisive factor in a decision to outsource. Police may be willing to bear additional costs in exchange for other benefits.

One of those benefits and another reason for outsourcing is the prospect of efficiency gains for police. In April 2005, the Boston Police Department decided to outsource the forensics work previously conducted by its own fingerprint analysis unit. The private firm to whom the work was outsourced found 109 fingerprints missed earlier by Boston detectives investigating crimes. Outsourcing the work was expensive, costing U.S. $30,000 per month, but clearly the benefits outweighed the costs. Those benefits included avoiding the ignominy of being responsible for a wrongful conviction and associated six-year imprisonment because of shoddy fingerprint analysis by the police (McPhee 2005). The City of Pittsburgh's outsourcing contract for wireless communications for police (of a similar nature to that of Western Australia Police, mentioned earlier) freed up police officers from paperwork that previously chewed up chunks of their time that was better spent on community policing (Schmitt 1997). Indeed, one of the major justifications for outsourcing by police (and other public sector agencies) is that it allows them to concentrate on the important (or 'core') parts of the job, and so has valuable flow-on effects for the public. This may account for the reluctance of police departments in Australia to outsource the more 'operational' parts of their workloads or to engage in "purchase-of-service" contracting.

Arguably, outsourcing may also result in higher quality services. As already noted, contractors may bring expertise and skills not available, or readily available, from within police ranks, and a private sector mentality of flexibility in terms of employment arrangements and responsive service delivery. Competition for business between

private service providers can ensure that a provider can be found to
suit particular requirements (Verspaandonk 2001: 9). But quality is
not guaranteed, as will be seen in the discussion later in this chapter
about the costs and risks that may be associated with purchasing.
However, police organisations do at least have some control over
quality issues where private contractors are employed. Performance
and delivery standards are usually specified in the outsourcing contract. The contract can be terminated on the basis of unsatisfactory
fulfilment of those standards whereas, if the task is being done in-
house, the whole situation may be much more complex for management to deal with, involving questions of workers' rights and of
who within the organisation should be held ultimately responsible.

Costs and Risks
Relying on outsourcing and procurement to supplement police
resources can also be costly and may bring about risk. Because policing
is a sensitive business, the costs and risks associated with these types of
interactions between police and third parties are sometimes greater
than they would be for other state agencies. Together with obvious
financial costs, possible costs and risks include overdependency on a
supplier, corruption and fraudulent practices, problems with quality
of outsourced services, difficulties over accountability of contractors,
police staff morale issues, threats to police legitimacy in the eyes of the
public and inequities in the provision of police services. Any one of
these factors, if serious enough, can cause significant embarrassment
to the police or to the government of the day.

Costs and the extent of risk involved in shopping activities will vary
with the size, culture and practices of the police department in
question. Size, in particular, matters. A small police agency with a
correspondingly small budget is likely to have little purchasing
sophistication and, perhaps, little motivation to acquire it. In the
United States, there are approximately 18,760 police agencies and
most of them are small.[11] With so many agencies serving

[11] See "Police Structure of the United States". Available at http://faculty.ncwc.edu/
toconnor/polstruct.htm (accessed 7 June 2006). According to this site, the average
size for a police agency is twenty-five sworn officers (that figure excludes
nonsworn officers or civilians).

communities of different sizes and natures (states, counties, cities, towns, campuses, ports and so on), the amounts of goods and services purchased and the types and degrees of risk that accrue to the processes connected with shopping will vary widely between agencies. For instance, overdependency on a single supplier may be a significant problem in smaller, more remote police agencies; by contrast, the risks associated with the quality of contracts and of the goods or services purchased under them may be greater in larger agencies that are dealing with more numerous and more complex transactions. In addition, opportunities for achieving economies of scale will be limited in such a fragmented market, so costs may be higher than in other more centralized jurisdictions.

Costs. The costs of finding and negotiating with private providers, and then of ongoing contract management, may be significant and may outweigh the cost of providing the service from within police ranks (DeHoog and Salamon 2002: 329). This is especially so, as noted above, where the service outsourced is a particularly complex one (Mulgan 2001). Savings may be 'eaten up' in monitoring and quality control.

Costs can also increase because of the need to train members of police organisations in the skills of contract management. This training, too, may be outsourced. Training may well be an ongoing cost, with some organisations having a high staff turnover in this area (Singer 2003: 154).[12] It is clearly essential that the costs of contract management and of any necessary training are taken into account when calculating the overall costs of outsourcing.

Overdependency. Where there are few suppliers, whether that is because the service or good supplied is highly specialised or merely because of geography, it is all too easy for the police organisation to become overdependent on a particular supplier. This may lead to an overly cosy relationship, perhaps even capture by the monopoly

---

[12] Singer writes about private military firms (PMFs). Because of the fact that both police and the military deal with security issues, many of Singer's observations about government outsourcing to PMFs are relevant to issues of police outsourcing.

supplier of that part of police business. This may be especially the case with information technology, where products may be incompatible and the transition between products of successive suppliers may be less than seamless. The problem with overdependency on a single supplier is that the police organisation cannot quickly replace the outsourced service if the contractor proves unreliable, goes out of business or decides that providing the service poses too many risks to their employees (the latter might be the case, for instance, with inherently dangerous tasks like prisoner custody and transportation services). Risks to the public may be the consequence, especially where the police have not retained, or never had, the skills themselves to undertake the outsourced services.

Another issue arising from too much dependence on a single supplier is that transition costs, that is, the costs of changing suppliers at the end of a contract period, will often be higher than the cost of contract renewal (DeHoog and Salamon 2002: 326). There is a temptation, then, to stay with a supplier, even if the service provided is not wholly satisfactory. Being 'too close' to a supplier clearly magnifies that temptation.

Corruption and fraud. Too intimate a relationship might also open a door to corruption and fraud. Allegations of bribery and favouritism emerged following the tender process for New Zealand's police dispatch system (CARD) in 1995. It was alleged that senior police officials had taken helicopter rides paid for by one of the main suppliers vying for the contract, Intergraph, and stayed at the holiday home of Intergraph's CEO. It was also suggested that the tender criteria were changed during the tender to allow tenders from companies which could not offer a 'distributed environment' (computers in separate cities in New Zealand), such as Intergraph. A member of the advisory panel of police technical experts claimed to have been pressured to favour Intergraph. And Intergraph was said to have extended a job offer to a member of the police procurement team (Hill 1997). However, the Police Complaints Authority investigation into the CARD tender found no evidence that police had personally benefited during the evaluation process or that the process was modified to favour Intergraph (National Business Review 1997).

A more recent example involving an Australian police department is also illustrative. In 1999, an unsuccessful tenderer complained of irregularities in the acquisition of a new digital communications system. A series of articles was published in a major daily newspaper alleging improper influence by the successful tenderer. The situation was complicated by the suggestion that, although the successful bid was indeed more costly and less compliant with specifications than the competitor, the successful bidder offered a significant discount on other products it was selling to the police, making the overall package preferable. An internal police investigation into the tender process recommended that a senior officer, the then commander of the police communications unit, be sacked and disciplinary action taken against thirteen other involved officers (Hills 1999c). Newspaper allegations of impropriety on the part of another senior police executive seriously damaged his reputation and gave rise to a successful action for defamation (*Jarratt v John Fairfax Publications Pty Limited* [2001] NSWSC 739; Australian Associated Press 1999; Hills 1999a, 1999b, 1999c, 1999d).

Potential poaching of personnel presents dangers during all phases of the procurement and outsourcing processes. Those involved may experience conflicts of loyalties and interest (Singer 2003: 154). This can potentially lead to an unfair process that delivers less than optimal supplies and services, causes resentment amongst vying suppliers and even damages the credibility of the organisation itself. Poaching can also increase the costs of procurement by forcing the organisation to "buy back the skill base at a private sector premium" (Australian Federal Police Association 2001). In the United States, the prevalence of the 'revolving door' syndrome, particularly in the military, has spawned legal rules regulating the relationship between contractors and government employees engaged in procurement activities.[13]

---

[13] The Procurement Integrity Act, 41 USC §423, requires contracting officers to notify their superiors if they are offered jobs by contractors and bans those who take such jobs from disclosing certain information about the government procurement processes. It applies a one-year ban on accepting compensation from a contractor to former federal employees who were engaged in procurement

Collusion between contractors and employees is the most common form of corporate procurement fraud,[14] but fraud can also arise from the activity of internal staff or through industry collusion (Australian Federal Police 2001). As the examples just discussed show, police organisations are not immune to perceptions of improper behaviour in the context of procurement and outsourcing activities. Over-charging and intentional cheating might also occur, a situation made worse for police where the service being purchased requires the private contractor to employ staff, as overpayments can then take place on a recurring basis (Singer 2003: 155). Issues of accountability, of course, pervade most areas of policing. In matters of procurement, as elsewhere, police have tackled these problems with guidelines and internal audits.

Primacy of profit motive. More broadly, whether or not collusive or fraudulent behaviour is engaged in, it is clear that the motivations of the parties to a procurement deal may influence their behaviour. Contractors are motivated mainly by profit, and in some cases this self-interest may trump the interests of those employing them. So, for instance, a contractor may elect to cut the costs involved in producing a final output by choosing technologies or methods according to their cost rather than their quality and value (Vincent-Jones 2000: 343; Singer 2003: 155). Such behaviour, although it may be perfectly legitimate, can lead to problems with service provision further down the track. Similarly, penetration pricing, or loss leader strategy, is a common practice in government contracting (Kelman 2002: 298) and is not unknown in the police procurement environment.[15] An initial bid is made intentionally below cost in order to gain the con-tract. Ex-post rent extraction by contractors may follow: after the contract is awarded prices may be raised in some way, such as through claims that further contracts, staff or pieces of equipment are needed. This practice is most common where high-technology purchases

---

activities. A summary of the provisions can be found at http://www.uah.edu/research/resadmin/information/integrity.html (accessed 4 July 2008).

[14] Paul Dopp, Senior Associate in a firm of corporate investigators headquartered in Dallas, Texas, cited in Australian Federal Police 2001.

[15] Personal communications to authors from police organisations.

are involved and it is relatively simple to make a case for updating that technology.

There is a danger that the benefits for police of putting the provision of a service into private hands could come at the expense of the public interest. Contractors in the United States supplying traffic safety cameras (also known as 'speed' or 'photo radar' or 'red light' cameras) are sometimes paid on a contingency basis, that is, the more traffic violation notices are sent out or the more violators are convicted, the more they are paid. Such was the case with Lockheed Martin in the 2001 case of *In re: Red Light Camera Cases, The People of the State of California v. John Allen, et al.*, Superior Court San Diego, County, 2001, No. 57927SD. Lockheed was paid $70, or 50 percent, of whatever San Diego City collected in fines from each red light camera citation, whichever was less. Lockheed had also been given the responsibility of fully operating the red light system, with almost no City involvement. The company was responsible for the entire process from installation and operation of the equipment, to reviewing the photographs to make the initial determination of the existence of a violation and whether the perpetrator could be identified, to printing and mailing of citations. The police were involved only in the latter stages in reviewing Lockheed's decision to issue a citation. The Superior Court judge found there was a potential conflict of interest between Lockheed's role as operator of the system and the contingent method of Lockheed's compensation and that this undermined the trustworthiness of the evidence used to prosecute red light violations. As a result, about three hundred tickets were dismissed.[16] However, the practices of contingency payments and of giving contractors powers of input over operational decisions such as the location of cameras still continues in some other U.S. states. For instance, ACS was in 2005 awarded an extension of contracts to continue running red light and speed camera systems in Washington, DC. ACS is paid a flat fee but also may be paid extra fees if the number

---

[16] In a similar case in Denver, Colorado, in 2002, a county court found that the City breached state law by delegating police department duties (the preparation of summons and complaint) to ACS, the contractor: *Denver v. Pirosko*, County Court of Denver, Case No. S003143859 (Jan. 28, 2002). The City dropped 446 pending photo-radar cases as a result of this case.

of citations issued exceeds a certain number per month. ACS is involved in processing tickets and also provides input on choosing locations for camera deployment (McElhatton 2005).

Clearly if police, through outsourcing, lose control over service volume or distribution decisions that influence the magnitude of contractor payments, there is scope for the contractor's self-interest to operate in ways that serve the public interest poorly. This is not to suggest that the public interest is always protected by police control over service provision. With technologies that lend themselves to revenue generation, such as traffic safety cameras, there can be the potential for abuse in either private or public hands. The U.K. London Safety Camera Partnership (LSCP) says, however, that safety cameras are employed not to generate revenue but to reduce casualty rates on the roads, so that falling revenue should be taken as indicative of success. As all revenue from that initiative goes either to the U.K. Treasury as general revenue or is channelled back to the LSCP to cover costs (London Safety Camera Partnership 2005), there is very little incentive in that country for either law enforcement or private contractors to attempt to increase that revenue.

Quality issues. As mentioned earlier, another risk associated with employing others to undertake tasks for one is that the service or good provided may not be the best quality. Quality may have implications for the safety of operational officers and of the public and, by extension, the reputation of the police department. Even selecting a reputable supplier does not guarantee quality. In New Zealand, IBM was selected in 1994 to develop an Integrated National Computerised Information System (INCIS) for the police. When IBM walked away from the project five years later, the parts of the system that had been completed were criticized for not operating as promised (Dore 1999). In the United States, new software was introduced in October 2004 to replace the local emergency dispatch, records management and jail administration systems in Washington state with a seamless system created by Intergraph Corporation. Problems with the quality of the new system have led to backlogs and inefficiencies, resulting in a call by an evaluation committee to make costly changes to both the system and its management (Fitzpatrick, 2005a, 2005b, 2005c; Trumbo, 2005).

Internal police difficulties. Of course, problems with outsourced contracts may not always flow from the unreliability of the chosen supplier. Sometimes the contract is poorly managed (so that, for instance, the supplier is not properly aware of expectations) or there are circumstances internal to the organisation that militate against the successful implementation of the project. The FBI outsourced to Science Applications International Corporation in 2001 the task of overhauling the Bureau's investigative systems, known as the TRILOGY User Application Component (UAC) project, costing U.S. $170 million. The aim of the project was to reshape the FBI's paper-driven culture and replace antiquated computer systems, something seen as critical to national security and the fight against terrorism. The project went over budget and ran behind schedule and is now unlikely ever to be fully implemented. An evaluation of the program in January 2005, costing U.S. $2 million, found that internal problems, such as a high turnover of IT staff, difficulties in finding the downtime from caseloads to implement the system and, most critically, a resistance amongst some agents to giving up pens and paper, contributed significantly to this result (Lichtblau 2005).

Legal problems. Large legal bills and rectification costs for police organisations and governments can result from poorly managed contracts, unreliable suppliers or unforeseen events associated with procurement and outsourcing arrangements. INCIS was three years overdue and N.Z. $30 million over budget when the New Zealand Government launched legal action against IBM relating to a dispute over contracted tasks. Problems with the financial management of a contract entered into in 1999 between Victoria Police and IBM Global Services (a joint venture between IBM, Telstra and Lend Lease) to provide mainframe and desktop services in up to 400 Victorian police stations resulted in lengthy disputes and a blow-out in outsourcing costs of more than $AUD100 million (Shiel 2003).

Information technology systems that provide an interface between government and third parties can spawn particularly costly legal problems when they fail. The Australian Customs Service recently replaced its twenty-year-old cargo clearance system with a new Integrated Cargo System designed to clear both import and export cargo much faster. New documentation requirements resulted in entire transactions being rejected and sent to the end of the processing queue, with the result that thousands of containers were left sitting for days and even weeks at Australian ports. In addition, there were reported security problems which allowed some customers to see each other's data. With evidence that Customs knew, at the time of approving the new software, that its old hardware did not have the requisite processing capacity, and in the absence of a compensation offer by the federal government, many affected businesses considered whether to take legal action against the government to seek compensation for the costs of storage, loss of business and staff overtime, and possibly employee stress (Bajkowski 2005; Australian Associated Press 2005; Hayes 2005).

Accountability and liability issues. Issues about accountability for poor service may also arise in relation to contracts for goods or services. Questions arise such as: who bears ultimate responsibility for the performance of contractors? Is there political as well as managerial responsibility? Do members of the public have access to redress for the actions or omissions of contractors and, if so, against whom? What remedies are available to them? And what mechanisms are available for investigation (internal police enquiries? Ombudsman? Auditor-General?) if things go awry? Mulgan (2001) points out that one cannot assume that accountability is a simple quantum that is increased, maintained or reduced under outsourcing – it will depend on the context. Certain activities generate very high expectations of accountability. Police matters tend to be one of these, because people see a direct connection between their taxes and spending on law and order matters, and also have high expectations of the probity of those entrusted with ensuring public security.

To bring to bear the complete array of public service accountability standards on private contractors may well diminish the gains in efficiency and cost made through outsourcing. To not do so may be politically unacceptable, especially in a sensitive area like policing.

"You can't outsource risk" was the belief expressed to us by one procurement manager of a large Australian police department. Getting the balance right in terms of accountability and transparency of process is a difficult task for police.

Police image and legitimacy. Police also have to contend with public perceptions that arise out of their procurement and outsourcing of goods and services. There is a risk that suppliers of services that were previously provided by police will not have the same high standards as police and that this will reflect badly on the police service as a whole. Similarly, the use by police of a particular brand of good (for instance, a particular vehicle manufacturer) could link police with the producer in the public's mind, something that could backfire if there is any subsequent scandal concerning that product or if police are called upon to investigate the producer.

Outsourcing of some services could present problems for police-community relations. Some members of the public may feel cheated if the person delivering a service (say, advice on home security measures or responses to emergency service calls or noise complaints) is not a police officer. Public demand for a more visible community-based police presence is increasing (Salmi et al. 2005; Crawford 2006b). The police themselves do not want to become 'harder to find'.[17] Yet services which do not fit a classical crime-fighting or law enforcement profile, those that are more community-oriented and preventative, are perhaps the services most likely to be classed as 'noncore' and so liable to be outsourced. This is particularly the case if decisions over which services are outsourced continue to be made with little or no public consultation (Davids and Hancock 1998: 51).

Staff resistance. Outsourcing worries many within police ranks, too. There is concern that outsourcing will cause a loss of police skills

[17] One submission to the New Zealand Review of Police Administration and Management Structures conducted in 1998, in discussing the possibility of outsourcing speed camera operations, stated, "The public see traffic cameras as police and often stop to report bad driving, accidents etc. Remove this and the police are even harder to find" (New Zealand Review Team 1998: 29).

(Singer 2003:161) or of police jobs,[18] and that officers will be rede-ployed without their consent or will leave the police to take up contract employment with suppliers. The Police Federation of Australia's (PFA) national policy relating to civilianisation of police forces and the use of unsworn officers "totally rejects the use of civilianisation/unsworn to downsize police numbers in any jurisdiction", arguing that the sole justification for the use of civilians and unsworn officers is to release limited operational resources to more effectively meet the community's needs. These same arguments were made by the PFA in discussions in relation to the outsourcing of those positions. The PFA also expressed concern that outsourcing may remove 'desk jobs' from police departments, leaving nowhere for sworn officers recovering from illness or injury to go during rehabilitation.

There are also more general concerns about the security of police information and systems, the effect on police relationships with the public and the overall cost-effectiveness and quality of outsourced services.[19] The occupational health and safety of police officers is also considered to be put at risk by outsourcing. There may be circumstances when civilian employees or contractors who engage in industrial action might place the safety of sworn police officers at risk. As a result of these concerns, staff morale is clearly an issue when outsourcing of services is being considered.

Inequities in service provision. Lastly, outsourcing also raises the spectre of inequitable distribution of policing services. A service that is no longer provided by the police could be outsourced in such a way that the supplier can charge for its provision. This would have obvious consequences for those who cannot afford these services. In

[18] Personal communication with Police Federation of Australia (PFA), January 2006. See also Australian Federal Police Organisation 2001.
[19] These concerns are drawn from submissions to the New Zealand 1998 Review of Police Administration and Management Structures Team that canvassed outsourcing of prisoner escort/custody, scene guarding, infringement processing, speed camera operation, document serving, commercial vehicle investigation, search and rescue, photography, video unit, lost and found, communication centres, information technology, property management, fleet ownership/maintenance, stores, payroll, management review and audit, accounting, records, cafeteria and welfare.

1998, a review of the management and administrative structure of the New Zealand Police considered the possibility of outsourcing the police's search and rescue function (New Zealand Independent Reviewer 1998: 19). The idea was ultimately rejected by the review team, mainly because there was no alternative organisation then in existence which had the expertise and experience to coordinate search and rescue activities. Likely charging of those who needed rescue, and the consequences of this, were raised as issues in submissions to the review (New Zealand Review Team 1998: 31), but this was not determinative, and the outsourcing of search and rescue was flagged as something that needed more consideration (New Zealand Independent Reviewer 1998: 47 para. 163). The effects of charging may be a willingness to take more risks (in terms of trying to rescue oneself) rather than pay. This may seem extreme, but in Grand County, Utah, where the Sheriff's department charges for search and rescue, rescuers have been asked by imperilled tourists about cost before being given permission to complete a rescue (Associated Press 2005).

Murphy (2002: 32) suggests that "focusing limited police resources on only core policing functions while cutting, limiting or selling other services, unfairly places the onus on citizens and communities either to self-police or hire private security; a strategy that favours the advantaged and weakens collective social relationships and obligations". Choosing to buy policing services may not just be a matter of necessity; it may also be attractive to some as a means of "distinguishing themselves (symbolically) from those who remain dependent for their security on a cash-strapped, seemingly unresponsive public service" (Loader 1999: 383). It is questionable whether police would wish to represent themselves as supportive of a system where those who cannot pay perhaps miss out on an adequate level of service.

On the other hand, there is no doubt that expecting police to do everything also can have consequences for the equitable application of policing services. Schönteich (2004b) notes that in South Africa the public is not now equally serviced by police, as the density of police and their willingness to intervene in violent situations is lower in less affluent areas. It may be, as he argues (p. 24), that outsourcing provides a wider choice of services at a lower cost, supplied more effectively and with less delay. Because of this, and because the state is better able to concentrate on its core functions, the poor may benefit rather than suffer from a rationalisation of policing services implemented through outsourcing.

Commodification of policing. The increasing focus on the bottom line in policing and the creative responses from management to resource acquisition and allocation that this has stimulated have been characterised as reflecting "commodification" of policing services (Loader 1999). Davids and Hancock talk about the shift in both language and approach in public policing, from regarding the public as citizens, part of the community, to regarding it as a collection of individual 'customers' to be 'sold' policing.

However, a private sector 'customer service' approach may just not be appropriate where citizens are just as concerned with more general outcomes of policing for society as they are with their own satisfaction (Davids and Hancock 1998: 60). According to Loader, when people recoil from commodification of police services it is because it entails a transformation of the police/public relationship that does not accord with their world views (or metapreferences), which include a concern that the common good be advanced and involve a "rejection of the idea that respect for human safety can be privatised, deregulated and generally be left to individuals to secure as best they can in the market" (1999: 388). The risk is real that, with an excessive focus on individual agreements, policing will omit to take account of broader societal interests. As Davids and Hancock point out, "there are other less obvious aspects of public and political accountability and public interest that are simply not mentioned in contracts" (1998: 57).

Safeguards
There is no doubt that shopping by the public police involves a number of risks for both the police themselves and for the communities they serve. But withdrawal of police from the market environment is not now a realistic option. However, a number of systems can be put in place to reduce the risks inherent in shopping. In

approximate chronological order of the procurement process, these include:

Before-the-fact open consultation on decisions to outsource services. The New Zealand 1998 Review of Police Administration and Management Structures attracted more than 560 submissions from police staff and persons outside the police. In addition, the Police Commissioner held meetings with staff around the country to get direct feedback on the draft Report. Whilst outsourcing was only one of five areas examined in the Review (along with governance, organisational structure, training and property management), it attracted a significant response; the majority of submissions dealt at least partially with the outsourcing issue. It seems that decisions about outsourcing of police services are of considerable import for both police and others because of their implications for the role of the police in society. However, few opportunities currently exist for lower level police or the public to have an input into those final decisions, with police management tending to make such decisions behind closed doors. A degree of transparency in decision-making in this area would ensure the airing of public interest considerations that might well be given too little attention in the more corporate environment in which the police now find themselves operating.

Such a process could lessen the risk of internal resistance, as well as enhance the wider public legitimacy of the acquisitions process.

'Good' contracts. Rules have broad application but they cannot deal with individual commercial relations at a sufficient level of detail to avoid or anticipate problems arising. 'Good' contracts are essential to avoid a waste of police resources in "constantly *'firefighting'* issues" with the contractor (Victorian Auditor-General's Office 2003b: para 2.168). Contracts need to be properly negotiated, with precise specification of tasks to be undertaken or results to be achieved (Kelman 2002: 305–6), and comprehensive provisions concerning monitoring, dispute resolution and termination. This would have obvious benefit in addressing the risks that legal and quality problems will arise.

Assistance in contract negotiation and management. As noted above, police (especially those in smaller agencies) often do not have the training or resources to properly negotiate and manage procurement contracts.[20] Training in these circumstances becomes critical. It is essential too that training is not simply focussed on the 'pointy' business end of the process (what is a fair price, what too low a price could mean for the future of the relationship, how to monitor the contractor and resolve disputes etc.) but also deals with the special issues that apply because of the nature of policing, such as the broader role of police in serving the public and what this might mean for the extent of discretion a contractor should be granted. Such assistance could provide quality assurance, as well as safeguard against excessive costs and overdependency.

Monitoring mechanisms for service contracts. Internal systems for monitoring the way in which contracted tasks are being performed need to be strong to keep contractors honest and avoid "shirking" (Kelman 2002: 302, 306). The costs of monitoring need to be included when considering the costs of outsourcing to particular suppliers.

Reporting mechanisms and internal audits. In addition to monitoring systems for the contractor, police systems to monitor the internal processes involved in procurement need to be in place. A lack of such systems will increase the risks of collusion between staff and contractors (Doherty and March 2005). The benefits of both monitoring and reporting mechanisms for accountability and corruption control are readily apparent.

Independent review of outsourcing decisions. A potential for independent review works to mitigate risks that arise from the intimacy that commercial relationships often generate.

---

[20] This problem is not exclusive to police, of course. In the Australian Capital Territory, the use of junior public servants to undertake purchasing for Territory Government Departments has been criticized by the Auditor-General, who said that such officers generally did not have the technical knowledge needed to ensure value for money: see Doherty and March, 2005.

> Transparency and group decisionmaking are important ways to
> reduce the danger of corruption, particularly in best-value source
> selections that give government officials greater discretion. It is
> relatively easy to corrupt even rule-bound officials if the grounds
> for decision can be kept secret. (Kelman 2002: 300)

Independent review could take the form of review by government
appointed auditors or, where outsourcing decisions are made public,
scrutiny by the media. Nations such as the United States and Australia
have established some institutions at federal level to perform such
oversight functions: the U.S. Government Accountability Office[21]
and the Australian National Audit Office. But with many police
departments located at lower levels (state, county and municipality),
particularly in the United States, there is clearly scope to further
consider more local forms that independent review could take in
these contexts, such as civilian oversight. A number of cities in the
United States have put in place civilian oversight mechanisms
designed to monitor police compliance with civil rights requirements
and to investigate civilian complaints. For example, the Los Angeles
Police Department uses independent monitors (Los Angeles Police
Department 2007), and in Albuquerque a 1998 Ordinance, the Police
Oversight Commission Ordinance, put in place a civilian Police
Oversight Commission and an Independent Review Office. Such
mechanisms may also be suitable for addressing policing policies and
practices that lead to police misconduct in the context of commercial
relationships.

Legislative oversight. Rules contained in legislation, delegated
legislation and formally promulgated policies and guidelines, like the
U.S. Procurement Integrity Act and the VGPB Procurement Policies,
are able to set standards in relation to fairness in selection of sources
and other questions of probity, ensure appropriate measures to
protect confidentiality are in place and prohibit fraudulent and collusive activities that might arise in the course of commercial relationships. Independent external oversight, provided by specialised

---

[21]   For an illustration of GAO oversight of procurement by the FBI, see Government
Accountability Office 2005.

audit agencies as well as by legislatures, can serve to enhance the legitimacy of the procurement process.

Conclusion

Police departments, and the men and women who manage them, are very different to their counterparts of a half-century ago. Developments in technology, and the increasing complexity of advanced industrial societies, have been accompanied by revolutionary changes in organisational life. This has entailed a diversification of the police function to include the acquisition of an increasingly wider range of goods and services. This in turn has necessitated a significant investment in the management of contracts and the monitoring of compliance with them. Police, like many other public sector organisations, are performing the role of meta-monitors (Grabosky 1995). Managerial skill is an essential prerequisite for appointment to the senior ranks. This new role has its benefits and its risks.

Thought has been given in many quarters to general principles to guide procurement and outsourcing decisions in the public sector, with transparency, accountability and the balancing of interests seen as integral to the process (Commercial Activities Panel 2002). The question is whether these principles translate directly to public policing. For example, should the police outsourcing framework "represent a balance among taxpayer interests, government needs, employee rights, and contractor concerns" as suggested is ideal for all government agencies in the United States (mission statement of the Commercial Activities Panel 2002: 7)? Or does the special nature of police work mean that policing is an area that requires distinctive measures? Decisions about what to outsource and to what degree a contractor should be granted discretion will perhaps be ones where police should give particular thought to how the public will be affected. Giving equal weight to contractor, police, government and taxpayer interests may not be appropriate here. Similarly, protection of confidential information may also be an area that requires more thought than in some other government agencies, given the sensitivity of information to which police become privy.

Decisions by police organisations about shopping for goods and services have very important ramifications for the public, for the scope of the police role and for the public's perception of public police and policing. When one considers the variety of risks to both police and the public interest that can arise in this context, it becomes apparent that transparency and accountability are critical. Sound and robust systems for risk management must be put in place, together with proper training and resourcing for police in developing and administering such systems. Most important, decisions about procurement and outsourcing need to be made in an environment where the links between the operational and non-operational sides of policing are both recognised and regarded as central. Consultation with those affected – police, members of the public and business – can help ensure that all relevant considerations are taken into account.

Such strategies as we have advanced in this chapter operate mainly at a modest and technical level. Issues about police legitimacy and image, about the implications of increasing marketplace activity for how the police see themselves and for the interests of the wider community, may not be so easily addressed. Increased police activity in the marketplace, of which shopping is an important part, represents a fundamental structural shift in policing driven by changing ideological, economic and pragmatic considerations. There can be no rapid-fire or simple solutions to the deeper structural risks brought on as a result.

What does the increasing shopping activity of police mean for the future of policing? For those who see an increasing pluralization of policing, the ascendancy of outsourcing may represent a transitional stage between policing as a state monopoly (as it largely was during the mid-twentieth century) and an increasingly competitive security market, where the public police will be but one among several players. For those who embrace a more state-centric model of policing, these new developments will liberate the police from dependency on their own resources, provide them with greater freedom of choice, and enable them to realise economies and thereby achieve more with less. But here it must be asked, are the police up to the job? How well the public police perform as shoppers will be indicative of their ability to manage the broader structural shifts occurring in policing. Can they rise to the greater challenge of performing in, as well as directing, a play with many performers? In a sense, the future of

policing will be foreshadowed in the competence of police as consumers.

PART 2: POLICE AS PURCHASERS OF INFORMATION

As Ericson and Haggerty (1997) have observed, a great deal of policing
is about managing information. The acquisition of that information is
an important policing task. Police acquire information in a number of
ways. They are informed when crime victims, or other members of the
public, call particular offences or other matters to their attention. Police
also collect information by observing what is around them. The astute
police officer will recognize anomalies that are imperceptible, or barely
perceptible to the layperson (Gladwell 2005).

But police also pay for information. They may engage the services
of information retrieval specialists, such as Jane's and ChoicePoint,
who collect open-source intelligence for a fee (Hoofnagle 2004) They
may offer rewards to members of the public who come forward with
information leading to the arrest and/or conviction of the perpetrator
of a (usually heinous) crime. Or they can pay individual informants[22]
to obtain information that might be useful in preventing crime or
prosecuting criminals. We focus first on rewards to members of the
general public, then on the engagement of specific individuals as
informants.

Rewards to Members of the Public

Offers of reward to citizens for assistance in enforcing the law have a
rich tradition. The professional sycophants of ancient Greece were
rewarded for disclosing illegality on the part of their fellow citizens.
In the United Kingdom, before the development of professional law
enforcement agencies, governments offered rewards for the capture
of criminal offenders, as did the offenders' more affluent victims
(Radzinowicz 1956a:112). Reward provisions were by no means

---

[22] Australian police organisations have chosen to replace the term "informant" with
"human source". The FBI refers to "assets". For the sake of brevity, we will here
continue to use the term "informant".

limited to what today one would call 'street crime', but extended also to regulatory compliance. A fourteenth century English statute specified that 25% of fines imposed on stallholders engaged in trade after the close of a fair be paid to citizens intervening on behalf of the King (5 Edw III, ch. 5 (1331); Boyer and Meidinger 1985, 948).[23]

Rewards to tax informers in France were made from the early eighteenth century. During the nineteenth century, the 'tax ferret', a subspecies of tax informer, was used to complement the administration of property taxation in Ohio and several other of the United States. Third parties informing on taxpayers who concealed assets from tax authorities were entitled to receive a percentage of fines or surcharges imposed on the offender (Herber 1960, Ch. 2).

Provisions for informers' rewards have existed under U.S. federal law since 1791. The U.S. Internal Revenue Service offers the prospect of reward to citizens who assist in the identification of individuals violating tax laws (IRC s.7623).[24] The U.S. Securities and Exchange Commission, under the Insider Trading and Securities Fraud Enforcement Act of 1988 (15 USC s.78u-1(e)), can award bounties for assistance in identifying persons engaged in insider trading. And in the aftermath of the Savings and Loan scandal of the 1980s, the Financial Institutions Anti-Fraud Enforcement Act of 1990 (18 USC s.3059A) provided for rewards to persons furnishing information to the government concerning offences relating to federally insured financial institutions. The precursor to modern U.S. environmental protection legislation, the Refuse Act of 1899, authorised citizen-informants to receive up to half of the amount of fine imposed upon a convicted offender (33 USC s.411(12)).

Another instrument of third party enforcement which is receiving increasing attention and use in the United States is the False Claims

---

[23] The cause of action whereby citizens were empowered to sue on behalf of the state became known as *Qui Tam* (*qui tam pro domino rege quam pro se ipso in hac parte sequitur*) which may be translated as "who brings the action for the king as well as for oneself" (Caminker 1989).

[24] The practice dates to the early days of the U.S. government. For a history of rewards to tax informers, see Herber (1960). The federal government has recently strengthened the tax whistleblower program in new provision Section 406 of the Tax Relief and Health Care Act of 2006: see http://www.taxwhistleblowers.org/main/page.php?page_id=14 (accessed 4 July 2008).

Act, which enables citizens who become aware of frauds perpetrated against the Federal Government to bring civil actions against the perpetrator (31 USC s.3730).[25] The Act was introduced during the Civil War to combat unscrupulous conduct by contractors to the Union Army. Since its reincarnation in 1986, the False Claims Act has served as the basis for numerous citizen suits, most of which have been brought by employees alleging fraud on the part of defence contractors, and more recently against perpetrators of large-scale medical benefits fraud. The government itself has the discretion to join the action, or it may remain at arm's length if it so chooses. In the event it joins and the action succeeds, up to 25 percent of the damages may be awarded to the citizen-plaintiff, with the majority going to the federal treasury. If the government does not proceed with the action and it is successful, the citizen-plaintiff receives up to 30 percent of the proceeds plus expenses.

Justifications. Justifications for the use of rewards relate primarily to their necessity, that is, the lack of a viable alternative means to acquire crucial information, and to the advantages for legitimacy that flow from their noncoercive nature. We deal with these in turn.

Necessity. Incentives may be necessary to enlist the assistance of the general public when conventional police powers and resources are inadequate to detect or investigate the misconduct in question. This is particularly so in many cases of organized crime generally, or of corporate or white collar illegality, where the misconduct in question is covert, and likely to remain beyond the gaze of enforcement authorities in the normal course of events. Where police resources are themselves constrained, third party assistance may be essential to the detection and investigation of the criminal behaviour in question.

Such assistance may not be immediately forthcoming, as the cost to third parties of assisting the police can at times be prohibitive. Under

---

[25] See also Barger et al. (2005); Callahan and Dworkin (1992); Caminker (1989). Individual citizen-plaintiffs stand to receive millions of dollars, depending upon the size of the fraud they challenge.

such circumstances, incentives may be necessary to encourage action that would entail extraordinary burdens or risks. Although one might question the morality of appeals to mercenary impulses rather than to altruism, the justification for offering monetary incentives to citizens who assist in the identification of tax evaders, fraudulent government contractors, or murderers rests in the recognition that these citizens are providing a valuable public service – one which could entail considerable expenditure if performed by public employees. The expense of private enforcement is such that third party assistance, whether in the form of citizen suits or the provision of information to law enforcement authorities, might not be feasible in the absence of some provisions for cost recovery. *Qui tam* actions are not costless undertakings; they may require years of preparation and many thousands of dollars in legal expenses (Phillips 1992: 65). Suits brought under the False Claims Act can be complex and resource intensive. When they are energetically defended, they can entail legal costs running into the millions.

One might also consider the situation faced by the employee who 'blows the whistle' on corporate illegality. The personal costs of this disclosure may be formidable whether in professional, social or financial terms (Glazer and Glazer 1989: ch. 5). The retaliatory power of the target individual or firm may be substantial; the whistle blower may be threatened, harassed or ostracised, and their financial security jeopardised. The threat of retaliation can be a significant deterrent to disclosure, and simple whistleblower protection mechanisms may be insufficient. The prospect of a reward can help compensate for these disincentives.

Coming forward with information can also be dangerous. In 1952, a young New Yorker, Arnold Schuster, provided information to police on the location of a notorious criminal, Willie "The Actor" Sutton. Schuster's identity and role in Sutton's arrest received media attention, and he was shot to death within a month.[26]

---

[26] The administrator of Schuster's estate sued the city of New York for wrongful death, arguing that police should have provided Schuster some protection in light of his visibility. *Schuster v. New York*, 5 N.Y.2d 75; 154 N.E.2d 534; 180 N.Y.S.2d 265 (1958 N.Y.)

Legitimacy. Incentives are more likely to be perceived as legitimate and are less likely to alienate their subject than coercion. The threat to legitimacy from coercive instruments of control, such as mandatory reporting requirements, was noted in Chapter 3. Absent careful management, coercive control through negative sanctions may produce feelings of resentment, alienation, and may lead to dysfunctional behaviour on the part of its recipient (Arnold 1989: 142). Rewards are easier to swallow.

The Downside of Rewards. The downside of rewards arises from their potential to 'commercialize' citizenship, from the risk that the administration of a rewards program may be less accountable, and from a culture of bounty hunting and mistrust that the institution of rewards can foster.

Negative Motivational Consequences. The availability of incentives implies freedom to choose, but this element of choice has its shortcomings. The function of reward as a signal that a particular course of action is desirable may also be perceived as a signal that a particular course of action is optional (Schwartz and Orleans 1967). As noted earlier, the discretion to forego activity which, because of its social desirability, might lead to reward is different from the decision to forego activity which, because of its potential for harm, might lead to punishment. With a reward, one can, quite simply, pass it up and go about one's business.

Goodin (1980: 139–40) argues that rather than supplementing moral incentives, material incentives tend to erode them. He alerts us to the risk that noble motives will be eclipsed by baser ones. Smith and Stalans (1991: 44) have also observed that the instrumental focus of reward tends to displace normative considerations, and that extrinsic reward can undermine intrinsic motivation. Geis et al. (1991: 79) speculate that cooperation with law enforcement authorities may become increasingly driven not by public-spiritedness but by financial consideration. These arguments are based on substantial evidence from social psychology. Research on incentive and motivation suggests that the availability of extrinsic reward does indeed diminish intrinsic motivation (Deci and Ryan 1985: 44–48; Braithwaite 2002: 16–17).

Another criticism of incentives, whether for direct compliance or for third party assistance, is based on the argument that citizens should not be rewarded for actions that are the normal responsibilities of citizenship. The idea of monetizing civic norms strikes one as no less preposterous than that of paying people to obey the law (Levmore 1986). Citizens should not be rewarded for doing their duty, but rather punished for failing to do so.

Just as instruments of public policy can foster or inhibit altruistic expression, so, too, can they contribute to the commercialization of citizenship. Acts are deprived of genuine self-sacrifice when they are turned into routine compliance with the law (Rudzinski 1966: 105). If legal compulsion deprives a virtuous act of its ethical basis, so, too, might payment. In his classic study comparing commercial and voluntary systems of blood donation, Titmuss (1971) argued that the existence of commercial markets for blood could contribute to the erosion of altruistic expression, and ultimately detract from the quality of human relationships. This suggests there is a real risk that cultural values will move away from the spirit of voluntarism and civic obligation toward those suited to a society of mercenaries as citizens. Few would favour any system of social control that is largely driven by opportunistic bounty hunters.

Accountability. Another reservation about the use of reward, and by no means a uniquely modern concern, is that of accountability. Reward systems have been criticised as less accountable than those systems based on negative sanctions. Activities of government that are explicitly coercive tend to invite more public scrutiny. If, as suggested by Freiberg (1986) and by Neiman (1980), losing a reward is tantamount to receiving a punishment, processes by which rewards are administered should be accountable and based on procedural safeguards. The best police services have in place a structured process to ensure that decisions about rewards are objective, consistent and made at an appropriate level.

Where accountability is lacking, an informant may take advantage of the situation. One of the potential risks inherent in reward systems is that of moral hazard (Levmore 1986: 886). The incentive to orchestrate an offence in order to claim a reward for its detection or prosecution is hardly a novel idea. One imaginative practitioner who succeeded for a time was the celebrated eighteenth-century thief-taker Jonathan Wild (Howson, 1970). Until his arrangements were discovered, Wild practiced at two complementary professions. On the one hand, he would recover lost property for a commission; on the other, he operated simultaneously as a receiver of stolen goods. Such ironies are by no means limited to eighteenth-century property crime. Prior to a recent amendment, it was possible for the architect of a fraud against the U.S. government to seek a reward under the False Claims Act (Phillips 1992: 72).

Some informants may be tempted to fabricate an offence, for a variety of reasons. And reward programs also carry the potential for blackmail. A prospective informer may demand payment from a violator as a condition of refraining from disclosure. As long as the amount demanded is less than the expected costs (financial and nonmaterial) which would flow from official knowledge of noncompliance, it will be in the violator's interest to pay "hush money".

Trust. A system of rewards to third parties for enforcement assistance poses a threat to interpersonal trust. Networks of surveillance supported by citizen informers were among the foundation stones of the totalitarian dictatorships of the twentieth-century. Among the greatest threats to political freedom in modern liberal democracies is the ethos of informing such as that which characterised the McCarthy era in the United States.

Overzealous citizens, encouraged by incentives, may transform society into one where no one can escape the intrusive gaze of others. It requires no imagination to understand how the availability of pecuniary reward can invite bounty-hunting. Even in the absence of material incentives, private citizens may not always be motivated by a sense of public service or civic virtue. The motivations for informing and the impacts on society are explored further in Chapter 6.

Paid Informants

There are additional circumstances in which citizens may contribute to criminal investigation and prosecution. They may do so freely, for purposes of revenge, perceived civic responsibility or 'just for the buzz'. The primary concern in this chapter, however, is with those in which the police offer a degree of remuneration or other inducement for

1. assistance of a covert nature; or
2. serving as a witness in criminal proceedings.

Individuals may be recruited to observe or to infiltrate a criminal enterprise, or to introduce an undercover law enforcement officer to participants in such an enterprise. Alternatively, a co-participant in a criminal enterprise may choose to abandon his or her partners in crime, and to offer, for a fee, to assist the government in the investigation and/or prosecution of the offence.

In some cases, essential intelligence or critical evidence may only be available through direct purchase. The Drug Enforcement Administration of the United States, for example, states that it could not effectively enforce the country's controlled substances laws without the assistance of informants (OIG Audit Division 2005). Organized criminal activity often involves parties other than reputable businesspeople, and is conducted under circumstances designed to escape the vigilance of police. In the imperfect world that we inhabit, few respectable citizens command detailed knowledge of the underworld, and those citizens who do command sufficient knowledge to be of assistance to enforcement authorities are unlikely to be selfless paragons of virtue. It is not uncommon for such knowledgeable people to offer to provide useful information, but only in return for some consideration. Knowledge of complex illegalities may also be limited to associates of the offender, and their willingness to disclose may come at a price.

The choice often faced by enforcement authorities in many cases is to pay up, or to forego enforcement altogether. To this end, U.S. federal law enforcement agencies budget tens of millions of dollars each year for compensation to informants (Marx 1992a: 199). Under the circumstances, law enforcement agents must engage in a cost-benefit calculus, to decide whether the information and assistance to be gained, or proceeds of crime which might be recovered, are worth the investment (Geis et al. 1991).

No knowledgeable citizen of an English-speaking democracy would seriously contend that their criminal justice system operates flawlessly. Among the more current concerns is the risk of mistake or caprice arising from the use of criminal informants for assistance in investigation or prosecution. As in many other areas of public policy, the use of informants for purposes of investigating and prosecuting criminal offences may entail unforeseen costs and unintended consequences.

The benefits of paid informants. The engagement of informants may be essential to the acquisition of certain critical information. The arrest of Ramzi Yusef – later convicted for the World Trade Center bombing in 1993 – is but one example (Kash 2002). Billingsley, Nemitz and Bean (2001: 5) observe that one third of all crimes cleared up by police involve the use of informers. They believe this alone justifies their use. One Australian police officer we spoke to referred to informants as "corporate assets".

The paid informant can be a more precise instrument of criminal intelligence and investigation than those that are conventionally available. Paid informants may be given specific tasks and directions beyond those that might be asked of ordinary citizens (Soto 1998; Hight 2000). Compensation may be made contingent upon performance of a specific act or upon the acquisition of specific information.

Using informants can also be a cost-effective technique. Obtaining the information by other means might be impossible or prohibitively expensive (Innes 2000; Kash 2002; Settle 1995; Ratcliffe 2002). A British Audit Commission Report (Audit Commission 1993) concluded that the use of informants was indeed cost-effective. Many notorious crimes have been solved because of crucial information provided by paid informants.

The hidden and not-so-hidden costs of paid informants. The use of paid informants is fraught with risk. Persons engaged as informants for purposes of assisting in a criminal investigation are hardly selected at random. If not recruited directly from the milieu that is the very focus of investigative attention, they tend to be drawn from compatible social circumstances. As such, they are likely to be practiced at the art of deception, if not criminals themselves. Some may indeed be skilled in treachery. Rarely are they paragons of virtue and honesty.

Informants are thus unlikely to be motivated by a commitment to efficiency and effectiveness in the administration of criminal justice, much less to the rule of law. Some will be driven by mercenary considerations. Others may be attracted by the ease of access to illegal commodities that their participation may provide. For others, who are facing or who could face criminal charges, the motive will be indemnity from prosecution or perhaps a reduction in charges. Others still may be driven by vengeance, and may seek to use their position to settle old scores. Still others may seek to eliminate competitors (Soto 1998; Bean 1996). One senior Australian police officer told us, "When you really understand a human source's motivation, you can manage them accordingly." Another put it more forcefully: "You *must* understand their motivation to manage them." But this fundamental contradiction between the interests of the informant and the interests of the government does pose numerous problems for police.

While the use of informants may strike some idealists as inconsistent with the basic principles of a free and democratic society, pragmatists will argue that informants are essential to combat a range of criminal activity, particularly that involving corruption or drug traffic. Rather than join this debate, we shall acknowledge that authorities have used and will continue to use informants. Our purpose here is to suggest how, given this continued use, the risks of collateral harm to innocent third parties, to the legitimacy of the police institution and to the rule of law may be minimised.

Criminal activity. The use of informants may create opportunities and incentives for illegal or otherwise unethical behaviour, by informants alone or in collaboration with police investigators. These risks highlight the importance of professional handling techniques.

Criminal conduct by an informant in furtherance of an investigation may take place at the conscious direction of a law enforcement officer, or with the officer's implicit condonation or passive tolerance. It may also be committed without the officer's knowledge, contrary to her explicit instructions. The extent of government complicity in an informant's criminality is a fundamental matter. This can entail putting law enforcement officers, or unwitting members of the public, in harm's way. Informants may also seek to deceive or to corrupt their police 'handlers.' Ultimately, these undesirable consequences may have adverse impacts on the legitimacy, and on the budget, of the police organisation. Is it all worth it?

CRIMINAL ACTIVITY AS DIRECTED. At one extreme, the government may actually solicit the commission of a crime, one that otherwise would not have occurred, in order to further an investigation. It may specifically direct the informant to engage in criminal activity or be vague in its instructions, leaving details to the informant's discretion. The issue at hand is whether the informant is 'creating' a crime that would otherwise not take place, or whether simply providing an opportunity for a predisposed offender to fall into a trap. Consider the 'reverse sting' where an informant sells contraband to a suspect who is subsequently charged. Here one may wish to make a distinction between a target chosen at random and a target selected on the basis of probable cause, or because of some apparent predisposition to commit the offence.

Not all offenders snared by informants are criminal masterminds. In one case, police used an informant to set up a drug factory. They provided him with equipment and chemicals necessary to begin production, and even provided the premises for the factory. The informant then enlisted the menial assistance of an individual who, although knowing that the activity was illegal, contributed no expertise, ideas, funds, or capital equipment to the enterprise. The menial assistant was prosecuted (*United States v. Twigg* 588 F.2d (3rd Cir. 1978)).

The most progressive jurisdictions specify the limits of permissible conduct in considerable detail. The United Kingdom's Regulation of Investigatory Powers Act 2000 Chapter II and the Australian Crimes Act 1914 Part IAB provide examples.

GRATUITOUS CRIMINAL ACTIVITY ARISING FROM OVERZEA-
LOUSNESS. In some cases, informants may get carried away by market forces. The inducement offered to an informant, whether monetary
or procedural, may be made contingent upon the success of an operation. Such use of contingent fee arrangements would appear to be
particularly risky, as it may invite overzealous conduct on the part of the
informant. In the event of a prosecution, these arrangements are likely
to be called into question by the defence.

Of questionable propriety are contingency fees offered to an
informant to produce evidence against a particular suspect for crimes
not yet committed, or those offered for the number of 'scalps' collected. In one Florida case, an informant was promised payment
contingent upon his successfully making criminal cases against others
to whom he was to sell cannabis (*State v. Glosson* 441 So. 2d 1178 (Fla
1st DCA 1983)). An informant engaged by the U.S. Drug Enforcement Administration testified that he received 25 percent of whatever
money the agency seized during those stings in which he participated. (*United States v. Estrada* 256 F.3d 466 (2001) at 471). In one
complex money laundering investigation, an informant was entitled
to a commission of 0.7 percent of the funds laundered during the
investigation, capped at US$10,000 per month (*United States v.
Cuellar* 96 F.3d 1179 (1996)).

Contingent remuneration or contingent immunity may provide
perverse incentives for an informant to commit perjury. Marx (1988:
134–5) cites an example of one informant who sought to fabricate
evidence of judicial corruption by subsequently adding the words
"That envelope on the table is for you, Judge" to a tape recorded
conversation which contained no other intimations of illegality.

There are also documented cases of informants having supplied
drugs for personal use to persons who were targets of an investigation, to the point that the target became addicted (*United States v.
Barrera-Moreno and Herndon* 951 F.2d 1089 (1991) at 1090).

GRATUITOUS CRIMINAL ACTIVITY 'ON THE SIDE'. Some informants, in the course of their engagement, may engage in criminal
conduct to establish their bona fides or credibility with the target of an

investigation. Assuming this activity is necessary, and not so egregious as to constitute government domination of the criminal
enterprise, one might regard it as acceptable. But there are limits, in
terms of quantity or quality, to the permissibility of such conduct. If
one or two drug deals are sufficient to establish credibility, can one
condone ten? Realising that police are not dealing with a society of
angels, and that some targets of criminal investigation are very nasty
people indeed, what if the conduct in question were to extend to
burglary, serious assault or homicide?

Criminal conduct may be entirely unrelated to the investigation for
which the informant has been engaged. Under such circumstances,
the more zealous police officer might argue that there is a degree of
collateral criminality that might be regarded as tolerable in order to
ensure the informant's continued cooperation. Others would regard
any such conduct as unacceptable. Again, one could perhaps overlook
one or two minor offences, but not serious crime.

Of course, paid informants, despite instructions to the contrary,
are often tempted to engage in crime 'on the side' for whatever
motives they might harbour. Marx (1988) describes how informants
may misuse false identification and credit cards, and in some cases,
may even seek to sell government property used in an investigation.
He notes one case in which an informant used his knowledge of an
operation in order to defraud a number of innocent businessmen and
women. In another case, an informant obtained a dummy $1.75
million certificate of deposit that he used as collateral for a bank loan.
The informant used the loan to purchase real estate, then defaulted
(Marx 1988:144–45).

Soto (1998) refers to an informant who used his position to obtain
car loans. He described the informant as "good on theft cases, but
with credit, ego (thought he was a cop) and money problems". The
informant contacted car dealers and claimed to be an agency
employee. The police officer managing the informant did not prosecute, whether from naiveté or embarrassment, but attempted without success to transfer him to another region.

Problems of informant criminality may endure long after the
conclusion of court proceedings. Persons who have been relocated
with new identities under a witness protection program may exploit

this opportunity to protect themselves from creditors (Marx 1988:158). They may also lapse into a variety of other undesirable habits learned in their earlier criminal career.

Risks of collateral criminality may be less in those jurisdictions where the limits of permissible conduct are made explicit. The Australian Federal Police advise their human sources in the strongest terms that if they break the law, they will be arrested.

IMPACT ON THIRD PARTIES. Some of the activities in which informants may engage during an investigation may be harmful to third parties, whether innocent bystanders or others who may be incidentally related to the target of an investigation. In one case, an undercover police officer and two informants, each of the latter "working off" criminal charges and earning weekly non-contingent salaries, planned to commit a break-in. They enlisted the 'assistance' of a willing suspect, known to them as an habitual participant in burglaries. The suspect acted as a lookout while the officer and the informants committed the burglary. The suspect was subsequently charged (*State v. Hohensee* 650 S.W. 2d 268 (Mo.Ct. App. 1982)). One might spare a thought for the victim of the break-in.

In another noteworthy case, the U.S. government engaged the services of an informant who conducted a flagrantly illegal search of a bank officer's briefcase, in order to obtain evidence that a client of the bank had falsified an income tax return (*United States v. Payner* 447 U. S. 727 (1979)). The errant taxpayer was convicted, but the officer managing the case was disciplined.

Unethical practice short of crime. Informants may also engage in a variety of conduct that, although not criminal, might be regarded as inappropriate. It may involve harassment, abuse, or invasion of privacy, or otherwise unconscionable conduct.

In one case, the government used an informant to introduce a drug dealer to undercover law enforcement officers. As a means of establishing rapport with the subject of the investigation the informant, who was a prostitute and drug user, developed an intimate physical relationship with him, despite repeated instructions not to by the agent in charge of the investigation. She succeeded in introducing the subject to undercover officers, a sale took place, and the subject was charged (*United States v. Simpson* 813 F.2d 1462 (9th Cir. 1987)).

In one famous case, the U.S. government enlisted the services of the vindictive former lover of Marion Barry, then Mayor of Washington, DC. The informant lured Barry, widely suspected of corruption and drug use, to her hotel room and provided him with cocaine. The room was wired for sound and vision, and the resulting raid was broadcast countless times over national television.

The use of such intrusive methods may be more palatable when investigating offences that have already occurred. Marx (1988: 61) refers to a case in which an attractive female informant entered a liaison with a murder suspect who ultimately proposed marriage. Exploiting her position of trust and intimacy, she probed the suspect about matters which might be burdening his conscience. He confided that he had killed two people. Their conversation was monitored by local police via a transmitter in the informant's purse, and the suspect was arrested soon thereafter.

The old saying that every man has his price suggests that a distinction might be made between being corruptible and being corrupt. Many of us have fallen victim to high-pressure salespersons during our careers as consumers. So, given the production pressures that law enforcement agencies sometimes face, and the variety of incentives that might be offered to informants to assist police in 'putting runs on the board', it is easy to envisage a situation in which an informant might bring to bear extreme pressure on a suspect. Repeated, persistent nagging in the face of a suspect's reluctance to engage in criminal conduct may ultimately produce acquiescence. At what point does such nagging become inappropriate? Would it matter if the informant had cultivated the suspect's friendship for the purpose of the investigation, and then exploited that friendship in order to induce the criminal act? Should similar pressure be applied to persons chosen at random, or should such operations be limited to targeted persons whom the police have reasonable grounds to suspect will commit an offence?

Informants may engage in extremely coercive practices in order to make a case against a suspect. In one instance, an entrepreneur, whose failing business was urgently in need of an injection of capital, was approached by an informant and introduced to a drug dealer, who told him he could make $60 million by financing a major cocaine transaction. The informant then introduced the entrepreneur to an undercover agent posing as a "banker," who offered to finance the deal. When the entrepreneur expressed reluctance to go through with the transaction, the informant threatened his life if he would not complete the deal (Marx 1988: 10, 130).

Unethical conduct by police in the recruitment and deployment of informants. Because of the necessity to produce a result in some cases, there is a risk that police may be tempted to indulge in unethical conduct in order to recruit informants or when managing them. What forms of coercion or inducement are appropriate in relation to the recruitment and deployment of informants? In addition to their access to targets of an investigation, informants may possess other properties that can be exploited by the government. They may be drug dependent. They may be emotionally manipulable. They may be financially vulnerable. They may be liable to prosecution, and to long terms of imprisonment. Some may be of very tender years. In one case, an officer executing a warrant at the house of a suspected drug dealer, while escorting the five-year-old son of the suspect to the toilet, promised the child $5 if he revealed the whereabouts of the drugs. He did, and the drugs were found. The mother was convicted, based on evidence obtained from the government's exploitation of the vulnerability of a five-year-old child. Moreover, the child never received the $5 that he had been promised (*United States v. Penn* 647 F.2d 876 (9th Cir.1980)).

In some jurisdictions, financial remuneration and the promise of indemnity from prosecution may be regarded as acceptable. But it may not be acceptable for the police to support an informant's drug dependence, either financially or by the direct supply of the informant's substance of choice, in return for the informant's assistance. The responsibility of a 'handler' to the informant raises many interesting questions. Beyond instructions to obey the law, how paternalistic should a police officer become? The handler may not be able to know, much less dictate, how the informant spends his or her money. And given the character of some informants, money paid to them by police may preclude the necessity of stealing it from an innocent third party.

And what if an informant were to obtain access to information that revealed the details of a suspect's legal defence? Is any degree of penetration, legal or illegal, of the lawyer-client relationship acceptable? In one case, investigators placed a 'body bug' on a defendant's lawyer and monitored conversations between the two (*United States v. Ofshe* 817 F.2d 1508 (11th Cir. 1987)).

If an informant has no enemies at the time he or she is engaged by the police, that very engagement is likely to create the potential for strong animosity in the event that the informant's identity is disclosed. Could it be acceptable for police, in order to exert pressure on an informant, to threaten to disclose an informant's identity or location, when such disclosure could result in the informant's death?

Fraud on police. Many, if not most, paid informants have made a career out of dishonesty. It comes as no surprise, therefore, that they may seek to defraud their police employers should the opportunity arise. In addition to the fabrication of evidence, as discussed above, informants may see themselves as double agents, and seek to obtain confidential police information for purposes of actually thwarting an investigation (Soto 1998; Marx 1988; Hight 2000).

Corruption of police. Hight (2000) also notes that informants have been known to record covertly their conversations with police officers with relative ease, later using the recordings to influence the relationship – for example, to induce corruption via bribery or blackmail. It is not unknown for informants to become involved in a sexual relationship with their police 'handler,' or for informants and police to become partners in crime (Clark 2000: 46–7; Marx 1988). Clark (2000: 38–40) describes a spectacular instance of informant-related corruption in the United Kingdom, where the informant ended up controlling the handler. The police officer disclosed confidential law enforcement intelligence to the informant for a fee. In another prominent case, it became apparent that a Special Agent of the FBI had been involved in an intimate romantic relationship with an informant whom he had been managing for eighteen years. The informant was actively spying for the People's Republic of China against the United States (U.S. Department of Justice 2006).

Physical danger to police. O'Connor (2006) notes that informants have killed police handlers, set them up for assault or robbery and made false claims of extortion or physical or sexual abuse. So risky is the interaction that he suggests at least two officers should be present at meetings with informants, and that meetings should always be held in safe places.

Informants as undesirable witnesses for the prosecution. The use of a paid informant as a witness in court is risky in the extreme, as that person's criminal history and remuneration arrangements would be fair game for a defence attorney. Any other ethically problematic practices might also be called into question. Some informants may appear convincing, but others will not. Informants are often perceived as inherently unlikeable souls, whose credibility may be doubtful. Their usefulness as witnesses in court thus has its limits, especially in cultures like those of continental Europe (Marx 1995) and Australia where there remains a cultural bias against informing or 'dobbing'.

Soto (1998) suggests that prosecutors should review deals with informants to ensure the information will result in a prosecution. He discusses the unreliability of information provided by informants, especially paid informants, stating: "in managing informants, NEVER TRUST THEM. Also, NEVER TRUST WHAT THEY SAY" (his capitals). Moreover, there always remains the possibility that reliance on information offered by an informant might result in the unjust conviction of an offender, or indeed, the conviction of a truly innocent person. High rates of wrongful convictions based on false informant testimony have been observed in the United States (Natapoff 2006: 109–10) and the Supreme Court there has recently begun to call for greater procedural safeguards on the part of the state and increased judicial scrutiny of the state's deals with informants in order to deal with this problem (see Natapoff 2006: 121–27 for a discussion of relevant cases). Because of the potential unreliability of an informant, neither an investigation nor a prosecution should rely solely on his or her evidence. Corroboration is essential.

Those cases in which the testimony of an informant *is* essential obviously entail substantial risk. In addition to the self-evident problems relating to a turncoat's credibility, informants have been known to have second thoughts about their roles. Key witnesses have been known to change their tune on the steps of the courthouse. A witness could recant in the middle of a trial. Even after the government succeeds in obtaining a conviction, an informant/witness may repudiate his or her testimony, thus paving the way for allegations of a miscarriage of justice. Provisions such as Section 21E of the Crimes Act 1914 (Cth), which permits the Director of Public Prosecutions to appeal against a reduced sentence when promised cooperation with law enforcement agencies has not been forthcoming, provide some disincentive to such conduct.

Long-term financial costs. Not all paid informants transform themselves into churchgoing taxpayers, or fade quietly into obscurity. The dysfunctional lifestyle embraced by many may not suit itself to unobtrusive reintegration into the community. Settle (1995) describes one person who had been engaged by police to assist with a murder investigation, and was given $9,500 to assist in securing legitimate employment. He was unsuccessful, and used some of the money to purchase a firearm. At the time of his arrest on a weapons offence, his funds were exhausted and he was living in a Salvation Army hostel.

Dunningham and Norris (1999) observe that any cost/benefit analysis of informants must take into account not only the quantum of payment, but also the often substantial operating costs entailed in managing the informant during and after an investigation. When the financial arrangements entail protection of the informant, the ultimate cost can be formidable. Settle cites a case involving two informants, one with a wife and child, who were protected by thirty-six police officers on rotating shifts. The costs of this protection ultimately reached AUD4.5 million. He also cites other cases in which the protection given was entirely inadequate (1995: 203–7).

Cost/benefit analysis can be vulnerable to misuse and misinterpretation. Some costs and benefits are exceedingly difficult to monetize. The loss of legitimacy that can arise from egregious malpractice is but one, as is not having one's integrity questioned. Some benefits and costs may also defy precise estimation. It is difficult to place a value on the interdiction of ten kilos of heroin, much less the avoidance of civil litigation and of harm to third parties.

Another problem of cost/benefit analysis is the duration of the activity under analysis. Some additional costs, and some additional benefits, may not become apparent until dust has begun to settle on a cost/benefit report. It may take a police organisation years to recover from a scandal, and the trajectory of a recovery may not be evident for some time.

Long-term loss of legitimacy of police organisation. In most countries with a free press, journalists will have a field day when a mishap involving informants comes to public attention. Simply being publicly associated with unsavoury characters can reflect adversely on police. But when a protected witness re-offends, or (failing adequate protection) becomes the target of retaliation by those whom he has betrayed, the adverse publicity can be painful indeed for police.

Because of the necessity for secrecy when protecting informants, and the silo mentality that traditionally characterized many large police agencies, mishaps can occur. Settle (2005: 207–8) cites a case of police receiving a tip that criminals were hiding at a particular location; they raided the place, only to discover that the residents were informants lying low. In another case, a politician unknowingly drove up to a house in which a key organized crime informant was hiding under police protection. The police stormed the visitor's vehicle, then persuaded him to depart.

Shoddiness in the management of informants can lead to the collapse of a prosecution. A large investigation of excise fraud in London was so poorly managed that the case was thrown out of court. In addition to the defendants going free, millions of pounds sterling were lost to the revenue (Butterfield 2003).

Safeguards
Designing appropriate reward systems. Busybodies, officious intermeddlers and individuals with grudges may wish to contribute to policing, but that role should be circumscribed. Incentives may send

the wrong signals. By contrast, compliance or assistance rendered under circumstances of great risk or sacrifice will necessitate some inducement, or will merit some recognition (Dunne 1990; Thagard 1992).

Authorities should be mindful of the possible side effects of incentives, including their potential for diluting altruistic motivation, and the risk that the mobilization of third parties in policing may serve to erode interpersonal trust. Authorities contemplating the use of incentives should also be wary of the vulnerability of a given incentive system to subversion or abuse.

Reward systems can be designed and administered in such a manner as to minimize their negative consequences. The rather discreet way in which the U.S. Internal Revenue Service dispenses rewards for information leading to the detection and punishment of tax offenders would appear not to encourage an ethos of bounty hunting. IRS employees are expressly forbidden to urge individuals to inform for the sake of a reward. Most claims are rejected, and the quantum of awards is of less than windfall proportions. The program is not widely publicized.

Problems of moral hazard which may affect third-party incentives may be lessened by certain safeguards. IRS guidelines provide for the rejection of claims where such action is deemed to be in the best interests of the government. Illustrative examples of situations warranting rejection include those in which informants themselves participated in tax evasion schemes or knowingly assisted others in such participation (Internal Revenue Manual 9371.7 (3)).

Rewards to members of the public at large for providing information should reflect contributions above and beyond the ordinary call of citizenship, most notably actions entailing extraordinary cost or risk. The quantum of incentives should be the lowest possible considering the degree of sacrifice involved. Because of the risk that the availability of such incentives might elicit overzealous or crassly mercenary conduct, publicity is best kept low key.

To paraphrase James Madison, if men were angels, no incentives would be necessary. Of course, one may infer from the current state of the world that men are not angels. Purists would suggest that the use of incentives will lead to an eclipse of moral judgment. In an ideal world, incentives would be replaced by moral suasion – the appeal for altruistic behaviour without the threat of punishment or the promise of reward (Romans 1966).

In our real world, however, public affirmation of good citizenship may be as important as denunciation of harmful conduct. And civic virtue may be more achievable when the costs of citizenship are not too great. The challenge is to design a regulatory ordering where the need for coercion is minimal, where conflict between private interest and the public good will be reduced, but where the choice to do good is not significantly driven by the opportunity to do well. As Goodin (1976: 178) reminds us, this is likely to entail a judicious combination of carrots and sticks.

Managing paid informants. The challenge faced by government is to manage informants in such a manner as to maximise their usefulness while at the same time minimising the risks of gratuitous criminality or otherwise questionable behaviour during the course of an investigation, as well as minimising opportunities for tactical advantage by the defence in criminal proceedings.

Commentators often focus on the complex systems needed to properly evaluate informants. The careful skills and knowledge needed to handle informants, coupled with the necessarily detailed guidelines regarding recruitment, management and termination processes, are time consuming and labour intensive. Thus paid informants who do not supply useful information can be a significant drain on resources (Soto 1998; Settle 1995; Hight 2000; Marx 1988; Bean 1996; Clark 2000). There is something of an art to maintaining a relationship that may yield valuable information in the fullness of time.

What arrangements might be put in place in order to achieve more rigorous scrutiny of the use of informants? Among the considerations which might determine whether or not to proceed with an operation are the following:

1. Will the benefits derived from the operation exceed any costs which the operation may incur? Whilst one must concede that it may be difficult for persons whose *raison d'être* is charging and convicting criminals to focus on a wider picture, interests

of justice and economy demand that this be done. It would appear self evident that informants, regardless of whether they are likeable or loathsome, should not be used gratuitously. Their use should be reserved for serious, not trivial purposes. The old injunction against "burning the house to roast the pig" is applicable here. When the gravity of the target criminality dictates, informants should be used only as a last resort. If conventional investigation methods will suffice, use them. Are there alternative, less invasive, investigative strategies that are as likely to achieve the goal of conviction? If so, they should be employed. If an informant can be of use in introducing an undercover officer to the target of an investigation, the use of the informant should be limited to that role. The informant's participation in the investigation should cease when the defined task is completed.

2. Is it likely that the foreseeable conduct of the informant will remain within the boundaries of tolerable behaviour? Investigations involving the use of informants should avoid using criminal or otherwise ethically questionable methods, where permitted, unless absolutely necessary. When the law permits and when necessity dictates their use, they should be used only as required. Officials responsible for managing investigations involving informants should be sensitive to potential harm to third parties. In the exceptional circumstances where the risk of such harm exists, it should be kept to an absolute minimum.

   The targets of investigations involving informants should be chosen with care. Informants should not be sent on fishing expeditions; investigations which might conceivably be seen to be politically motivated or in some way discriminatory should be considered with the utmost caution.

3. What safeguards are in place to minimize the risks identified here of using informants? Such investigations are not, after all, conducted in a vacuum, for their own sake. They are undertaken to produce evidence sufficient to achieve a successful prosecution. The whole purpose of using an informant may be defeated if he or she engages in behaviour which is gratuitously illegal or

unethical, or if their engagement creates more problems for police that it solves. Safeguards can be put in place to cover all phases of an informant's employment by police, from recruitment through to the criminal trial based on the investigation and beyond.

Recruitment. Proactive recruitment of informants is the norm. However, clear guidelines establishing a hierarchy of transparency and accountability within the police organisation can spread the load of decision making about the need for informants in any particular case as well as about the details of their handling. In one Australian police organisation, money payments are assessed at very high levels, bearing in mind the value of the particular informant as well as his or her culpability. In addition, there is immediate supervision up the line of all informant handlers. The liability of police for situations that 'go wrong' and the protection of the community are paramount.

Prior to engaging an individual as an informant, his or her potential for criminal conduct and, if appropriate, his or her reliability as a witness should be carefully assessed. Trott (1988: 124) suggests that information should be secured "on the witness' background, mental problems, probation reports, prior police reports, and prior prosecutors who have either prosecuted the witness or used him in court. What do they think about his credibility? How did the jurors react to him?" Any history of medication or drug use should also be explored with a view toward neutralizing a potential challenge to the witness' credibility.

Informants who are recruited for assistance in a criminal investigation should be carefully instructed about their role and their responsibilities. Particular attention should be accorded the boundaries of permissible conduct. A bright line should be drawn between that conduct which is acceptable, and that which is not. As noted earlier, the Australian Federal Police advise their human sources in no uncertain terms that if they break the law, they will be charged.

During the operation. In the United States, the Attorney General's Guidelines Regarding the Use of Informants are mandatory rules governing police/informant relationships (U.S. Department of Justice

2002). The U.S. guidelines incorporate a great many of the suggestions made by commentators as ways to manage risk. They include
formal procedures attaching to approval of payments (requiring that
a Department of Justice officer authorise any payment, with the level
of seniority of the officer dependent on the amount of the payment),
documentation of the payment with two law enforcement representatives, notification of payments to the tax authorities and cooperation with the prosecution where possible.

The guidelines also make it clear that informants are forbidden to
engage in certain types of illegal activity. They specify that a junior
officer may never authorise illegal activity, but that a more senior
officer, in consultation with a prosecutor, may do so. This authorisation can occur only where the activity is necessary to gain vital
information or prevent death, serious injury, or significant property
damage. The guidelines set out the risks such agents will consider
when making their decision.

Limiting the authorization of illegal activity, and ensuring that
certain risks are considered by the agents with authorising power,
effectively minimises the risk of what Hight (2000) called the 'tunnel
vision' approach, where an officer allows informant activities without
considering peripheral factors that could impact the case later. Even
with guidelines in place to minimize the risk that informants will
misbehave, an informant may yet engage in conduct, criminal or
otherwise, which is so unconscionable that it indelibly taints an
investigation. How should police respond when an informant acts in a
way that brutalizes, abuses, harasses, invades privacy, or otherwise
intrudes to an unacceptable extent upon people's lives? What is the
appropriate course of action for the police in such a case? Does one
turn a blind eye? Rebuke the officer or officers responsible? Refuse to
introduce any evidence derived from the improper conduct? Where
police do not act, they may attract the unfavourable attention of the
media, elected officials, and the various tribunals and authorities that
may exist to investigate police misconduct (Goldsmith 1991).

Monitoring. The activities of informants should be closely monitored.
Whenever possible, checks should be made to corroborate information provided by the informant. This may entail both human and

electronic surveillance. Some consideration might even be given to the use of polygraph examinations of informants for purposes of verification. Problems of reliability inherent in the use of polygraphs, especially with sociopaths or persons devoid of conscience, would suggest that their usefulness is limited. As one prosecutor notes, "Mistrust everything; look for corroboration on everything you can; follow up all indications that he may be fudging" (Trott 1988: 124). One senior officer of an Australian police organisation we spoke to affirmed that corroboration is essential and acting on single source information simply does not occur in that organisation.

It may be argued that a prosecutor should be an integral part of an undercover operation from its inception through to its conclusion. A prosecutor would be in a position to advise whether the practices in question are legal, ethical, and likely to produce the evidence required. Once in progress, the operation itself should be frequently reviewed by a monitoring group that includes prosecutorial representation. This group could review evidence as it emerges during the course of an operation, and participate in the planning of strategy and tactics as the operation unfolds. Not all jurisdictions involve prosecutors in criminal investigations to this extent. In Australia for instance, prosecutors stand mostly at arms length from police investigations, although this situation may be slowly changing.

Preparing for a prosecution. The informant's capacity for treachery was noted earlier. It has been said that one should say nothing to an informant that one would not wish to read in the newspapers or hear in open court. Indeed, 'co-operating' witnesses have been known to act as double agents, disclosing the identities and tactics of undercover officers.

Those officers managing the investigation should maintain sufficient contact and support to ensure that cooperation remains forthcoming. As one prosecutor experienced in these matters put it, "If you neglect the baby-sitting aspects of this business, you will get burned" (Trott 1988: 127). The potential for double dealing by informants cannot be ignored.

Perceived generosity to an indemnified witness may be seen by the jury as an inducement to lie. Defence counsel will seek to discredit an informant by portraying past or future compensation as the basis of his or her testimony. The smaller the inducement the better. Any linkage between performance and reward should be structured with great caution. It may also be preferable to structure an agreement with a cooperating witness in such a manner that there remains an incentive to perform well. Trott (1988: 126) suggests that police should "Hold something back. The witness must perform first. If you give him everything to which he is 'entitled' before he testifies, you may be unpleasantly surprised when he disintegrates on the witness stand. I prefer if possible to have such a witness plead guilty before testifying and sentenced afterwards". Some jurisdictions try, as a matter of practice, to withhold financial payment until the defendant has been convicted and all appeal avenues exhausted.

Given the jaundiced view that many jurors have of criminals as witnesses, there are a few strategic observations which one might make. It might already be obvious, but the witness should not be more culpable than the defendant. The accused should not look good by comparison. This means that 'little fish' should be used against 'big fish', not the other way around.

Furthermore, the presentation of evidence must be considered. The testimony of a police officer is likely to be received with less incredulity by a jury than is the word of an informant. Police officers tend to be more accountable than informants.

From this discussion, it might be concluded that the use of an informant in the course of an investigation is one matter, and the use as a witness for the prosecution in a criminal case is quite another.

Afterwards. Whether or not the informant/witness is in custody, there may be significant risks to his or her safety. These risks may be posed by those who stand to lose from the testimony, or by those who find informants abhorrent in principle. Informants may also place themselves in harm's way through reckless behaviour. It is obvious that police must act to protect informants to the extent possible. "You don't compromise the identity of a human source," said one Australian officer we spoke to. In that organisation, the area where information about informants is kept is the most secure area in the premises: only five officers have access. Clear avenues of communication with other police organisations can help to avoid mishaps arising from a lack of knowledge of an informant's protected status.

It might also be appropriate to consider remedies that could be made available to third parties who suffer harm as a result of an informant's criminality, whether collateral or in furtherance of an investigation. In some jurisdictions, innocent citizens are entitled to recover damages for losses suffered at the hands of an informant during the course of an investigation, or at the hands of a protected witness for the duration of his or her protection. A purist might even argue that the remedy should extend even to those losses that were not foreseeable to the agency that had engaged the informant's services.[27] In any event, one imagines that governments would be disinclined to hold themselves to a standard of absolute liability for damages inflicted by wayward informants.

Conclusions

What conclusions might then be drawn from this discussion?

1. Rewards to members of the public should be commensurate with risk or sacrifice, and should be proffered sparingly. Their use should be subject to guidelines to ensure transparency and accountability.
2. Paid informants should be used only as a last resort. As a U.S. federal prosecutor once put it, "The best way to control informants in undercover operations is not to use them at all" (McDowell 1988: 108). When they are used, the risks that this entails should be managed with great care.
3. Where possible, the use of paid informants should be limited to facilitating investigations. Their use as prosecution witnesses should be limited to those cases in which their evidence is absolutely necessary to establish guilt. In those cases, the use of pre-trial reliability inquiries (similar to those beginning to be used in some states in the United States, see Natapoff 2006: 113) should be contemplated.

---

[27] For a less charitable view, see *Powers v. Lightner* 820 F.2d 818 (7th Cir. 1987).

4. They should be used to investigate only where the public interest is compelling; usually this will be in relation to the most serious offences.

5. They should not be used in circumstances which entail a risk of significant harm to themselves, to police or to third parties.

6. Clear guidelines to assist police in assessing each situation, as well as close monitoring of informants' activities, are essential to ensure that the key aim of achieving the arrest and prosecution of targeted criminals is achieved. As one senior officer told us:

> What are required are strong management strategies. These include clear and unambiguous rules, a robust audit process and tight security measures. It requires objective management focused on the subject and not distracted nor blinkered by general policing requirements or practices. Despite what many believe, professional human source management is a specialised area and not suited to everyone. The higher the level of human source, the more specialist skills are required from the handlers (hence dedicated Human Source Management Teams and management oversight). (Houghton 2007)

Prosecutors may have an important role to play in ensuring that the use of informants remains legal and ethical. This, of course, assumes that prosecutors themselves are ethical.

Informants, along with surveillance and the manipulation of trust, may be necessary tools for law enforcement, but they are double-edged tools. If they are to be used at all, they should be used not indiscriminately, but surgically, in accordance with established principles and procedures. Inappropriate use of these most intrusive of investigative methods may contribute to the further erosion of trust that is the cement of an open and democratic society.

Police will continue to pay for information. Whether the providers of this information are members of the general public, or criminals working under contract, these commercial exchanges entail risk. Assessing these risks, and weighing them against potential returns, has become a central challenge of contemporary policing.

CHAPTER FIVE

SALE – SELLING

Police also engage in the act of selling their own goods and services in order to bring in financial resources to the police organisation. In this chapter we consider, in Part 1, police selling their services, what is sometimes called 'user-pays' or 'fee-for-service' policing. Part 2 looks at the sale by police of the police 'brand' in the form of merchandise and intellectual property.

PART 1: POLICE AS COMMERCIAL SECURITY VENDORS

Police are not only purchasers but also vendors of security. A market in crime control is far from new, as is made clear in histories of state police (Radzinowicz 1956b; Critchley 1972), but, as Zedner points out, the scale is changing. Today's market reaches all corners of the globe rather than being constrained by local or national borders (Zedner 2006: 83–84). This market includes state and non-state providers of security that are engaged in both domestic policing and military activities (Singer 2003, 2005; Avant 2005, 2006). In exploring this market, the principal research focus has been on the activities of private security companies. Much less attention has been devoted to the activities of state police organisations as players within the market (for exceptions, see Reiss 1988, Blair 1998; Wood 2000; Johnston 2003; Crawford and Lister 2006; Johnston 2006). What is particularly significant about the police as commercial security vendors is that, when their services are paid for by non-state entities, the police retain their legal status and the access this provides to the legitimate use of physical, including deadly, force (Stenning and Shearing 1979; Law Commission of Canada 2006).

In 2000 Jeremy Gans comprehensively explored the legal framework of privately paid public policing, concentrating mainly on common law jurisdictions, and examined in some depth the motives of the parties. Building on this, we look at the prevalence and diversity of what has come to be known as 'user-pays' or 'fee-for-service' public policing today, the benefits and risks of these developments, and the implications for the future of policing as a whole. As the literature on this subject is uneven, our coverage is somewhat limited. However, we believe that it nonetheless provides grounds for some conclusions to be drawn.

The first part of this chapter deals briefly with the historical background to the practice of police selling their services to private interests. The various types of user-pays policing are then examined, drawing examples from different, mainly western, jurisdictions, with particular emphasis on Australia. We consider how this fits with the image of public police as a public service, concluding that the two are not necessarily inconsistent. The events user-pays policing scheme of one Australian police force is used as an example of public policing for private interests and the way in which such policing can be used to serve the wider public interest. The case study also illustrates the place of user-pays in the broader context of the overall commercialization of public policing. The chapter then canvasses some of the risks that can and do arise, and concludes with some thoughts on the implications of police participation in the marketplace as security vendors.

Background to User-Pays Policing

The public police as we know it had its origins in a combination of two related streams: the system of self-policing, involving constables, warders and watchmen and the community itself (through the hue and cry and the court leet) as documented in the 1285 Statute of Winchester (Critchley 1972: 6–7), and the private policing and prosecution business that established itself in early-mid eighteenth century London. This business was conducted by 'thief-takers' and their recruits for personal profit, and involved the use of violence, extortion, and blackmail, as well as the manipulation of specialized

knowledge of the law. According to McMullen, it 'linked the underworld of London crime, the private trade in police services and the
administration of criminal justice into a mutual toleration and protection society' (1996: 93). Today such activity would likely be thought
of as state-sanctioned, perhaps even state-sponsored, corruption.
Even when, in 1750, Chief Magistrate Henry Fielding undertook to
rationalize and modernize existing practices and garnered some
public funding for his new force of trustworthy 'thief-takers', later to
become the Bow Street Runners (Critchley 1972: 32–33), this
remained for some time an essentially for-profit enterprise largely
funded by private interests (mostly rich and powerful individuals,
businesses and government institutions), and one that still sometimes
operated at the margins of the law (McMullan 1996: 93–98). When
London's public police force was progressively established by Robert
Peel after 1829, there was great public opposition. However, this
started to wane once those who benefited from the private enterprises
that preceded the force's creation began to see the public police as a
way of shifting costs onto the public purse (Benson 1994: 259).

　According to the majority of the House of Lords in the 1924 British
case of *Glasbrook Brothers Ltd. v Glamorgan Country Council* [1924] 1 All
ER 579 at 587, the practice of police charging for their services dates
from the mid-nineteenth century. According to this account, the
public police had not been long established before a need was identified for the re-introduction of private funding for certain functions.
In *Glasbrook*, fees for policing services came before the courts for the
first time when a mine owner requested and was granted a long-term
garrison of police to protect the mine's 'safety men' (whose job was to
ensure the mine was not flooded) from picketing miners. The owner
refused to pay a charge levied by the police for the 'special services' he
had requested. In the opinion of the superintendent of the local
police, a garrison was not necessary; a mobile column of police would
have been adequate protection. The majority of House of Lords
justices upheld the police position. The decision revolved around the
concept of police 'duty'. Police, said the majority, could go beyond the
scope of their absolute obligations to the public (which were in this
case to provide such a force as was adequate to protect life and
property) and give protection of a 'special sort', as long as that could

be done without interfering with the fulfilment of their obligations elsewhere. In so doing, police could set conditions, including a fee. The legality of charging a fee for special services was said to derive from tradition, and the fact that it was against neither the law nor public policy. However, not until 1964 was the authority to charge for policing services codified in legislation (U.K. Police Act 1964 s. 15(1); now Police Act 1996 s. 25).

Forms of User-Pays Policing
Discrete and general policing services. Today, the extent of the user-pays component of policing varies from jurisdiction to jurisdiction, as do the kinds of policing services for which fees are levied. There are still some jurisdictions where charging for services is not generally practised, such as New Zealand and the Netherlands. In some others, demanding fees for law enforcement services is part of a pattern of petty corruption (International Crisis Group 2001). Here we concentrate on lawful and formal user-pays schemes.

The policing of events organized by private interests, particularly those intended to make a profit, is a service for which a fee is commonly charged, but this is by no means ubiquitous. Such events include sporting competitions, parades, festivals and concerts. Police also frequently require payment for:

- traffic control services where the beneficiary is a private business (film shoots, escorts for long or wide loads, road closures at construction sites etc.);
- guards and escorts;
- criminal history and probity checks of potential employees requested by government and nongovernment agencies;
- incident and accident reports provided to insurers, solicitors and individuals;
- certain technical and forensic services (e.g., photography);
- attendance at false alarms; and
- the provision of training.

An example of the last is the courses run by the Australian Federal Police Protective Service for government agencies and other security practitioners in aggression management, bomb threat management, property security escorts and security x-ray screening and interpretation (Australian Federal Police 2006b). The AFP Commissioner has a wide discretion to charge persons other than those employed by the Commonwealth, such as defence establishments on Australian soil and major galleries and museums, a fee for providing Protective Service security, but the amount charged must be reasonably related to the cost of providing the services (see s. 69E of the Australian Federal Police Act 1979).

Some user-pays schemes are more unusual. Northumbria Police in the United Kingdom charge fees to writers, broadcasters and film makers for whom they provide police expertise in the form of advice, premises, chaperoning, labour and equipment, in relation to the production of non-documentary material or documentaries that are not focused specifically on Northumbria Police (Northumbria Police 2006). Similarly a media production company paid the full-time salary of an officer of one Australian police organisation to act as advisor for the entire run of a police television drama (approximately ten years) (Williams 1998; Victoria Police 2006). Services provided by dog units, mounted police or police bands may also be subject to payment of a fee in some jurisdictions. The sheriff's department in Grand County, Utah, charges lost and stranded hikers and rafters for the cost of search and rescue missions, a practice also undertaken in some counties of Idaho, Hawaii and New Hampshire and at some ski resorts in Washington, Oregon and Colorado (Associated Press 2005). Some police departments have discretion to charge for whatever services they deem to be appropriate even if those services are not specified in legislation (see, for example, s. 96(2) *Police Service Act 2003* (Tasmania)).

The problems caused by alcohol consumption are often one reason for user-pays initiatives. In Halton, Canada, it is a condition of liquor licences that the costs associated with any extraordinary deployment of police to ensure safety and security at licensed premises can be charged to the licence-holder (Scott 2005: 402). Pubs and clubs in some areas in England and Wales have banded together to pay for extra police patrols at busy times for their businesses, such as weekends (Borland 2005). In the United States, the Century Council, a not-for-profit organisation funded by brewers, vintners, distillers and wholesalers, pays the overtime costs for police to work undercover in liquor stores to prevent the illegal sale of alcohol to minors. Police

departments in more than forty states and campus police in many
locations have implemented this 'Cops in Shops' program (Gallagher's Beat 1994; The Century Council [nda]). In Michigan, defendants in drunk driving cases are required by law to pay the costs to
police of processing their cases (see, for example, Ingham County's
Ordinance Providing for the Reimbursement of Costs associated with
Violations of Certain Offenses, adopted June 2003, Article 5).

Extraordinary discrete occurrences that attract police attention
may also invite police to consider recovery of costs. In January 2008, a
Melbourne, Australia, couple departed for a holiday, leaving their
sixteen-year-old son to mind the family home. The son decided to
throw a party, and, as the word was spread via e-mail and text messages, some five hundred guests arrived at the venue on a quiet
suburban street. Concerned neighbours called police, and dog
squads, transit police, divisional vans and a critical incident response
team were mobilized – thirty police officers in all. A helicopter was
even used to disperse the crowd. Police were considering the possibility of billing the teenager up to AUD20,000 for the intervention
(Rood and Schneiders 2008; ABC News 2008).

A number of police organisations are now 'hiring out' police officers for patrol functions in specific public, private and public/private
spaces (such as shopping malls and airports). Crawford and Lister
(2006: 176–181) recount how, in 2000, a community on the periph-
ery of York, England, contracted through its housing trust with local
police commanders for an additional twenty-four-hour per week
community patrol service to the village, with the intention of
addressing residents' concerns about a perceived lack of beat police.
Such extra paid policing is not unusual in the United Kingdom.
Legislation allows police to trade with other designated public
authorities (s. 18 Police Act 1996) and to provide, "at the request of
any person, special police services at any premises or in any locality in
the police area for which the force is maintained, subject to the
payment to the police authority of charges on such scales as may be
determined by that authority" (s. 25 Police Act 1996). Large shopping
complexes like the MetroCentre in Gateshead and Bluewater in Kent
use contracted police (Crawford and Lister 2006: 168–69). The Royal
Devon and Exeter Hospital contracted for two officers to patrol its

buildings and grounds (Gibbons 1996: 22). Officers have also been contracted to provide focused patrols to housing estates in various locations, for example, Bierley Estate in Bradford (Gibbons 1996: 23–24), Dennistoun in Glasgow (Patience 2005) and Broomhouse housing scheme in Edinburgh (Mooney and Mather 2005). In Scotland, Lothian and Borders Police Board recently approved a user-pays scheme whereby private companies such as Lothian Buses are able to pay for additional police cover (Hamilton 2003). In 2005 the Edinburgh Council contributed £1.3m a year over three years towards dedicated squads of police called 'youth action teams' and 'safer community units' to patrol particular areas of the city and tackle antisocial behaviour (Roden 2005). In 2003 West Midlands Police received £30,000 for a transport liaison officer from Travel West Midlands (Hamilton 2003).

In Kenya, the Administration Police is a branch of the Kenyan Police Force and hires itself out as an armed force to clients such as embassies, banks and supermarkets. The private security industry in Kenya also hires the services of the Administration Police to protect cash-in-transit (Abrahamsen and Williams 2005a). In Sierra Leone, the Operations Support Division (OSD) is the armed division of the unarmed Sierra Leone Police. OSD wages are sometimes supplemented by private security companies that pay a premium in exchange for the OSD co-manning private security vehicles and assisting in the protection of cash-in-transit and the security of banks, diplomatic missions and the diamond industry (Abrahamsen and Williams 2005b). Most private security companies in Nigeria are permanently supplemented by armed Mobile Police Officers (MoPol), who are contracted out by the Inspector General of Police. These officers assist in a range of duties such as cash-in-transit, armed response, guarding duties and so on (Abrahamsen and Williams 2005c).

Cities and towns with a population of over five thousand in Alberta, Canada, are responsible for providing their own police services. Very often the Royal Canadian Mounted Police (RCMP) provides these services under contract (Alberta Government 2006). In fact, the RCMP provides policing services under contract in all provinces and territories of Canada except Ontario and Quebec, and this involves almost half of RCMP uniformed personnel (Royal Canadian

Mounted Police 2006). Ontario Provincial Police also provide a contract policing service in different municipalities within Ontario (Law Commission of Canada 2006: 4).

In some U.S. cities, police officers are assigned to foot beats in shopping malls, usually in addition to the mall's own private security contingent. The police in Montclair, California, developed a solution to the problem of high levels of juvenile crime in Montclair Plaza, concluding an agreement with the Plaza's management for 50 percent funding for a full-time police officer to patrol the Plaza and give training to the private security staff. The Plaza agreed to provide the officer with an office and equipment (Geason and Wilson 1992). As this example suggests, 'payment' for police services may well be in kind. In Cannington in Western Australia, Westfield Carousel Shopping Centre provides computer, fax, video interviewing facilities and office space in the Centre to the Western Australia Police Service (Western Australia Police Service 2000: 14) in return for a police presence on the premises. A number of shopping malls in Victoria have in place similar agreements (Victoria Police 2006). Whether these kinds of arrangements can be regarded as user-pays policing or as a form of gift to police is a question of perspective, and perhaps depends on whether it is the police or the management who instigates the arrangement (Grabosky 2004: 73).

Off-duty services. User-pays policing has not only taken the form of officially providing on-duty police officers' services for a price. In his 1988 study of the private employment of public police in the United States, Reiss (1988: 2) found that in many police departments the number of police officers 'moonlighting', that is, performing police duties when off duty,[1] exceeded the number officially on duty. As with

---

[1] There are a number of different activities that might be and are in the literature called 'moonlighting', including:

- Taking secondary employment when off-duty – no police permission sought.
- Taking secondary employment when off-duty with police knowledge or permission-officer involved arranges this and keeps the income.
- Taking secondary employment when off-duty with police knowledge or permission – officer involved arranges this but police organisation gets a commission.

other forms of user-paid policing, moonlighting police officers retain their police status and hence their powers. In some jurisdictions, such as in many parts of the United States, moonlighting is officially sanctioned and only creates a problem if the opportunity to work a second job is abused (as when police 'double-dip', that is, work the second job while actually on duty). In Jakarta, Indonesia, 'moon-lighting' seems to have a semi-formal status, in that it appears to be allowed provided that the officer's unit commander is informed in advance and a commission is paid to the police from the contracted officer's wages (Anon 2004a). In Australia, as in many other jur-isdictions, the taking of employment outside the police organisation is strictly regulated. In general, secondary employment is allowed with the permission of the police department provided it does not involve a conflict of interest with police duties.[2] Security work, for instance, may or may not be permissible depending on the circum-stances. In 2002 the New South Wales Police Minister, Michael Costa, launched a series of trials at several locations in the state, wherein approved private businesses such as shopping centres would be able to 'rent' off-duty police officers who would be fully equipped and possess all their on-duty police powers. The businesses were to pay the New South Wales Police for this labour, which would then pay the officers' wages (and possibly retain a commission: Phillips 2002; but see Costa (Hansard 2002) referring to the trials as a "not-for-profit operation"). The trials sparked controversy (Vincent 2002), but supplementary policing was eventually included in the New South Wales Police Cost Recovery and User Charges Policy (New South

• Taking secondary employment when off-duty under the auspices of the police department – police organisation arranges this and pays the officer involved (may keep a commission).

Secondary employment may be limited to employment involving policing duties.
[2] For example, s. 10.9 of the Queensland Police Service Code of Conduct provides that:
  Members may not engage in any employment outside the Queensland Police Service whilst on leave or otherwise if such employment:

  i.   interferes with the effectiveness of the performance of their duties;
  ii. creates or appears to create a conflict of interest; or
  iii. reflects adversely on the Service.

Wales Police 2004) as a category of service for which charges are levied. Supplementary policing was seen by the New South Wales government as a way both of regulating secondary employment (Vincent 2002) and of meeting community demands for increased police visibility (Hansard 2002).

More permanent institutional arrangements. Sometimes there is a more permanent 'user-pays' arrangement in place. In London as early as 1798 the Marine Police Force was set up to police ports along the Thames. This force was originally funded jointly by shipping interests (the West India Merchants and Planters Company) and the government, with Ship Constables being appointed and controlled by the Marine Police Force but paid for by ship owners. In 1839, the Marine Police Force amalgamated with the Metropolitan Police to become the Thames Division of the Met (now the Marine Support Unit).[3] Today there is no privately funded water police for the Thames but there is such a force for the British rail network. Around 95 percent of the British Transport Police (BTP) budget is provided by the rail industry (train operating companies, the infrastructure operator Network Rail, and the London Underground), with the rest conferred by government grants. Police Service Agreements between the BTP Authority and individual rail companies cover payment for 'core' policing services.. Companies can also contract with the BTP for 'noncore' services and enhanced levels of core police services (Department of Transport 2006: 57–58). In Los Angeles County, the Sheriff's Department has a separate bureau that provides policing under contract to the Metropolitan Transportation Authority, which operates the public transit system (light rail and bus), and to the Southern California Regional Rail Authority, Metrolink (heavy rail) (Los Angeles County Sheriff's Department 2007).

In Western Australia, the Gold Stealing Detection Unit (GSDU) of the Western Australia Police has been in existence since 1907. This Unit of 6 or 7 detectives, based in Kalgoorlie, has responsibility for investigating gold stealing offences and deterring organised crime

---

[3] See http://www.the-river-thames.co.uk/police.htm;http://www.eastlondonhistory.com/ the-river-pirates-on-the-thames/ (accessed 21 July 2008).

infiltration into the gold industry. It is funded entirely by members of the WA Chamber of Minerals and Energy through its Mines Security Trust Account (MSTA) (Chamber of Minerals and Energy 2005; Western Australia Police 2007a). The Unit also provides personal services to MSTA members in the form of regular mine site inspections and security reviews, security advice and training. The MSTA funding covers salaries, accommodation, equipment, infrastructure, travelling allowances and overtime – costs that are not included in the WA Police budget. GSDU accountability is split between the WA Police Executive for operational matters and the MSTA Committee for financial and administrative matters.

Also in Western Australia, two police officers are permanently stationed at the Argyle Diamond Mine. The mining company meets the cost of providing and maintaining buildings, equipment and accommodation for these officers but not their ongoing operating costs, which come from the WA Police budget. The Argyle police officers provide services to the nearby Balgo Aboriginal community as well as to the mining operation (Western Australia Police 2007b).

On a grander scale, in Nigeria, oil companies pay and control a public police entity, the Supernumerary or Spy police. This force was specially recruited and trained by the Nigerian police at the behest of the companies to provide unarmed security, mainly guarding at oil company facilities. Abrahamsen and Williams note that there are well over two thousand Supernumerary officers employed by companies in this capacity (Abrahamsen and Williams 2005c: 13).

In the Northern Territory of Australia, Aboriginal Community Police Officers are posted to remote Aboriginal communities that partly fund the positions by providing vehicles, accommodation, infrastructure and office space (Northern Territory Police 2006).

University campus police in the United States provide an interesting example of what might be classified as user-pays policing, given the links that exist between some campus police organisations and local police agencies, and their legal status as police officers. The Michigan State University Police Department (MSUPD) essentially functions as a municipal police agency in the state of Michigan, with its authority deriving from the State Legislature. However, it obtains most of its funding from the university, which allocates it from its general appropriation. Each MSUPD officer is fully trained as a police officer, armed with handguns, tasers and pepper spray. MSUPD vehicles are equipped with MP5 patrol rifles. The department has a large K9 program and operates one of only four computer forensic units in the state. It is in daily close contact and cooperation with the East Lansing Police Department and the two departments use the same radio frequencies and dispatch centre, and have a joint special weapons and tactics team. Although MSUPD's main focus in the Michigan State University campus, its officers are deputized to function off campus if needed.

Public Policing and User-Pays Policing: The 'Fit'

The dramatic growth of private security over the last few decades (Shearing and Stenning 1983; Stenning 2000; Forst 2000: 21; Law Commission of Canada 2002, 2006; 10; Pastor 2003; Sarre and Prenzler 2005), together with the drive by governments across the industrialized world to integrate private business mentalities and strategies into the provision of public services, has changed the very conception of what it means to provide a public policing service today (Wood 2000; O'Malley and Hutchinson 2006). The traditional wisdom is that public policing is a public service; that is, a service provided by government to the public at large, to which each member of the public has equal access regardless of income. Having described it thus, one might expect there to be a couple of corollaries: first, that policing is a 'public good' in the economic sense of that term; and second, that policing for a private interest is not consistent with the notion of public policing.

Policing is generally thought of as a public good; that is, as non-rivalrous (in that its consumption by one person does not prevent it being available for consumption by others) and nonexcludable (in that its benefits are shared by all, whether they pay for them or not).[4] This idea of policing has been widely discussed in the academic

---

[4] As Drahos (2004: 324) points out "The non-excludability of a good is a contingent matter". To say that a good is nonexcludable is not to say that the good can never be made excludable; rather that, because of the nature of the good, it is difficult and perhaps costly to do so.

literature in recent years (for example, Benson 1994; Hope 2000; Loader and Walker 2001, 2006; Shearing and Wood 2003, 2005; Crawford 2006a). Benson (1994), for example, rejects the idea, considering instead that policing is, like highways, a free-access common pool – a good that is rivalrous and non-excludable – and so, because individuals do not bear the full costs of their personal use, it tends to be overused. The resulting congestion in turn suggests a need to ration policing in some way. Crawford (2006a: 99–120) identifies some of the forms of rationing that are now taking place. Writing about the recent changes in the nature of public policing, he states (2006a: 112) that "we are witnessing the further residualization of policing as a public good through processes of capture, as well as the enclosure and collectivization of security as a 'club good'". In economic terms, a club good is one that is excludable but non-rivalrous, at least until the point of congestion occurs. Crawford argues that policing is more and more being provided through and by collective club arrangements, leaving public policing to deal with the resulting negative externalities (the displacement of crime and disorder) and to police those excluded from club membership (2006a: 121).[5]

What is clear from these analyses and others is that policing, including public policing, now comes in many different *economic* forms. Police departments perform a variety of functions, some of which may be classified as pure public goods, some as club or toll[6] or common pool goods ('impure' or 'quasi-' public goods), and some as purely private goods (Fixler and Poole 1988: 109). Where do user-pays forms of policing fit into this scheme? Is policing for

---

[5] Security clubs tend to display themselves in geographical space as enclosures or enclaves, such as gated communities or other 'mass private property' (Shearing and Stenning 1983; Crawford 2006: 125). As Kempa et al (2004: 573) point out, the clubbing of security in these 'communal spaces' has the effect that public police are left to deal with not only the displaced, but also the spaces between enclaves that the displaced inhabit and that must be traversed to move between communal spaces, resulting in a 'conduit policing problem'.

[6] Like a club good, a toll good is excludable but nonrivalrous. The difference lies in the mechanism employed to exclude others – a toll payment (as on a highway) or the formation of a club (for instance, to play golf) – both mechanisms work to ensure that the utility derived from use of the good by an included individual is maximized.

a private interest consistent with notions of public policing as a public service?

There is no doubt that requiring payment for policing services can be seen as a form of exclusion: only those who can pay can access the service. There may, therefore, be implications for the equitable distribution of services. The chargeable service perhaps fits the definition of a toll good (excludable but nonrivalrous). But sometimes, too, policing *is* rivalrous: more policing for one means less for others. It may be the case, for instance, that if a number of police attend a major privately organised event, there will be a dearth of police to attend to normal duties. In economic terms, this would be a negative externality for the public of policing the private event.

However, private interests and the public interest do not always conflict. Sometimes serving a private or otherwise parochial interest will benefit the public interest (Shearing and Wood 2003), as when police ensure that a minority is free to go about its business, be it religious worship or a street march. Higher interests in freedom of worship or expression are served, together with the private interest in safety and free speech. Public policing of an event may similarly have wider public interest ramifications in terms of public safety, even if it is the private promoter of the event for whom the policing is technically provided. There is every reason for the police to be interested in the policing of such events. It may provide wider social or economic benefits (positive externalities) for the community. Thus even the provision by the police of services with the attributes of private goods, like excludability and rivalry, may be in the public interest.

In such circumstances, policing at the behest of a private interest may well be consistent with the notion of public policing as a service provided to benefit the public. A further way to reduce negative externalities is to charge for the service. Where police lack resources to perform a service in the light of other demands, charging can pay for replacement resources to be brought in to satisfy the total demand. The same may be said of many chargeable policing services other than events policing. If I ask the police for an accident report for my personal use, I am asking them to expend time and energy on an activity (locating, copying and sending me the report) that may well reduce the resources they can devote to other activities that have more widespread implications for community security (like criminal investigation). Paying for the report may enable additional resources to be found and deployed. Charging may also discourage frivolous applications and so reduce wastage of police time. In a sense, then, levying fees for public policing services may help secure equal access to policing services for all, regardless of ability to pay.

Events Policing – A Case Study

Some may argue that, if policing should be available to all because it is funded by the taxpayer, charging particular taxpayers extra for public policing services is both unfair and unethical. However, take a situation where a private interest is responsible for generating an activity that could spawn the necessary conditions for criminal activity (for instance, by drawing together large numbers of people in a limited area) and will profit from this activity. Is it unreasonable to expect from that private interest a larger contribution to the public policing effort involved in public safety than from the general taxpayer?

Police organisations, as we have seen, have adopted a variety of approaches in answering this question. We look more closely now at one of these: the scheme adopted by Victoria Police in Australia to deal with the issue of public safety at events. Victoria Police answer the above question 'no', but with qualifications. Fees are charged for events policing, but there is also in place a scheme for the waiver of fees. The following information is largely based on discussions with the police involved.

The law and policy in relation to charging for police services is set out in the *Police Regulation (Fees and Charges) Regulations* 2004 and VPM Instruction 107–2. The Regulatory Impact Statement for the Regulations states the police case for charging: "The application of charges for certain police services recognises the community"s right to have first call on the resources of the Victoria Police, compared with organisations or individuals who may seek to divert these public goods for private and/or commercial purposes" (Regulatory Impact Statement for *Police Regulation (Fees and Charges) Regulations* 2004, s. 5.4).

The Victoria Police scheme for events charging is relatively new. Although user-pays for events has been around for sixty or seventy years in Victoria, previously all income went to the State's consolidated revenue fund and the Minister responsible for justice matters made all decisions concerning waivers. Only since the introduction of the new regulations has the responsibility for waivers transferred to police. Police also now keep revenues over a certain threshold, as a result of intragovernmental agreement. That revenue is pooled centrally and submissions may be made by regional police officers for funding from the pool.

Victoria Police charges are levied in relation to sporting and entertainment events that fit within one or more of three types: first, events where admission charges are made (whether to view or participate in the event); second, events that are commercial in nature; and third, events that are commercially promoted or sponsored (reg.4(1)). The charges are levied not only for police services at the event itself but also those used in the planning of the event and the supervision and support of the personnel involved. The fees charged are set out in the Regulations. Fees are imposed in relation to equipment (vehicles, dogs, horses etc.) as well as police time, on a cost recovery basis. The revenue raised, while significant in absolute terms, is relatively minor in the scheme of overall police revenue.[7]

A request for assistance by the organiser of the event is not a prerequisite for police attendance and the rules on charging will apply whenever police attend an event of the specified type (unless the event can easily be policed using personnel ordinarily on duty at or near that location). Event organisers are expected to approach the police before the event to discuss the number of police officers to be deployed. Organisers are also expected to take into account police recommendations on a range of issues relating to safety, security and public order at the event. Negotiations may cover, for instance, plans for the engagement of private security, start and finish times, limitations on alcohol availability and manner of service, water provision, traffic management, setting up of barricades and space design issues. Once satisfactory discussions have been had, police will provide the organiser with a quote for the needed police resources so that

---

[7] The revenue from events charging in 2004–2005 was approximately AUD3.4m. The total revenue for Victoria Police in 2004–2005 was over AUD1,352m (Victoria Police Annual Report for 2004–2005, Appendix J).

'the organiser can budget for police just like any other expense associated with the event'.

Because Victoria Police regards the policing of such events as part of general duties, and therefore as something they have an obligation to provide, sometimes they, in their own words, "impose" themselves. This may be necessary if an organiser neglects or refuses to come to the police before the event, or where the arrangements proposed by the organiser do not, to the police's satisfaction, properly address the issues of public safety and order. Organisers may be provided with and charged for numbers of officers they may not necessarily have wanted or budgeted for because the police consider this is necessary to fulfil their public obligations. An element of compulsion therefore lies behind these commercial arrangements.

After an organiser has been provided with a quote, some can apply to the Chief Commissioner for a waiver of fees. A waiver is seen by Victoria Police as a government subsidy (Victoria Police 2005). If an event is profitable, waivers are not usually given. A waiver is normally available only where the event organiser can demonstrate that the imposition of police charges would threaten the viability of the event or its staging in Victoria. Waivers will also almost always be partial (an exception was the event staged to raise money for the Indian Ocean tsunami victims in 2005, when a 100 percent waiver was given).

In determining the eligibility to apply for a waiver (that is, whether application of police charges would threaten the viability of the event or its staging in Victoria), the Chief Commissioner considers not only the presented financial details, but also asks questions about whether the organiser could have done more to increase viability, better manage the event and comply more satisfactorily with police suggestions. Where eligibility is determined to exist, there is then a complex matrix of criteria applied to the question of the amount of waiver that should be given. As well as purely financial considerations, questions such as whether the event is a recurring one, what kinds of benefits it brings to the community and the effects of the identified funding deficit on the event or organiser are given weightings with a view to determining the percentage waiver that should be awarded. That percentage may then be further reduced if, for instance, unnecessary police resources were consumed because of organiser mismanagement, if the event had attracted waivers in previous years, or if the organisers have not taken the advantage they should have of private security.

According to one officer we spoke to, decisions about charges and waivers "are not light decisions – if you make the wrong decision it affects real people ... you need to understand the event and the impact of it". And such decisions can become 'political footballs' as well. In 2005 it was proposed that the organisers of a rural fishing competition, held annually for the previous thirty two years, would, for the first time, be charged fees for the police who were to patrol the river bank for the weekend of the competition. Outrage greeted the news that the organisers could be liable to pay up to AUD40,000. The organisers were incensed, too, that they did not get any choice about accepting police services or about the number of police to be deployed. Ultimately a decision by the Chief Commissioner to waive all but AUD560 of the fees was hailed as a "reprieve", but not before the parliamentary opposition had accused the state government of deliberately engaging in a revenue-raising exercise that would put at risk many rural and regional activities across Victoria (Dalton and Sellars 2005; Sellars 2005; Kingsley 2005; Delahunty 2005).

Victoria Police's user-pays scheme for events makes an interesting case study for two reasons: first because, although cost recovery is the proclaimed primary purpose of the scheme, other factors play a part and, second and related, because of the place user-pays occupies in Victoria Police's future strategic planning.

While the charging of fees for the policing of events is indeed about cost recovery, an important underlying objective (and a reason behind many of the extensive negotiations between police and organisers) is to educate event organisers about how to manage events from a security perspective and how to improve their management over time. An important element here is the 'responsibilisation' (O'Malley and Palmer 1996; Garland 1996) of organisers so that they will manage events in ways that limit demands on police resources. This is also part of the rationale for reducing waivers progressively for recurring events. If the organiser learns how to better ensure public safety and security, the reasoning goes, the event should become increasingly self-regulating so that fewer and fewer police resources will be required. An organiser who is reluctant to learn and thinks it is cheaper to pay for public policing than to implement police recommendations will find they are paying more and more for policing because of the reducing percentage of waiver. In other words, police are here engaged in engineering solutions to the deficit in policing resources with which they grapple every day. The scheme is an example of Cheng's 'structural' methods of regulation in that it establishes "mechanisms or procedures that push citizens [in this case, event organisers] toward compliance by making the undesirable behavior less profitable or more troublesome. ... Unlike fiat, structure does not regulate undesired behavior directly through ex post penalties. Rather, it regulates indirectly and ex ante by subtly shaping the physical, social, or other arrangements that enable the behavior to occur in the first place. Its philosophy is more preventive, rather than reactive" (Cheng 2006: 655, 662).

That is not to say that all is 'smooth sailing' in these responsibilisation attempts. Resistance to the payment of user fees is found not only among those being charged fees (as in the fishing competition example), but also among police themselves. Charging sometimes makes life more difficult for local police who are seeking to build partnerships within their communities, and who see community events as a part of their 'patch' rather than anything discrete or special. Many argue that user-pays and community policing are not happy housemates. A 1988 report by the National Police Research Unit in Australia identified charging for police presence as an initiative that could "dissipate the unique closeness between the public and the police fostered by such events" and negatively affect public opinion of police (Berwick 1988: 9).

However, the events-policing fees scheme, and user-pays more generally, is at present established policy, and is centrally managed and decided upon. It sits within a broader context of an increasingly financially aware and business-savvy policing organisation. The Victoria Police organisation has approximately fourteen thousand staff and AUD1.4b in annual government funding. As one officer put it, "We're a large business". While there is little government support for general commercialization in the policing arena, and certainly not for user-pays as a principle for day-to-day or 'core functions' policing, it is evident that Victoria Police appears to be cautiously positioning itself for a more business-oriented future. The organisation already engages in some activities of a clearly commercial nature; for instance, it breeds its own dogs and sells any surplus. In the last few years, research has been conducted within Victoria Police into the best way to manage both income generation and expenditure. A variety of business 'tools' (consisting of decision-making frameworks and templates to analyse work, output and cost flows and the impacts of changes) have been created and some have been least partially implemented as part of an 'integrated management framework'.

Police officers are being trained as business managers, and recruitment of persons with prior business experience is ongoing. Victoria Police seems to be ahead of many other policing organisations in its willingness to consider innovative solutions to the question of police resourcing for the future, with user-pays being only one element. But it is not alone, as evidence from locales such as Canada's Ontario Provincial Police makes clear (Wood 2000).

Risks and Future Directions for User-Pays Policing
While there may be clear public benefits to user-paid policing that serves private interests, the practice is not without risk and concerns. Risks can be categorized as relating to efficiency, equity and legitimacy.

One efficiency-related risk is of neglect of public policing because of the demands of private policing. Police simply do not have the resources to do everything that the public thinks they should be doing. Choices are constantly made about work priorities – discretion is an essential feature of public policing. Some police forces, for example, have withdrawn from responding to home alarms unless on-site verification of criminal activity has taken place (this in the case in our home town of Canberra, for instance, and also in Las Vegas and Salt Lake City in the United States). The policing of private interests, whether those involve events, special services like escorts, or services to a particular industry such as provided by the GSDU in Western Australia, consumes resources that may not always be replaceable. Similarly, fees may not always adequately cover the costs of replacing those consumed resources.

Police acceptance of private sources of funding also carries with it risks that public safety and security may be sacrificed to private agendas. In 'marketing' security services, police could be regarded as acting like private security firms. The problem with that, of course, is that private security owes its primary allegiance to the paying client. When police are faced with the choice between investigating an alleged fraud on a large company that is willing to contribute towards the cost of the investigation (say, by providing overseas travel) and investigating an alleged fraud of a smaller company that is unable to pay, the risk that police will choose to provide a better service to the former is not an imaginary one. After all, apart from the possibility of personal benefits for involved police officers, there is a revenue benefit for the organisation and possibly also a reputational benefit if the case is a high-profile one.

There is a risk, too, that the reputation of the police organisation may suffer. In some countries, such as Australia, the tradition of taxpayer-funded public policing is a long and honoured one. Anything different provides fertile ground for suspicion and speculation that corruption may be afoot. Transparency of user-pays processes is therefore essential to protect the legitimacy of police.

Police in many jurisdictions deal with the risks to efficiency, equity and legitimacy that are presented by user-pays policing in a variety of ways, including through limits on the types of services they will charge for, the amounts of the fees that are levied, and qualifications on charging (such as the Victoria Police waiver scheme). Often they will develop detailed policy guidelines covering these and other issues. However, the very variety of user-pays formats on a global scale suggests that there is still plenty of scope for new arrangements to arise carrying their own risks, such as types of policing that sit on the ambiguous border between public and private security.

Some bodies, particularly in the United States, are already occupying this border area. The city of San Francisco in California hosts an organisation separate from the police department, known as Patrol Special Police (SFPSP). SFPSP officers are appointed and regulated by the Police Commission, trained at the Police Academy to the standards of peace officers (the same standard as a police reservist) and supervised by the San Francisco Police Department.

Once designated by the Commission as the 'owners' of a certain beat or territory, they are funded entirely by businesses and residents who contract for their services within that beat or territory. Services provided include patrol (including patrolling the private property of businesses that have hired them), escorts and alarm response, but they also respond to regular police calls within their area. This special force has a long history, dating from the gold rush days of 1847 when merchants established it to tackle the activities of Barbary Coast criminals. One might ask whether the SFPSP is best described as user-pays policing, as corporate sponsorship of a police service or as private security providing a service outsourced by the public police.

As Shearing points out, policing has had both a public and a private face for as long as public and private aspects of the social world have been recognised (1992: 402). But for most of the time since public policing came into being, these have, in the main, been regarded as separate spheres, capable of cooperation and conflict but still discrete ventures. However, border-area forms of policing such as discussed above represent a blurring or merging of the two faces that has been ongoing for some time.[8]

Where public and private security meet and mix like this, the complex questions of responsibility and accountability that already exist in relation to commercial involvement by public police are magnified. Who is responsible if a privately paid but publicly trained and commissioned officer misbehaves or is negligent? Indeed, what are the scope and limits of such an officer's duties and powers? To whom is he or she accountable? Where do the legal rights and liabilities lie? The risks that public-private forms of policing will result in greater inefficiencies and inequities in the distribution of policing services to a society increase even further as the soup is stirred and the

---

[8] Shearing (1992: 409ff) identifies the RAND Corporation report of 1972 examining private security in the United States and the follow-up study by the Hallcrest Corporation in 1985 as the beginning of a reassessment of the role of private security in policing (including public/private policing partnerships and privatization of public policing functions) that is still ongoing. See further, for example, Marx 1987; Johnston 1992; Sarre and Prenzler 2005; Jones and Newburn 2006.

ingredients (public policing, private security) lose their distinct identities.

Conclusion

User-pays or fee-for-service policing is a common and longstanding phenomenon in many jurisdictions. Charges are levied by police for a variety of different services, ranging from the simple provision of information, to special policing services provided for one-off events or on a longer term basis, to services to a particular industry or sector provided by a specialist body of public police. A critical implication of user-pays, per se, is for police resourcing. Charging fees for public policing services to private entities enables police to at least partly recover the costs of providing them.

Just because public policing now encompasses newer economic forms like user-pays does not *necessarily* detract from its nature as a public service. As we have argued, there is no necessary disjuncture between addressing local or private concerns and more general or public ones. User-pays policing can be, and often is, compatible with public interests and the provision of public goods. When this is the case there may be sound reasons for supporting it. User-pays policing does, nonetheless, raise the possibility that private interests might have more influence on service provision than is appropriate. The charging of fees for service may also be an early step in movement towards a more extensive commercialization of public policing. It may even result in the wholesale transformation of public policing into private policing, such as occurred when the U.K. port constabularies in Harwich, Felixstowe and Tilbury were sold in their entirety to port companies (Hinds 1994: 185).

Some authors have warned of potential negative effects of this 'commodification' of policing, that is, of its packaging and promotion as a thing that can be traded (Loader 1999; Newburn 2001; Murphy 2002; Crawford and Lister 2006). These include the risk that it will create inequitable or 'tiered' policing, with taxpayer funded public policing constituting 'a second tier form of provision, more geared to coercive law enforcement and the residual policing of those left behind' (Crawford and Lister 2006: 184; see also Loader 1999: 383–4). Loader (1999: 383) also suggests that police budgets may suffer in circumstances where a market in police services encourages the affluent to spend on paid services and to resent subsidizing through their taxes the provision of services to those who cannot afford to pay (see also Crawford and Lister 2006: 184). Resulting inequities in the delivery of services would inevitably endanger the legitimacy of public policing itself.

Crawford and Lister (2006: 186) remark that "Left to its own devices, the market will foster competitive tendencies among plural providers that are unlikely to fit with broader conceptions of policing as a universally available 'public good'". Our Victorian case study, however, suggests that when it comes to selling their own services, not all police are leaving the market to its own devices, nor are they necessarily interested in competing there. Charging can be used by police in some circumstances as a market regulator, a means of engineering the marketplace: forcing private interests to consider more seriously their consumption of police resources and how they can consume less by minimizing the risks to safety and public order of their activities. For police, this represents a way of obtaining much needed resources with which to continue to do public policing, not as a residual service but as their main game. Requiring people to take more responsibility for the law enforcement aspects of their actions enables police to gradually retreat from involvement in private policing, rather than pushing out into that market as competitors. So Victoria Police can be regarded as involved in a balancing act: supporting events (particularly those with a strong community benefit) by being 'on the ground' and maintaining order, whilst also making those persons organizing these events progressively take more responsibility for their conduct. To do this, Victoria Police use a combination of informal police training (negotiations and recommendations), charging and graduated reductions in waivers.

In some jurisdictions, such as Australia, careful thought is being given to the appropriateness of police involvement in various types of commercialization. Without clear government support, commercialization of the public police is bound to proceed only slowly. Furthermore, it seems that adopting a business culture is not easy in policing organisations where techniques for business analysis, strategy formulation and risk management are not built into officers' training.

Caution with respect to their own activities in the marketplace is a sign that police may be heeding commentators' warnings about the risks of commodification. But, despite that caution, it seems likely that increasingly hybrid forms of policing will continue to appear (albeit at different rates in various cultural contexts). These may encompass not only cooperation between, but a merging of, the public and private faces of security. As Swanton forecast some time ago (1993: 8), the career paths of those in the "protection domain" (by which he meant both public police and private security) frequently cross each other, with police often taking up careers in private security once retired from the police service, and private security increasingly being formally entrusted with more public policing powers (this is happening in the United Kingdom, for instance, through accreditation of private security firms under the Police Reform Act 2002). Commercialization of public policing services may well make these cross-overs more common by equipping the various public and private policing bodies with knowledge and experience relevant to the others. New forms of policing will challenge conceptions of state centrality in the 'protection domain' and raise questions about the extent of state regulation that is needed and about the appropriate loci of accountability and responsibility for the services provided.

PART 2: SELLING THE POLICE BRAND

For most people, association with the police carries a degree of prestige. Trading on this, police have found ways to raise funds by selling the police 'brand'. In many jurisdictions, quite apart from selling their services, police engage in merchandising, selling products explicitly or implicitly related to the organisation. The licensing of individuals and institutions to use police intellectual property is also becoming more common.

Merchandising
It is often but not always the police organisation itself that is involved in selling police merchandise. Sometimes only a part of the organisation is involved, such as the police band. Sometimes the vendor is a police association or union (such as the Australian Federal Police

Association (AFPA)) or a police foundation (such as the Chequered Ribbon Association in Australia, the Vermont Troopers Foundation or the New York City Police Foundation). It may even be a private commercial entity. In these cases the revenue from merchandising may not go directly to the police organisation itself. However, it may still benefit police because the money is used to support the activities of the association or foundation. Or a private company (such as the Mounted Police Gift Shop in Canada) may purchase the products it sells from a licensee of the police organisation which has of course paid the police organisation, association or foundation a fee for that privilege. In certain cases, merchandise is only available to employees of the organisation (e.g., the CIA, the FBI[9]) or the sale of products to particular buyers is strictly regulated (e.g., the AFPA).

Police may have a retail outlet in a police museum or other police premises (as in Tokyo and Melbourne), or license a particular retail outlet or outlets to sell official merchandise for them. Sometimes merchandise is only available online (e.g., Band of the South Australia Police[10]). Most merchandise will carry either the police organisation's name or logo, which may be obvious or discreet (the Swiss Police merchandise, for example, bears only a small logo). Clothing of various types (t-shirts, hats, sweaters, ties, sportswear, sleepwear etc.) is probably the most common merchandise sold, along with novelties like toys, mugs, pens and key rings. Glassware, clocks, coasters, spoons, flashlights, magnets and plaques are also popular. Some police organisations sell books relating to their organisation or jurisdiction (for example, the Royal Canadian Mounted Police). Hong Kong Police sell (through a licensee) an amazing array of products, including umbrellas, card holders, musical jewellery boxes, buttons, calculators and chopsticks. They sell warrant card holders, police badges and truncheons. They even offer an array of crystal items such as batons, rank insignias, a model of the police HQ and a very personable uniformed robot.[11] The Swiss Canton of Valais police

---

[9] See "Corporate Store Strategies", article No. 9560 on the Sales Marketing Network, available at http://www.nyirr.com/resources/9560–Corporate-Store-Strategies.16.html/ (accessed 10 July 2008).

[10] See http://www.bandsapolice.com/returnindex.htm (accessed 10 July 2008).

[11] See http://www.yorkview.com/diyhp/3/xml/index2.html (accessed 10 July 2008).

specialize in wooden products.[12] The Australian Federal Police Association (AFPA) offers a stubby holder adorned with the Australian Federal Police (AFP) logo (a stubby is a small beer bottle, and the holder is made of an insulating material to keep the bottle cold). The Western Australia Police Pipe Band complements its similar offering with a stubby opener.[13] Police bands sell mainly CDs, videos and DVDs although some also offer clothing and other items (the Victoria Police Band sells thumb cuffs and the Pipes and Drums of the Edmonton Police Service kilt pins).

Merchandise may be readily identifiable as relating to the police even though the name or logo of the police organisation on the product is discreet or non-existent. Constable Kenny Koala in the Australian Capital Territory (ACT) is a community personality within the ACT region and instantly recognisable by most ACT children. There are Kenny soft toys and his image adorns a range of other merchandise. Similarly, the RCMP sells uniformed toy 'Mountie' bears, moose and other Canadian wildlife.

Sometimes a particular program is promoted through merchandise. Queensland Police offer products carrying the Neighbourhood Watch logo, including stickers and tote bags. In 2005 the same police organisation sold merchandise relating to the Queensland Police Games. The Community Supporting Police (CSP) organisation, which is financially supported by Queensland Police and appears on its Web site, sells soft toy koala police officers, model police cars and tea-towels, all carrying the CSP logo. The funds are used to help provide emergency accommodation to police and their families in times of crisis.

Sometimes police even sell items relating directly to law enforcement. The Osaka police sell purse snatching prevention covers for bicycle baskets[14] and the Miyagi police sell bicycle antitheft devices.[15]

---

[12] See http://www.vs.ch/navig/navig.asp?MenuID=4380 (accessed 21 July 2008).

[13] See http://www.wapol.com.au/merchandise.html (accessed 21 July 2008).

[14] See http://www.info.police.pref.osaka.jp/ps/habikino/top.html;.http://www.info.police.pref.osaka.jp/ps/joto/2oshirase.html (accessed 21 July 2008).

[15] See http://www.police.pref.miyagi.jp/hp/so1/hittakuri/bousi/bohangoods_h.htm (accessed 1 March 2007).

Managing Use of Intellectual Property

Police merchandising is often accompanied by a realisation on the part of police organisations of the importance to revenue streams of properly managing police *intellectual* property. The Metropolitan Police in London provide a good example. The head of the Met's Resources Directorate was quoted as saying "The Met has always been able to raise sponsorship – but our aims are changing to long-term income generation." This is in line with a recent exhortation by the Police Forum for Income Generation (PolFIG) (2003/2006: 44): "Where possible Forces should seek to maximise the commercial potential of all material." A new unit within the Directorate, the Events and Income Development Unit (EIDU), was launched in 2003 for just that purpose. Together with merchandising and sponsorship, the EIDU looks after licensing the use of the Met's intellectual property. This includes images of Met assets and activities used in print, film or television. There is a charge for the use of IP at approximately £200 per hour with a minimum charge of £250 per license. These charges include the cost of administration and preparation of the license (Metropolitan Police Service (nda)). In 2003, it was reported that the Met had plans to raise up to £1m by selling its backlog of CCTV footage, including car chases and the Millennium Dome robbery recordings, to production companies. The funds were to be reinvested into projects such as Neighbourhood Watch and Operation Sapphire, which deals with sex crimes in London (BBC News 2003). PolFIG (2003/2006: 44) reports that both the Met and Hertfordshire Police also promote the use of police premises for films and documentaries and the provision of police staff or officers to assist with filming on location. In a similar vein, as mentioned in Part 1 of this chapter, an Australian police organisation 'lent' a media production company an officer to act as advisor for the entire run of a police television drama (approximately ten years), in return for funding for the officer's full time salary.

Auctioning Seized and Unclaimed Found and Stolen Goods

Police may also raise funds through the auctioning of goods. These may include goods that are surplus to requirements, that have been confiscated under proceeds of crime legislation or impounded, that are recovered stolen goods that have not been claimed by the rightful owner, or that have been found and remain unclaimed. Police auctions are generally conducted by a third party private auction house, although in some cases the police department itself or another government agency will conduct them.

In the United States, it is quite common for firearms to be sold at police auctions. Generally, confiscated firearms can only be sold to licensed firearms dealers, members of the public licensed to possess firearms or other law enforcement agencies. In Kentucky, weapons confiscated by state and local law enforcement agencies are sold by the state's Division of Surplus Property. The funds are distributed through a grant program run by the Governor's office. Grants are given to purchase body armour for officers and canines (Kentucky Government 2006). In Missouri, only a court can order the sale of firearms following the conviction of the offender who used the weapon to prosecute a felony, but the proceeds of the sale become the property of the police department or sheriff's department responsible for the defendant's arrest or the confiscation of the firearms and ammunition.[16] In Indiana, any proceeds from auctions and sales returned to law enforcement agencies must be used to defray the costs of firearms training for police officers (Indiana Code 35–47-3 s.2(D)).

Benefits
The benefits to police of selling their brand include revenue raising, image and awareness promotion, and in some cases, direct crime prevention.

Revenues. While income raised through selling merchandise, seized and found goods and police intellectual property is unlikely to be significant to the scheme of overall police revenue, every little bit helps in an era of tightening budgets. Moreover, if the funds raised are used to support particular programs or activities, they may be of

---

[16] See   http://www.house.mo.gov/billso71/biltxt/intro/HB0180I.htm   (accessed   5 March 2007).

significant benefit for that program or activity. Proceeds from the New South Wales Police Shop, for instance, go to the Police College "to provide equipment and facilities for the exclusive use of students" (New South Wales Police Force 2001). If a police brand is particularly strong, revenues can help police to finance new initiatives. The New York Police Department, through the New York City Police Foundation, has been able to use the sale of merchandise such as action dolls and toy rescue dogs "to turn the flood of affection for the NYPD [following September 11] into revenue" (Weissenstein 2003). These revenues, along with donations to the Foundation, have been used to fund counter-terrorism initiatives.

Revenues may be reduced by licensing others to produce and sell merchandise. However, licensing allows police organisations to retain some control over quality and content of merchandise, while still being free to concentrate on their 'core business'. The City of Chicago sees trademarking of the Chicago Police insignia and subsequent licensing of its use on apparel as a way to boost revenues for the city (some of which may end up in the police budget) (Meyer 2006).

Image and awareness promotion. Police we have interviewed have spoken about their "reputational assets" as the most important assets they hold. Merchandising sensitive to this fact can promote an image of the police that they want the public to see. Soft toys dressed as officers, for instance, can promote the 'friendly and helpful' image, particularly the idea of police as adults that children can safely and easily approach when anxious or afraid. This is one of the main aims of the AFP's Constable Kenny Koala campaign (Australian Federal Police 2003: 53). Action figures can promote the 'brave and daring hero' image. Clothing carrying a police organisation name or logo, or the name or logo of a particular police program, may simply raise awareness of the existence of the organisation or program.

In the same way, the media may act as an agent to protect the image of police. The Los Angeles Police Department, in charging licence fees for the use of its badge and logo in television police dramas, is looking for a balance of "creativity and representation of the LAPD in such a way that it does not damage our image and reputation"

(Tribune Media Services 2002). If the use of intellectual property is carefully controlled, the police image may even be enhanced. This is why, for instance, the Metropolitan Police in London would refuse to licence a drama production that portrayed all the police characters "taking drugs, then racially abusing other characters and perpetrating crimes", but might consider it if only a small number of the police characters were doing so and "the production depicted correctly the practice of the organisation by showing that the actions of the officers were regarded as criminal and that the behaviour was neither tolerated nor condoned" (Metropolitan Police Service (nda),.

Although police are not overtly trading on their brand in selling surplus, seized and unclaimed goods at police auctions, the fact that the vendor is a police organisation may make some difference to the willingness of purchasers to trust in the integrity of the vendor, and so enhance the appeal of the goods. One might expect an ex-police car, for example, to have been well maintained, and that an electrical item purchased at a police auction has been properly checked for safety. One might trust that the police will not tarnish their own image by hocking faulty goods. However, some police auctions are indeed conducted with a caveat emptor warning, with clear publicity that goods procured there may come with liens or other such encumbrances. Sales by the Insolvency and Trustee Service Australia (ITSA) of assets confiscated by the Australian Federal Police and other agencies under the *Proceeds of Crime Act* 1987 (Cth) are subject to just such warnings.

Direct crime prevention. As mentioned above, some Japanese prefectural police sell merchandise that assists in crime prevention. Most police organisations seem to leave this kind of product to specialist security companies, but one can certainly imagine there would be a market for police-branded security goods such as locks, alarms and security lighting.

Risks

Any commercial venture by police carries risk. With the sale of police goods and the licensing of police intellectual property come the risks of counterfeiting, misuse and damage to the police organisation's reputation.

Counterfeiting. After 9/11, there was an explosion of merchandise bearing the logo of the New York Police Department (NYPD) (among others). Licensing industry analysts estimated that, if that merchandise had been authorised and its production licensed by the NYPD, it would have brought in millions of dollars to the organisation (Lauro 2002). Licensing, of course, does not halt the flow of goods that carry the police logo without authorisation or that imitate police property. The internet has made trading in such goods even easier. The NYPD and other police organisations deal with this by using a special label that indicates that the item is official merchandise, by notifying retailers of the identity of their authorised producers, and by law enforcement action against unauthorised producers and dealers. However, the production of unauthorised merchandise cannot be halted altogether, and the risk remains that the police organisation is missing out on potential revenue.

By authorising any production of goods, a police organisation puts goods into the public domain that can be easily reproduced. However, if consumers are aware that police are selling merchandise, they may well be attuned to the difference between official and unauthorised merchandise, and choose to buy the former because of its authenticity, thus limiting the market for the unauthorised versions. Of course, consumers may also choose to buy the latter because of its generally lower price.

Misuse. One of the problems with any police merchandise is the potential for it to be misused. In general, most police organisations are very careful about the range of products they sell, ensuring that items do not imitate real police uniforms or equipment. Hong Kong Police may be an exception, given that, as is mentioned earlier, it appears possible for citizens to buy police clothing (but not official uniform), warrant card holder, badge and even a truncheon.

But many police organisations also recognise that *any* merchandise bearing the organisation's logo might be misused to "lend a regular citizen an air of authority" (Lauro 2002), or worse. The AFPA certainly acknowledges this in its Merchandise Policy, where it states:

> The AFPA maintains a policy of the proper and secure handling of merchandise that may be used by members of the public in an attempt to break the law, or for an improper purpose of misleading the public. As a result we strictly regulate the availability of merchandise in accordance with this policy. The AFPA reminds all purchasers of their obligations with respect to the proper use and handling of any AFPA merchandise that may have affixed or included a replica AFP logo and accepts no liability for misuse.

The AFPA deals with the issue by a combination of action and threat:

> ... The AFPA reserves the right to refuse sale to any purchaser at its discretion and will refuse sale to any purchaser who may or may be perceived to have the intention of misusing any AFPA merchandise. The AFPA also has an obligation to contact the relevant law enforcement agency in the event that it perceives that there has been a misuse of any AFPA merchandise, or the person making the below attached declaration has provided false information in the declaration.
> ... Some items may be restricted from general sale at the discretion of the AFPA. Some specific items may only be available to police employees or employees of law enforcement agencies eg DEA. (Australian Federal Police Association 2008).

To prevent misuse, collectors of police memorabilia are also in some jurisdictions (such as New South Wales) required to be licensed.

In the United States, there has been criticism of the sale of firearms for having the potential to rearm the criminals from whom the firearms were confiscated in the first place, or others like them. For this reason, some states have made it illegal for police to sell confiscated weapons and police are required to dispose of them, generally by transferring them to another law enforcement agency or to a forensic agency for research purposes, or by destroying them.[17]

---

[17] For example, House Bill No. 1172 was introduced in Indiana in 2000 for just this purpose, see http://www.in.gov/legislative/bills/2000/IN/IN1172.1.html (accessed 21 July 2008).

Reputational damage. The most concerning issue for police about both unauthorised merchandise and the misuse of merchandise (whether authorised or not) is the effect its existence and use will have on police legitimacy. Unauthorised merchandise may not be designed with "the style and quality befitting its [the police organisation's] image" (Lauro 2002). The misuse of merchandise, say, to commit a crime like fraud or robbery, will similarly do little to promote the police organisation in the eyes of the public. Just behaving inappropriately (such as fighting or being drunk in public) whilst wearing police-branded apparel runs the risk of bringing the police organisation in question into disrepute by association.

Even merchandise sold with complete police approval may pose hazards. Any item carries the usual product liability risk. However, barring an unlikely negligence action, selling some items such as mugs and coasters involves little risk to the police image. However, this may not be the case with less conventional items. In the words of one licensing consultant (with particular reference to police action figures and other items on sale after 9/11), police may "run the risk of cheapening the essence of what they stand for, and their heroic message by doing novelty merchandise" (Lauro 2002). The same might be said of the broadcasting of police-in-action scenarios on programs that are essentially the television equivalents of tabloid newspapers. This is an issue not about the use or misuse of an item or a piece of intellectual property, but about the nature of the item and whether this is in keeping with the desired police representation at a fundamental philosophical level.

But there is a further issue here about the practice of merchandising itself. A police organisation that is seen as resourced so inadequately that it needs to generate revenues through merchandising may be perceived as lacking in central government support, which in turn may raise questions in the public's mind as to whether it is deserving of that support. Public belief in the legitimacy of police is clearly essential to their continued effectiveness.

Conclusion
Merchandising and related sales by police organisations are part of the general commercialization progressively taking place in public policing. As with all forms of commercialization, police need to assess

the costs and benefits for their organisations before embarking on the sale of goods and intellectual property. On the one hand, there may be benefits in the form of additional revenues, the potential for image promotion and enhancement and the possibility of directly contributing to crime prevention through the marketing or licensing of particular products. On the other hand, these benefits must be weighed against the risks that police legitimacy may be tarnished by misuse or counterfeiting of merchandise carrying the police brand, and that the products being sold or licensed, or indeed the very act of selling them or licensing others to use them, will not give the right message about the police. To properly make this assessment presents a real challenge for police organisations.

CHAPTER SIX

GIFT

The primary focus of this chapter is the third form of exchange relationship, donation or gift. Our concern here is with gifts to the police organisation, rather than to individual members. This can entail the giving of cash grants, or the provision of complimentary goods and services to the police organisation, usually in return for acknowledgment or recognition.

Part 1 of the chapter examines private sponsorship of public policing and its increasing importance to police organisations as a means of enhancing their resources. Part 2, similarly, considers the growing reliance of police organisations on the voluntary assistance of people who are not police officers.

PART 1: PRIVATE SPONSORSHIP OF PUBLIC POLICING

Introduction

While the notion of private sector subsidies or sponsorship of public police agencies and operations might strike those who favour a large state apparatus as less than desirable, the idea of private sponsorship of governmental functions is not at all new. Let's start with some easy cases:

- *Funding for the arts*: Many works of art are donated to public museums by private citizens. Many public art exhibitions are sponsored by corporations. The Louvre, traditionally resistant to naming galleries after benefactors, announced in 2007 that it will name a wing after Sheik Zayed bin Sultan Al Nahyan, President of the United Arab Emirates and the Ruler of Abu Dhabi (Riding 2007).

- *Funding for education*: The tradition of private universities is perhaps greatest in the United States, where many universities are named after wealthy founders or benefactors (Carnegie-Mellon, Duke, Stanford, and Rockefeller are but some of many). Lesser contributors may have their names on buildings or lecture halls, or endowed professorships. But even public schools have begun seeking sponsorship. A small public primary school in New Jersey has auctioned naming rights to its gymnasium to a local supermarket (Pennington 2004).
- *Funding for health and medical research*: The United States has its National Institutes of Health, as well as the Scripps Foundation for Medicine and Science, the Robert Wood Johnson Foundation, and the Bill and Melinda Gates Foundation. Individuals also make donations for medical research direct to medical establishments. The late Kerry Packer, then Australia's richest man, donated millions to the Institute for Child Health Research at the Children's Hospital in Sydney. In this, except for the quantum, he was not alone. The Hospital receives thousands of individual gifts each year.

More recently, Michael Bloomberg, the Mayor of New York City, has energetically pursued sponsorship arrangements for city institutions. The Metropolitan Transportation Authority began to consider proposals to sell naming rights to subway stations, bus lines, bridges and tunnels (Luo 2004).

And, if present trends continue, private sponsorship of functions that have thus far been largely, if not exclusively, governmental is likely to become even more prominent. Where will this end? In January 2001, then U.S. Senator Jesse Helms advocated that foreign aid be distributed by private and religious groups rather than the U.S. Agency for International Development (Schmitt 2001).

As governments withdraw from many areas of activity which were previously regarded as core public functions, they are making explicit and implicit pleas to commercial and non-profit organisations to fill the vacuum. The federal government of Australia previous embarked upon a program of promoting philanthropy. A recent prime minister of Australia has argued that "if business prospers from a stable society and a well run economy … then there's some obligation to put something back, and increasingly businesses are doing that" (Howard 2000).

> Our purpose is to build a new social coalition of government, business, charitable and welfare organisations, and other community groups—each contributing their own particular expertise and resources in order to tackle more effectively the social problems that directly or indirectly affect members of our society in one way or another. (Howard 1999)

A recent prime minister of the United Kingdom has similarly spoken of harnessing private sector expertise in reforming the British public sector (Blair 2001). And in the United States, President George W. Bush indicated his intention to encourage private contributions to the resolution of social problems:

> … the Federal Government should do more to encourage private giving—from individuals, corporations, foundations and others—to the armies of compassion that labor daily to strengthen families and communities … . America is blessed with social entrepreneurs who see a problem and set about with energy, ingenuity, and organisational savvy to provide solutions. Foundations provide private support for the public good. This is civil society at work. At the least, government must be sure not to harm such efforts by over-regulation or providing insufficient legal protections for good-faith volunteers, nonprofit groups, and philanthropic companies. (Bush 2001)

In South Africa, President Mbeki has also spoken of the need for the involvement of businesses in South Africa's development:

> … government recognises the fact that it does not have all the resources it needs to meet its obligations to the people. Accordingly, it is interested to attract resources that are in the hands of the private sector, through mutually beneficial public-private partnerships, to increase the capacity of the government to respond to the needs of the people. At the same time, business respects the right and duty of the government to set clear and stable policy and regulatory frameworks that determine how our people and all their

institutions, whatever they are, operate within the context of the rule of law, governed by the precepts contained in our Constitution. (Mbeki 2002)

Application to Policing

The question is, are these developments generalisable to criminal justice? Corporate and private contributions to criminal justice activities are by no means without precedent (Grabosky 1992). Indeed, the New South Wales Police published detailed guidelines for sponsorship in 1992, some time before the development of guidelines for engaging and managing police informants (New South Wales Police 1992). The academic treatment of the issue of sponsorship of policing began well over a decade ago (Bryett 1996).

Sponsorship of policing is becoming increasingly common around the world.[1] In the United States, with its tradition of philanthropy towards public institutions, it is particularly well developed. It is becoming more widespread in the United Kingdom. In Australia, however, it has been relatively uncommon until recently. The growth of sponsorship in the area of policing is part of this broader trend for governments to allow others to perform functions for which they were previously responsible.

What do we mean here by 'sponsorship'? In his anthropological overview of gift giving in pre-industrial societies, the French sociologist Mauss suggested that gift-giving represents a mixture of motives on the part of the giver, including the desire to feel that one is doing one's duty, the desire for prestige that may result from giving, and the expectation of return gifts (Mauss 1950; Dillon 2003: 40–41).

With this in mind, gifts may be imagined as located on a continuum of increasing return on investment for the donor. At one end of the

---

[1] Sponsorship of policing occurs at an international level, too. A state may choose to provide resources (both financial and in terms of training or other assistance) to another state's police force, as the United States has done in Latin America as part of its 'War on Drugs' and as Australia does in its capacity as a regional peace-keeper. Many of the same issues of risk we deal with in this chapter that arise for police organisations in accepting corporate and private donations (such as risks of influence on police agendas) also arise for the governments and police organisations accepting these state 'gifts'. See, for example, Bowling 2006; Bayley 2006: ch. 6.

continuum is pure donation, where the donor does not expect anything in return, except perhaps a private word of thanks. An example
might be the donation by community groups of needed equipment,
such as the topographic maps donated to Queensland Police Service
by local Lions Clubs to assist with search and rescue. Moving along
the continuum, donation becomes sponsorship when the relationship
becomes more of a commercial arrangement and public recognition
of the donor by the recipient is an important, and sometimes the
primary, motivation for the gift. The corporate donation of vehicles
to police might fall into this category, the display of the company's
name on the vehicle sufficing as acknowledgment of the company's
generosity. At the far end of the gift continuum is a grant of resources
that is made subject to conditions by the donor concerning its use. For
instance, in the U.S. state of Virginia, under the HEAT (Help Eliminate Auto Theft) program, insurance companies return a percentage
of liability insurance premiums to the criminal justice system, earmarked for auto theft reduction (Pilant 1998: 44). And in Florida and
several other U.S. states, Purdue Pharmaceuticals has provided funds
to investigate diversion of its prescription painkiller Oxycontin and
for police training on prescription drug abuse.

The benefits for companies of sponsoring police or their activities
are obvious. Reputational association with the 'good guys' can bring
great cachet to a company, and by so doing increase their profits.
For police, sponsorship carries the lure of much-needed resources.
However, there are potential disadvantages to these arrangements
both for police and for the public. It has been suggested that corporate sponsorship of police vehicles with its associated advertising
will create the risk of conflicts of interest for police, distortion of
police agendas and even of corporate capture, and will undermine
the symbolic authority of police (Fleury-Steiner and Wiles 2003:
447–49). This chapter explores the risks and possible consequences
of arrangements involving gift-giving on all parts of the continuum.
The types of concerns we identify are generalisable to most forms of
police sponsorship. As we have seen, the same kinds of concerns
have been raised in relation to relationships of sale, such as user-
pays policing.

Varieties of Gift-Giving

We have said above that gift-giving to police may come in any form ranging from 'pure' donation through sponsorship to conditional grants. The givers may be individuals, community organisations, other government agencies or businesses, and the gift may be a one-off or result from a more permanent arrangement. In South Africa, an organisation called Business Against Crime (BAC), funded by business organisations, provides training and materiel support to police agencies as well as influencing criminal justice strategy, policy and priorities (Bhanu and Stone 2004; Singh 2005). Many police organisations obtain resources from foundations and charitable trusts set up specifically to assist them. The New York City Police Foundation, for example, has raised money for police health screening, scholarships and training, amongst other things. By the end of 2006, over twenty constabularies in the United Kingdom had established their own registered charity or charitable trust (ACPO 2006: 22).

The following brief survey of gift-giving in a number of jurisdictions giving examples from each provides some indication of the breadth of gift-giving arrangements across the world.

The United States. In the United States, small and under-resourced municipal police services exist in a climate of philanthropy arguably more generous than that prevailing in most nations of the world. In the 1960s, in the context of interracial unrest, the Ford Foundation threw its considerable material support behind policing institutions such as the Southern Police Institute at the University of Louisville, the Police Foundation, the Police Executive Research Forum and the National Organization of Black Law Enforcement Executives (Stone 2002), as well as providing grants for research into the policing of minorities. An even more vivid and current example of corporate support for policing is to be found in the generosity of the W.W. Caruth, Jr. Foundation Fund of Dallas, Texas. This family foundation donated $15 million to the Dallas Police Department over three years. The gift was used to purchase new equipment, including 520 video cameras, 532 police-car partitions, 50 bullet-proof vests and at least 400 cell phones, in addition to maintenance and the services of consultants (Bernstein 2005). However, even the support of average citizens for police organisations can have widespread effects. A child in Pittsburgh, Pennsylvania, raised money to buy a local police dog a bullet-resistant vest. As a result of the enormous number of donations received, she was able to start a program of canine vest purchases that has since grown into the nationwide Vest-a-Dog Inc. Foundation.

Business in the United States also provides substantial financial support for police. Many gifts are directly tied to particular police activities that relate to the business of the donor. Microsoft, in cooperation with the U.S. Secret Service and the FBI, has established an Antivirus Reward Program, providing funds for use as rewards for information leading to the arrest and conviction of persons releasing viruses and worms on the Internet (Microsoft 2003).

The El Cajon, California, City Council accepted donations totalling $5,000 from local tow truck operators and community businesses to the Police Canine Acquisition Trust Account (El Cajon City Council 1998). In Los Angeles, Allstate Insurance Company has sponsored the recruitment and training of reserve officers for the LAPD (Allstate Insurance 2001). General Electric has funded the acquisition of closed circuit television cameras linked through the internet to the local police station (Gallagher's Beat 1994; Los Angeles Police Department 2004). In New York, under the stewardship of Mayor Michael Bloomberg (himself a noted philanthropist), the New York City Police Department received contributions to build a $1.2 million counterterrorism centre, and to create a mobile chemical and bio-logical detection lab (Steinhauer 2003).

Sometimes an overt acknowledgment of sponsorship is required by sponsors. Explicit commercial advertisement through police facilities is more widespread than one might suspect (Fleury-Steiner and Wiles 2003). Government Acquisitions (GA), a private company located in the U.S. state of North Carolina, arranges corporate sponsorship of police vehicles. A company pays for a vehicle, which it donates to a public police organisation under an arrangement negotiated by GA. In return for the donation, the company may feature advertisements on the vehicle's hood, boot and quarter panels for three years. Police officials have final say over sponsors' identities and the design and placement of the graphics (Government Acquisitions 2004). GA's service has proven very popular with cash-strapped municipal and county police departments, but has also attracted considerable criticism, on the basis that putting police cars 'up for sale' suggests that police and justice are similarly for sale (Mollenkamp 2003: 81).

A similar scheme, at a more local level, is to be found in Crown Point, Indiana. Local businesses donate $1,500 each to provide communications and other equipment for patrol cars. Under the Adopt-a car program, the cars may bear the message "This vehicle is equipped by 'XYZ company' " on the back of the car (Pilant 1998: 44).

General purpose organisations also exist in the United States. Perhaps the most significant of these is the New York City Police Foundation, established in 1971. This is an independent, non-profit organisation dedicated to strengthening the Police Department and promoting public safety in New York. In some respects, it operates in a manner analogous to a 'blind' trust, in that donations are pooled, and cannot be directly earmarked by the donor. Over the years, it has received tax-exempt donations from prominent (and less prominent) corporations and citizens, including Merrill Lynch, Tiffany, Motorola, David Rockefeller, and The New York Times Company. The Foundation in turn contributes funds to support programs which can not be funded through the City budget. The Foundation sponsors a Horse Donation Program for the Mounted Police Unit, has launched a campaign to raise $2 million to provide bullet-proof vests for police officers and has organised a series of networking and educational activities involving leaders from the corporate community to promote the professional development of women members of the Department. In 1996, the Police Foundation obtained a state-of-the-art computer system to facilitate crime analysis.

Australia. The annual reports of some if not all Australian police services contain lists of private donors/sponsors, and may refer explicitly to the nature or purpose of the gift. The New South Wales Police Annual Report for 2005, for instance, indicates that the Service received fifty-two separate donations valued at AUD2,000 or more from a diverse range of donors including numerous motor vehicle dealers, a major insurance company, a large shopping centre developer, local government councils, and the Korean Presbyterian Church (New South Wales Police Service 2005: 61–62). The gifts in question ranged from cash for specific crime prevention projects to 'covert vehicles', fingerprint cameras, petrol, and bicycles. In 2003, Alfa Romeo supplied a car for the crime prevention patrol at Bondi. The vehicle attracted more attention than would a standard police car (Wilson 2003). Similarly, improving relations between car enthusiasts and police was the reasoning behind the recent acceptance by Sydney's Bankstown Highway Patrol of the loan of a high-performance Lotus Exige (N.R.M.A. 2007). We noted above that the Westfield Carousel Shopping Centre donates computer, fax, video interviewing facilities, and office space to the Western Australia Police (Western Australia Police Service 2000: 14).

It is not only state police organisations that receive donations. The Australian High Tech Crime Centre, an organisation in which all Australian police agencies participate and which was set up to provide a national coordinated approach to combating serious, complex and multijurisdictional technology-enabled crimes, includes analysts and investigators from Australia's major banks whose salaries are paid by their employers, and who work side by side with police officers (Keelty 2006). This phenomenon of business lending people to assist police in areas where business has expertise is dealt with further in the next part of this chapter on people as a policing resource.

Sometimes specific police activities or investigations are sponsored. The Western Australia Police Macro Task Force, investigating a series of murders of young women in Perth, was subsidised in part by donations from members of the public.

Just as in the United States, a sponsor will sometimes receive public acknowledgement for their sponsorship, as did a large department store chain and a local radio station that awarded prizes to Victoria police officers who successfully participated in the organisation's health and fitness program (Arnold 2006). Other sponsors may receive a concession from police in addition to or instead of acknowledgment. In return for a donation of aerial surveillance camera equipment for the Victoria Police Air Wing helicopter fleet, Melbourne's commercial television stations received not only acknowledgment in the form of an article in the police magazine, but also permission to broadcast pictures of events involving police via a digital microwave television downlink (Miller 1999).

South Africa. The crime problems which confront post-apartheid South Africa are overwhelming by any modern standard, and have given rise to a very large private security sector. But not everyone in South Africa can afford private security services, and economic development requires a degree of security more than the market can deliver. So it is that former President Nelson Mandela invited the South African business community to assist the public police.

After Business Against Crime was established, it organised R8.5 million worth of gun-proof hi-tech closed circuit television (CCTV) cameras monitored twenty-four hours and linked to emergency services (Business Against Crime – Western Cape, and the City of Cape Town 1998). Business Against Crime has also offered management courses to police in certain stations (Minnaar 2004: 23). It even provided assistance in drafting the white paper on Safety and Security (Department of Safety and Security, South Africa 1998).

Businesses have also been individually active. Philips SA contributed R500,000 for the refurbishment of a court house near their headquarters. According to CEO and Chair Wouter Dronkers: "Business has an important role to play in the development of this country".[2] AECI, a major South African industrial group and leading supplier of chemicals and related products, has sponsored training of police management teams in a BAC-instigated leadership development program for the South African Police Service (Business Against Crime 2006). Police tracking computers have been fitted to the vehicles and aircraft of a number of police units throughout South Africa courtesy of a private tracking company, Tracker. These computers enable police to pick up a signal being emitted from the tracking unit fitted to a hijacked or stolen vehicle that is activated by the company or vehicle owner, and to recover the vehicle. Tracker has also provided training on vehicle tracking to police members in the relevant units (Minnaar 2005).

[2] See http://www.info.gov.za/speeches/1999/9910271106a1003.htm (accessed 10 July 2008).

Some communities in South Africa also make donations to assist the usually over-burdened, under-resourced local police. Items such as fax machines, two-way radios, computers and even vehicles have been donated (Minnaar 2004: 23). Some communities have established non-profit companies in order to by-pass Treasury regulations with respect to police receipt of donations. The development of Business or City Improvement Districts in a number of South African cities has prompted a more standardised cooperative relationship between the police and the private sector. For instance, in the city of Cape Town the Cape Town Partnership, as part of its agenda to revitalise the city, opted for the use of private security to improve security in the CBD. This in turn prompted the development of relations between private security and the police through joint operations, linked radio communication, and joint patrols, sometimes in private vehicles (Berg 2004a).

The People's Republic of China. Modern China does not have a significant tradition of philanthropy. In the post-Mao era, those who have become affluent tend not to call attention to themselves, for reasons of privacy, security, or modesty. There is, however, a rich tradition of voluntarism. Police foundations are very common in China, where they serve in the absence of workers' compensation insurance as a safety net in the event of death or injury to police members. By 2006, twenty-eight such foundations had been formed at the provincial level across the country. Donors included private citizens, business, governments, and police members themselves. The Shenzhen City Police Foundation was founded in 1995, and as of January 2005 had received donations exceeding 30,000,000RMB (approx. U.S.$4 million). The Tsing Tao Brewery Group's Distribution Branch in Shenzhen made a large donation. More than a quarter of the received donations have been used on health checkups for police officers and on police officers who had died, been injured, or fallen ill due to their duties (Southern City News 2005).

In China, one can see the early stages of the evolution of gift into arrangements that are more commercial. At the Twentieth National Public Security Conference in 2003, Zhou Yongkang, the Minister of

Public Security, called for "using market forces to build a timely insurance structure for police officers who die or are injured on duty". After the Twentieth National Public Security Conference, public security organisations in Shaoguan City bought accidental personal injury insurance for serving officers and have also been actively sourcing funds to set up police foundations (Guangdong Provincial Public Security Department 2005).

The Henan Provincial Police Foundation was formed in February 2006 after gaining a large grant from the government. The Provincial Public Security Department called on police officers to join the foundation voluntarily by making a donation depending on their official level. After obtaining membership, all members pay a yearly membership fee of 30RMB. Benefits depend on one's status and the severity of one's disability. Educational assistance for children of officers who die, are injured, or who otherwise suffer hardship is also available.

Elsewhere in Greater China, more traditional forms of corporate largesse are evident. In Taiwan, a producer of medicinal plants donated an ambulance to the police station of Tainan County. A large manufacturer of industrial and household paper products has made gifts to police that have included fire-fighting equipment as well as condolence money for police wounded on duty (Anon. 2004b; 2006).

Other jurisdictions. In other places, it is not uncommon for police organisations to have been established for the protection of the state rather than of its citizens. In many developing countries, especially those in the post-colonial era or whose post-independence government structures tend toward the autocratic, engineering a cultural change in police-community relations is a significant challenge. In Kenya, the Nairobi Central Business District Association has worked with police to develop community policing programs with a customer focus. In India, some local business leaders are seeking to improve the living and working conditions of lower-ranking police officers with a view towards improving morale. Other business people in Mumbai and Delhi are working with local police executives to create "islands of excellence" in policing (Bhanu and Stone 2004).

Road safety, which has become core police business in many countries, is one area that lends itself to widespread private sponsorship. In India, a petroleum company and local vehicle man-ufacturer co-sponsored a workshop on transporting school children, in collaboration with the Delhi Police. In Bangalore, Infosys has donated police vehicles and breathalysers. Police officers in Ottawa and Toronto in Canada have been sponsored by the community organisation Mothers Against Drunk Driving (MADD) to set up roadside checkpoints to crack down on drink impaired drivers (CBC News 2005). The insurance industry, too, has an obvious interest in road safety. So it is that the Accident Compensation Corporation of New Zealand donated four compulsory breath testing buses, referred to as "ACC Stop Buses", to New Zealand Police (Global Road Safety Partnership [nda]).

The Risks and Consequences of Accepting Gifts

It may be asked whether there really is such a thing as a 'pure' gift as we have suggested in our continuum model. Mauss (1950: 3), in his anthropological overview of gift giving in pre-industrial societies, distinguishes between gifts that are voluntary, disinterested and spontaneous on the part of the donor and those that are linked in some way to the donor's interests. He observes that, in some cultures, the receipt of a gift creates an obligation on the part of the recipient. Mauss (1950: 11) uses the term "contractual gifts" to refer to such cases. He also observes the function of gifts in maintaining mutually satisfactory alliances (1969: 94).

Even the anonymous clandestine philanthropist derives a 'warm inner glow'. But there are those donors who give in order to display, and/or who receive some form of prestige or recognition for their gift. And some energetically seek such recognition, so much so that, but for the anticipated acknowledgment, the gift would not have been forthcoming in the first place. Ostentatious giving by indigenous community leaders in the Pacific northwest of North America served as an expression of the donor's superiority (Mauss 1950: 95). The most extreme position is that of Derrida (1991: chs. 1–2), who argues that true gifts are impossible.

In the words of a former Chief Constable of North Yorkshire Police: "There are dangers. Sponsorship will never provide a massive amount for the police service. Not only because the legal restrictions will never allow it, but because there is only so much money that an organization will be willing to put into something before getting any real return" (quoted in Potter 1997: 31). It is this need for return on the donor's part that means acceptance of gifts by police will almost always carry some, sometimes hidden, 'catch' – some risk or consequence which it is important for police to identify and understand. Clearly, some police organisations do understand the dangers: the UK limits police sponsorship income to 1% of gross budget (Police Forum for Income Generation 2003/2006: 6). Similarly, to their credit, many Australian criminal justice agencies have devoted a great deal of thought to processes by which sponsorship may be managed with integrity (for example, New South Wales Independent Commission Against Corruption 2006; New South Wales Police Service 2001; WA Police Sponsorship and Donations Policy AD 54).

Some of the costs and risks of gifts as a resource for police are dealt with in the following paragraphs.

Costs. Some gifts may be more trouble than they are worth. The cost of administration or oversight may not be immediately apparent. Something as seemingly simple as a donated or loaned vehicle may entail insurance and service costs that must be borne by the recipient. Furthermore, not all donations will be of the highest quality. Some items may require repair or ongoing maintenance. Some items will be donated not out of any desire to assist police but because the donation is advantageous to the donor as a way to get rid of an unwanted good or because it brings tax concessions. As Stellwagen and Wylie (1985) note, "Law enforcement departments must be careful that they do not become glorified thrift-store depositories."

Skewing of police priorities. Police may need to contemplate carefully any gift arrangement which is tied to a particular activity undertaken by police. Does it result in a diminution of their discretion? Even acceptance and use of a donation of work space, for instance, an arrangement which suggests very little interference by the donor with the police agenda, may suggest a police presence is expected at that location, not down the road. Any provision of funds that comes with conditions attached needs to be carefully considered to ensure that acceptance of the 'gift' does not distort the police organisation's own agenda. It could also be suggested that corporate sponsorship of an investigation, for instance, might compromise its integrity, in that the investigating agency might lose its independence and be guided more by the preferences of the donor rather than the rule of law. One might consider the scenario of a cash-strapped police force that is investigating six unrelated murders being given a substantial donation by the family of one of the victims. The 'conditions' might not be explicit, but the effect of skewing the investigation might nevertheless be the same.

Private sponsorship of certain other investigations may be less controversial, however. As noted above, Western Australia Police received donations from individuals and service clubs to support the Macro Task Force, a serial murder investigation. Most of the donors in this case were unrelated to the victims; the distinction between public and private interest was more clear-cut.

The courts have had to deal with the question of the effects of private sponsorship on police investigations. The Alberta Energy Corporation in 1998 provided the Royal Canadian Mounted Police with computer equipment, software and technical support to enable it to investigate a particular instance of 'oilpatch vandalism'. In the subsequent prosecution of the alleged vandal, the court found that the donation did not compromise the integrity of the investigation (Law Commission of Canada 2006: 12, fn. 5). In another Canadian case, an Ontario businessman sued an insurance company over an outstanding claim relating to a hotel destroyed by fire. He was placed under electronic surveillance by local police. The wiretap was financed by insurance companies and by a private investigative agency. Counsel for the businessman, who was subsequently charged with arson and fraud, contended that the interceptions assisted the insurance company in its civil claim and that private sponsorship of the investigation was repugnant (McLeod 2000).

A similar case in the United Kingdom involved payments solicited by Hampshire Constabulary and made by insurance companies in furtherance of a fraud investigation (*R. v. Hounsham and others* [2005] EWCA Crim 1366, [2005] Crim LR 991 26 May 2005). The Court frowned upon the practice:

> In our judgment, soliciting by the police of funds from potential victims of fraud, or any other crime, quite apart from being ultra vires police powers, is a practice which is fraught with danger. It may compromise the essential independence and objectivity of the police when carrying out a criminal investigation. It might lead to police officers being selective as to which crimes to investigate and which not to investigate. It might lead to victims persuading a police investigating team to act partially. It might also lead to investigating officers carrying out a more thorough preparation of the evidence in a case of a "paying" victim; or a less careful preparation of the evidence in the case of a non-contributing victim. In short, it is a practice which, in our judgment, would soon lead to a loss of confidence in a police force's ability to investigate crime objectively and impartially.

Notwithstanding their unambiguous disapproval of the payment, the Court dismissed Hounsham's appeal.

Police services, at least in theory, are beginning to understand and recognise these risks. The U.K. Police Forum for Income Generation notes, "It should be recognised that sponsors will usually seek to maximise the benefit obtained from any association with a Force. Great care must be exercised to ensure that a correct balance is maintained between the legitimate business aims of the sponsor and the interests of the Force" (Police Forum for Income Generation 2003/2006: 32).

Appearance of partiality arising from personal benefit. Clearly, acceptance of gifts by individual police officers, whether on behalf of the organisation or not, could result in the appearance of partiality toward the donor. This is perhaps less problematic than in earlier days, with the now very common requirement in many police organisations' guidelines and policies that any individual member or members of the police service not benefit personally from any sponsorship agreement to which their service becomes a party.

The New South Wales Police, among many other police organisations, has a code of conduct relating to acceptance of gifts or benefits. For individuals, the decision "to accept a gift must not influence or appear to influence your ability to act impartially in the discharge of your duties" (New South Wales Police Service 1992: 52).

Dependency, capture and inequity. The risk of dependency on private largesse may also be an important consideration for police when considering the acceptance of gifts. A group that solicited the $15 million contribution to the Dallas Police Department launched a campaign shortly thereafter to persuade one hundred thousand citizens to contribute $25 each to further support the Dallas police. A spokesperson for the campaign was quoted as having said "We hope this brings up the morale of officers on patrol when they see 200,000 bumper stickers on cars throughout the city" (Trahan 2006). One hopes these bumper stickers would have no effect on the exercise of discretion in traffic enforcement. That may be why some police organisations, such as Seattle Police, reject the idea of bumper stickers that would identify donors.

One must also consider the real threat of 'capture' of the police organisation by the donor, or at least the appearance of a conflict of interest. Is there any risk that the police agency will provide, or will be seen to be providing, a degree of service different from that delivered to similarly situated non-donors? A police service which enjoys a degree of private sponsorship must ensure that its services are delivered in the public interest, that there is no actual or apparent conflict of interest and that as a result of the sponsorship there is no unfair distribution of policing services. As the court in the Hounsham case (quoted earlier) points out, its legitimacy will be under threat if it does not do so. The existence of other regulatory or contractual relationships between the prospective donor and the recipient may render a sponsorship agreement suspect.

Actual or perceived endorsement. Another consideration is whether sponsorship is perceived as an endorsement by the police service of the sponsor and its products. The relatively detailed guidelines developed by the New South Wales Police and published in 1992 explicitly stated that acknowledgment of sponsorship must not confer naming rights on the sponsor (New South Wales Police Service 1992: 9). Guidelines developed by the U.K. Police Forum for Income

Generation require a standard disclaimer to this end (Police Forum for Income Generation 2003/2006: 32). Police services may be concerned about being seen, explicitly or implicitly, to endorse a donor's product. Not only are they concerned about commercial exploitation, where a provider invokes the police connection for business advantage, there may also be a risk of liability on the part of the police service in the event of product failure.

But the acquisition by a police service of a particular brand of product, from Glock pistols, to Holden cars, to BMW motorbikes, could be regarded as an implicit endorsement of that product in what is often a very competitive marketplace. Ironically, those who sell goods and services to the police, whether pistols, tyres or intelligence software, are certainly able to advertise that fact. Would this endorsement carry any less weight when the product is given as a gift rather than in a commercial transaction?

Association with certain interests. There are certain industries with which some police services may prefer not to be publicly associated: alcohol, tobacco, gambling, firearms, and the sex industries among them. Those industries, even where they are legitimate, are of such a nature that either they may find themselves subject to a degree of regulation or at least monitoring by police, or their externalities may entail a degree of tension with government policy (e.g., tobacco).

Some donations certainly raise questions about not only motivations but also the provenance of the gift. One retiring police chief in Indonesia donated a number of cars and motorcycles to his own department (International Crisis Group 2001). Whilst the donors themselves may be unimpeachable, a police organisation may still suffer if an undesirable historical source of the gift becomes publicly known.

The use of foundations or charitable trusts to receive donations on behalf of police organisations may serve to protect against the appearance of impropriety that might emerge from a direct donor–recipient relationship. But it is no guarantor. Ironically, it may have just the opposite effect. For example, if a police foundation is able to raise and spend money on behalf of a police department, it may be able to circumvent basic procurement safeguards. These

arrangements appear to have operated in Los Angeles to fund con-
sulting contracts with former associates of the Chief of Police. In the
words of Professor Erwin Chermerinsky: "It's a way of the government spending money but not following all of the procedures for
competitive bidding. ... When the police foundation goes out and
buys things on its own, or hires consultants on its own, all of those
protections are not followed" (quoted in Weissenstein 2003). The
vulnerability of participants to allegations (justified or not) of
impropriety is obvious.

However, Los Angeles Police Foundation makes it very clear to
prospective donors that there is no quid pro quo for donations to the
Foundation. Contributions are generally sought from the most
affluent citizens: people who "don't need special treatment". It is
considered important to choose carefully with whom the Foundation
associates. 'Wannabees' and 'cops buffs' who want their pictures taken
with police are avoided "like the plague". "If you get into bed with
fleas, you expect to get bitten" (Bratton 2006).

Of course, the police organisation can always refuse a gift where the
circumstances may provoke controversy or pose any risk of adverse
publicity, or where the costs or risks are too great. Some gifts, such as
the gift of a corporate aircraft, may entail maintenance costs that are
prohibitive and so, instead of providing a resource boon, may constitute a drain on police resources. At the end of the day, police need
to decide whether a gift is in their interest and/or in the public
interest.

Long-term effects on police funding. It is possible that sponsorship of
policing will have long-term effects on law enforcement agencies in
instances where the police organisation, like the Western Australia
Police, are permitted to retain all operating revenue as part of its
appropriation agreement with government. For instance, there could
be a reduction in core government funding. Or treasury bureaucrats
may seek to cap such revenues or to 'confiscate' the excess for general
revenue. The flow-on effect of reducing a police organisation's budget appropriation may be to eliminate any incentive to raise additional revenue for fear of the consequences for the next year's
appropriation.

Alternatively, just as 'efficiency dividends' and 'capital use charges' have induced a degree of resourcefulness on the part of public sector managers, so too might changes in government funding provide incentives for police services to supplement their appropriations with other legitimate sources of revenue. As a former chairman of the (U. K.) Association of Chief Police Officers Finance Committee put it, sponsorship and private finance initiatives are not without risk: "The danger of these is that they both give the opportunity for the Treasury to say it's down to forces to raise the extra funding they need, either from local funding or private companies" (quoted in Potter 1997: 31). Such incentives may serve as an invitation to chase paying police work at the expense of other police work that does not bring those rewards, with adverse consequences for the public interest, possibly distracting police attention from their core business or leading to inequalities in the delivery of services. Such longer term effects of private sponsorship are clearly an issue that both police organisations and governments need to consider.

One might also note that the very existence of private sponsorship of policing may provide some unscrupulous people with an opportunity to exploit this for illegal purposes. Solicitations from the public by individuals claiming some police affiliation may be fraudulent.[3]

Political risks. As is the case with fee-for service or user-pays policing, the existence of private donations to police may invite exploitation for labour relations or political purposes. In 2004, when it became apparent that the Queensland Police were in receipt of various gifts such as furniture, topographic maps for search and rescue work, and veterinary services for the Dog Squad, a Queensland Police Union spokesman was quoted as saying "they shouldn't have to go begging to be provided with what is essential equipment" (Murray 2004). And the state's Sunday tabloid weighed in with editorial comment:

It is absolutely ridiculous that police should be expected to go blue cap in hand to businesses and individuals to provide everyday

---

[3] See http://www.nyc.gov/html/nypd/html/iab/iabpdinf.html (accessed 30 March 2007).

items such as office furniture and a few workplace comforts. ...
And it is downright frightening that they should have to beg maps
to perform search-and-rescue operations, and jet skis to patrol
waterways. (Sunday Mail 2004)

Conclusions

Other countries may not follow directly in the path of the United States
or South Africa, but it seems likely that corporate or other private
sponsorship of policing may increase in years to come. Whatever the
circumstances, if the idea of a social coalition persists, one can expect
that public donations to public police will at least remain with us. If
corporate philanthropy in furtherance of law enforcement increases to
any significant extent, changes in the quantum or the conditions (if
any) attached to these gifts will require a re-examination of the procedures through which they are sought and received.

Understandable concerns about maintaining integrity and minimizing perceptions of irregularity or favouritism by police have
raised some interesting issues. It was suggested to us more than once
in the course of our research that private actors should have an equal
chance at participating in sponsorship arrangements with police. As
such, some might regard the traditional bilateral arrangements,
initiated either by the prospective sponsor or by the police organisation, as inferior to more formal, transparent arrangements similar
to those governing purchasing or acquisition. In other words, sponsorship arrangements should only come about through a process
similar to open tendering. Guidelines to this end were developed by
the New South Wales Independent Commission Against Corruption
in 2006. As we will see in a later chapter, the line between gift and
commerce may become obscured.

In most cases, wise decision making (for instance, in relation to
choice of sponsors), clear policy guidelines and thorough contract
negotiation and management by police organisations will ameliorate
any possible undesirable effects. Clearly, there is a balance to be
sought in these gift arrangements, between protecting the law
enforcement agency's reputation and integrity, ensuring that the
arrangement satisfies both the sponsor (in terms of its return) and the
agency's need for resource enhancement, and serving the public

interest. Endorsing a product, for instance, may not necessarily damage a police organisation's credibility or reputation, but there are certain industries with which police would be prudent not to be publicly associated. Similarly, police involved in sponsorship arrangements need to be concerned not only about the effect on police reputation of commercial exploitation, but also about the possible risk of liability if the product is defective. It is not only the police who will be concerned with the consequences of such arrangements for their legitimacy. It will also be in the sponsor's marketing interest to be cautious that that legitimacy is not undermined.

Police need to be aware of their own bargaining power over the parameters of sponsorship relationships, with this power lying in the reputational advantages for sponsors of association with law enforcement. Police should use this power to secure the kinds of arrangements they want or, if that is not possible, to walk away from a sponsorship that threatens their legitimacy or their ability to equitably and independently provide policing services.

But whatever risk amelioration policies and practices are adopted, there remains the fundamental question about public perceptions of police who use private money to do their jobs. A number of criminal justice specialists, responding specifically to the practice of commercial advertisements on police cars, have suggested that the perceived impartiality of law enforcement is compromised when police officers are seen to act as marketing agents for corporations. They argue that the moral authority of police is compromised when they are seen as "hucksters on wheels" (Commercial Alert 2002). In Western democracies at least, police are an important and powerful symbol of public security. It is appropriate for such symbols to become commercialized? Might it be risky for them to do so?

In other words, legitimacy may be contingent. And legitimacy has a direct effect on the ability of the police to perform their role. The notion of policing as a public good, available to all, and paid for by all through the system of taxation and government appropriations, might be argued to have faded considerably. Perhaps it was an illusion all along, as those who claimed that there was one system of justice for the rich and another for the poor were fond of telling us. In any event, government's ability or willingness to provide what was once known as "the basics" seems unlikely to expand in the short term. What are the limits of corporate sponsorship of public policing? How much is desirable? How much is feasible? As Davis (2000: 9) reminds us, there are good gifts and bad gifts, and those that are not really gifts at all.

Australia's most celebrated horse race, known for a century simply as the "Melbourne Cup" became the "Foster's Melbourne Cup" and, more recently, the "Emirates Melbourne Cup". One wonders whether we will one day see a Microsoft Computer Crime Squad.

PART 2: PEOPLE AS A POLICING RESOURCE

Introduction

Over a decade ago, Grabosky (1992) identified a resurgence of citizen involvement in crime control. The focus in this chapter is on one aspect of that trend, the donation by people not of money or equipment, but of their own time, energy and labour. Citizen involvement in law enforcement has a long history, dating back a thousand years or more (Critchley 1972; Blue 1992; Greenberg 2005). The recent revival of interest in community involvement in policing is reflected in discourse and practice relating to community policing and "the police extended family" (Johnston 2003). Citizens are just one limb of the policing tree; other branches are other private and public actors (public police, private security, business, government agencies and so on). This new hybrid governance of policing (Grabosky, 1995) itself reflects wider societal shifts from state-centric 'government' to 'governance' by a wide variety of agencies (Rhodes, 1997). Citizens are, then, only one node of many in 'networks' of policing governance (Loader, 2000; Newburn, 2001; Shearing and Wood, 2003; Fleming and Wood, 2006). From the point of view of the police, however, they are significant as a resource that might be harnessed to further police objectives. One could also argue that the use of this resource is becoming essential in the light of the increasing financial pressures under which police departments are struggling. Yet the use of non-police human resources varies greatly between and within jurisdictions.

However, the police are not always in control of this node of policing (Johnston, 2003: 188), despite their efforts to ensure police sovereignty over local security networks (Johnston, 2003: 199–200). Voluntary citizen participation in law enforcement, whether it be carried out within public police organisations, in cooperation with police or purely as a citizen initiative, is a gift to police that carries with it not only benefits but also risks. Along with the increase in policing resources the gift represents, there may be follow-on benefits to security, including a greater degree of self-regulation exercised by citizens, improved policing as a result of greater communication between police and citizens and the creation of social capital within communities which itself may bring about a fall in crime rates. But side-by-side with these benefits are risks, ranging from the potential for breaches of confidentiality and privacy that accompanies the increasing presence of citizens within police organisations to the dangers posed by vigilantism and a society increasingly focused on surveillance. For police, harnessing unpaid citizen resources in a way that maximizes benefits and minimizes risks presents a real and stimulating challenge. Beyond those current issues, the independence of many of the gift-givers also raises questions about the future shape of policing.

Forms of Exchange Relationship Involving People

The resource that is people may come to police as a result of a variety of exchange relationships between police and others: the relationships of coercion, sale and gift to which we referred earlier. People are often legally compelled to assist police (see Chapter 3). For example, they may be by law required to assist officers when asked or to rescue those in distress, to report when they suspect there has been a breach of the law or to themselves police compliance with laws relating specifically to their business environment. The assistance of nonpolice people may also be 'bought' by police. The use of informants, for instance, will often involve a commercial transaction, just as it may involve an element of compulsion (see Chapter 4). Similarly, the services of experts are often purchased by police, particularly in areas where police are not traditionally strong, such as information technology and finance (see Chapter 4).

People may also present themselves, their powers of observation, their time and energy, to the police as a gift. Such a gift will sometimes be driven by a desire to help, verging on altruism. Motivation is a complex thing, particularly when it comes to social activism of one sort or another, including volunteering (Wilson, 2000). Tyler and Fagan (2005) point out that willingness to help police to fight crime (either proactively, or just by complying with the law) is more likely to exist if police are seen as legitimate (entitled to be obeyed), and that legitimacy judgments are shaped by people's views about the fairness of the processes the police use when dealing with members of the public (procedural justice). However, police legitimacy is only one factor at work in personal gift-giving to police. Patrick Carr's recent work (2005) suggests that a deteriorating law and order situation may provide the impetus for people to collaborate with police in setting up better mechanisms for informal social control within the community. But motivations may be even more personal. A person's willingness to participate in community patrol may stem from frustration with, resentment of or anger at the police for their lack of action in dealing with 'yobs' and 'vandals'. Another person, a victim of crime, may see reporting it as a way to wreak revenge on that wrongdoer or those of his ilk. Yet another may volunteer to work within the local police organisation in order to further her own career aspirations, to fill in time or because she is attracted to the thrill and power associated with policing. Nevertheless, whatever the motivation, from the point of view of the police, all these people come at little direct financial cost and may be regarded as a gift.

Mapping Forms of Personal Gift
Personal gifts come in a variety of guises, as discussed later in this chapter. They may be formal, in that they are carried out under a formal arrangement with the police or in cooperation with police, or informal, in the sense that they are citizen-initiated. They may involve a donation of a person's body, in terms of active labour, or merely the gift of a person's senses, their powers of observation and a willingness to pass the information on to police. In either case, the giver is undertaking a policing task. Taken together, these gifts of bodies and senses allow law enforcement more opportunity for

percipiency and hence a greater claim to omniscience than if they
were to rely on the bodies and senses of police alone. These gifts act as
a force multiplier, dramatically increasing the reach and effectiveness
of the police,[4] who rely on citizens for much of the information that
allows them to identify and investigate crime (Ericson and Haggerty,
1997; Sampson, 2004: 110; Brodeur and Dupont, 2006).

People as police officers. In a number of jurisdictions, police organisations make provision for enabling citizens to volunteer to become
unpaid police officers. Such volunteers are known as police reservists
(e.g., in South Africa and some police organisations in the United
States), auxiliary police (e.g., in Toronto, the New York City Police
Department and the Northern Territory of Australia Police), volunteer police (e.g., in Germany and the Netherlands) or special constables[5] (e.g., in the United Kingdom, New Zealand, Singapore and
some states of Australia).

In New Zealand, volunteers were in the past used as a temporary
measure to deal with threats or instances of public disorder. In 1913,
a waterside workers strike at various ports around New Zealand was
effectively dealt with by the employment of Special Constables
recruited largely from the ranks of the farming community. As Casey
and Collinson (2005) record, unlike during previous strikes, Special
Constables were used not just to protect scab labourers but to enforce
a kind of state of emergency in a number of urban areas. There were
violent confrontations between armed foot and mounted patrols and
crowds of strikers and their supporters. The Special Constables
became known as 'Massey's Cossacks' in reference to the then prime
minister, W. F. Massey, and to the elite cavalry used by the Russian

---

[4] The term "force multiplier" is usually used in relation to military operations.
Strength of numbers is only one example of a force multiplier. An increase in
morale, which may happen as a result of gifts of assistance to police relieving the
pressure on individual officers, is another.

[5] Not all "special constables" are volunteers. The term "special constable" is
generally used to designate a person, whether paid or otherwise, having a legal
status that carries with it limited police powers or police powers confined
geographically. They may or may not be considered to be public police officers.
For instance, in Canada, paid "special constables" provide security on some
university campuses and at some nuclear power stations; Law Commission of
Canada 2006: 27–28.

tsars to keep the working classes in their place. Almost all of the 'specials' involved in the 1913 strike were volunteers (Casey and Collinson 2005: 20).

A similar recruitment occurred at the height of Apartheid, in the late 1980s, when the South African Police appointed a few thousand special constables or 'kitskonstabels' (literally, 'instant constables') as part of a 'black-on-black' policing strategy to help contain the political unrest that was occurring mostly in the townships. The kitskonstabels were given only a few weeks training. As a result they became renowned for their heavy-handed tactics and brutality. As this did little to appease the tense relations between the police and the community, the police were prompted to improve training and raise entrance criteria (Rauch 1991).

In contrast to jurisdictions where special constables are recruited in emergencies or for particular jobs, the United Kingdom has a standing volunteer Special Constabulary within the police organisation, with its own parallel ranking and administrative structures. Volunteers must work a minimum of sixteen hours each month. They often work alongside regular officers, and their powers are the same (although they may have a more limited geographical reach), as are their uniforms (except for insignia) and equipment. The kinds of jobs allocated to special constables vary according to the particular police department, with regular patrols being a common task for reasons related to the rise of 'reassurance policing' in that jurisdiction (Home Office 2006). Theoretically at least, 'specials' can be required to undertake anything their regular colleagues do. In practice, they may be more often employed in a supporting role involving anything from attendance at public events to assisting detectives in a major case, such as a murder investigation.

Sometimes volunteers are recruited for specific jobs that the police find themselves unable to perform, such as digital forensics. In Hillsboro, Oregon, the Police Reserve Specialist (PRS) Program recruits individuals with high-technology skills as reservists for a minimum of two years and trains them in the requirements and constraints of the criminal investigation process, such as those related to the gathering of legally admissible evidence (Harrison et al. 2004). These volunteers from industry and academia work under the direction of a case officer to access, analyse and preserve computer information relevant to the investigation. They also advise regular officers on technical issues generally and sometimes act as expert witnesses in prosecutions. Cases include fraud and forgery investigations.

People in police organisations. There are other ways to work within police departments that do not involve becoming a police officer. Volunteers-in-Policing (VIP) programs are fairly common around the western world. The motto of the Tempe Arizona Police Department volunteers-in-policing program expresses the relationship between the volunteers and the police themselves: "We are not an arm of the police; we are the heart of the community". Police, too, are keen that volunteers are seen as a link to the community served. The New South Wales (Australia) VIP program describes volunteers as helping "deliver an even better service to the local community", and the first of their listed duties indicates that volunteers will spend time "assisting police in community policing initiatives". The roles of VIPs can be very diverse and may overlap with those of police volunteers (reservists, specials etc). Many of the tasks volunteers undertake would fit the community policing model, for instance, community bike patrols, assisting in school programs, distributing information about the police at community events and answering citizen phone enquiries.[6] To 'enhance public confidence' and 'increase public satisfaction' were explicit strategic objectives of the West Yorkshire Police's VIP project (Christmann, 2003).

Sometimes volunteer programs operate at the national level. The Israeli Civil Guard, established in 1974 after a series of terror attacks and initially having a terrorism focus, is conducted under the supervision and control of the Israel National Police. It now comprises around seventy-five thousand volunteers (Weisburd et al. [forthcoming]). Volunteers are involved in an enormous array of tasks ranging from administrative work, Neighbourhood Watch, local patrol and traffic duties to guarding schools and public transport,

[6] For a list of possible tasks for VIPs in the United States, see http://www. policevolunteers.org/volunteer/what.cfm (accessed 21 July 2008).

setting up roadblocks, helping tourists, policing compliance with environmental regulations, conducting search and rescue missions, surveillance and other detective activities, assisting bomb disposal experts and clearing-up after terrorist bombings. Generally officers of the Guard do not wear police uniforms, but some members of specialized volunteer units within it may do so.

In some countries, the recruitment of volunteers to help with policing tasks mirrors that of specials or reservists but without the police status. The Department of Home Affairs in Indonesia established Hansip (civil defence units) in 1962. Hansip comprised volunteers in three groups, Wanra, Linmas and Kamra, the latter being the security element allocated to the police. Hansip were supposed to be mobilised only for special events like elections, disasters, sporting events and domestic conflicts, but over time became employed by local governments more generally. Hansip have now been disbanded in most areas and former members have joined other local security groups such as private security firms and paramilitary troops.

In other arrangements, industry sometimes lends employees to the police to assist them with tasks in which industry has special expertise. The Joint Banking and Finance Sector Investigation team (JBFSIT) within the Australian High Tech Crime Centre (AHTCC) is made up not only of federal and state police but also of investigators from major banks. The team investigates online banking fraud, including phishing[7] and the dissemination of malicious software. A similar body in the United Kingdom is the Dedicated Cheque and Plastic Crime Unit (DCPCU) that investigates plastic card counterfeiting and various types of fraud, including cash machine, cheque and identity fraud. The DCPCU is wholly funded by the banking industry and staff from that industry work with police on investigations. In each case, the gift of their employees by the banking industry is clearly of benefit both to the industry and to the police.

---

[7] "Phishing" is a fraud perpetrated on the Internet (often through e-mail) whereby a user is tricked into revealing personal or confidential information (such as bank details and credit card numbers) that the 'phisher' can use illicitly.

People in partnership with the police. Increasingly the police are entering into partnerships with community organisations and private companies which involve the said partner in police business. For instance, one-to-one relationships between business leaders and police executives have been established under the Leadership Exchange London, a partnership set up in 2001 between London First and a number of London police forces, and the similar Partners in Leadership Program of the Police Service of Northern Ireland (Business in the Community 2004). The objective of such schemes is that, through meetings, business leaders can share their expertise in business and management with their equivalents in the police, passing on skills that are sorely needed in twenty-first-century policing (such as those relating to financial, personnel and information technology issues). Similarly, in order to keep pace with advances in cybercrime, certain branches of the South African Police Service involved with bank-related crime are working closely with the technical staff at different banks to improve arrest rates as well as promote skills and knowledge exchange (Sikwane 2006).

Business Against Crime is an active partner of the South African Police Service. Together with the Department of Education, BAC and the police have partnered to launch both an awareness-raising, drug reduction program and a school-based crime prevention project called *Tiisa Thuto* (meaning 'Strengthening Education' in Sesotho), which "combine[s] the expertise, energy and resources of all role players ... " (South African Police Service 2006). However, the South African government and business sector have taken their co-operative relationship a step further. In November 2006, a joint Leadership Forum was set up. The Leadership Forum meets bi-monthly and is attended by Ministers, Deputy Ministers and Directors-General of six government departments involved in justice, crime prevention and security as well as officials from Business Leadership/the Big Business Working Group and Business Against Crime. The purpose of the Forum is to develop solutions and interventions to address the crime wave in South Africa as well as to 're-energise' the partnership between government and the business sector. Recommendations are to be made to parliament and cabinet on the resolution of crime problems (South African Press Association 2006b; Ministry of Safety and Security 2006).

At a grass-roots level, the South African Police Service frequently engages with the Metro Police and the private security industry in blitz operations as well as more long-term partnership operations. One such operation, called *Siyabopha* or Gotcha, involved the zero-tolerance style policing of inner Johannesburg by the state and metro police, private security and surveillance companies, and resulted in 166 arrests for a range of offences as well as plans for a surveillance company involved to set up a CCTV system in one of the suburbs targeted (Enoch 2006). Another joint operation, *Kwano*, between the South African Police Service and the Pretoria City Council, involved the hiring of private security guards to patrol tourist destinations and protect tourists and shoppers in the CBD. It developed into the Kwano Forum, resulting in the implementation of more patrols, the establishment of specialist units and agreements between police from local stations and Metro Police to meet on a weekly basis to coordinate activities. Kwano is funded by stakeholders from the Pretoria Inner City Partnership, one of a number of partnerships in various cities in South Africa established as private, non-profit companies aimed at revitalizing urban spaces (Minnaar 2005).

Sometimes private organisations that specialise in investigating particular illegal activities will choose to assist the police directly. Software Security, a Czech company dealing with software piracy, investigates suspicious transactions that may indicate piracy but will hand their findings over to police for further action. In 2005, that company assisted police in catching nine pirates and seizing over seven thousand CDs containing pirated software (Kopic 2006). In Japan, private detective agencies will often inform police of cases of stalking coming to their attention (McNeill 2004).

People policing the community. Much of the assistance given to the police happens quite outside the formal strictures of police organisations. In some cases, this involves a time-consuming commitment of the giver to policing tasks within the community, with varying levels of involvement from the police. Of direct assistance to the Dog Section of the Thames Valley Police (TVP) in the United Kingdom, for example, are the people who volunteer as "puppy socialisers", caring for the puppies bred by the TVP for up to ten months and ensuring they get used to the sights and sounds of the world before the beginning of their training as police dogs.

Voluntary forms of policing may be very attractive in countries where there is a perception that crime rates are rising or that police do not have the resources to deal with this. Baker reports on the case in Uganda where law and order has been increasingly decentralised since the assumption of power by the National Resistance Movement following the 1986 civil war. With the introduction of community policing in 1989 came the establishment of various forms of citizen participation in law enforcement and crime prevention, amongst them Crime Prevention Panels which have been set up in a number of districts, consisting of volunteers trained in crime prevention for the purposes of empowering the local community and making it more responsible. The Katwe Crime Prevention panel in Kampala consists of thirty thousand volunteers trained by the panel and the police in crime prevention. These supplement a police division numbering not much over four hundred (Baker 2005a).

Other forms of community policing by citizens are outlined in the following paragraphs. Although these citizens have been categorised as 'patrollers', 'watchers', 'reporters' and 'actors', it is acknowledged that there are quite significant overlaps in some cases between these categories. For example patrollers are by definition watchers, and watchers are often also reporters.

The Patrollers. Patrols by citizens of their communities are becoming increasingly common. While many are undertaken in formal coop-eration with the police (and might be classified as a 'partnership'), others are wholly citizen-initiated and operate with only tacit state support or none at all.

In the Ginza district in Tokyo in 2004, for example, kimono-clad 'mamma-sans' (hostesses) hatched a plan to conduct evening patrols in groups of six, accompanied by a police officer. Initially the idea was to remove cards left by sex-industry touts in telephone boxes and generally tidy up the streets. But it was felt that the patrols also gave Ginza the appearance of being under surveillance and so deterred bag snatchers and other undesirables from moving into the area (Lewis 2004). In another area of Tokyo, fifty volunteers operate night patrols out of a 'private koban', a shop space located in a municipal apartment complex borrowed from the city government (Yomiuri Shimbun 2006). This is one of over two thousand volunteer groups for crime prevention in Tokyo alone (Ishihara 2005).

A large scale community patrol operation conducted with police cooperation and support takes place in New Zealand. Community Patrols of New Zealand (CPNZ) is the umbrella organisation for eighty patrol groups throughout the country involving between four thousand and five thousand volunteers, who patrol their communities with the specific aim of assisting the police to apprehend criminals and increase safety. The police are closely involved in this operation, vetting applicants for patrol membership and providing patrols with information about suspicious activities and trouble spots on which they could focus. CPNZ takes pains to stress that its members are not doing the job of police, but are simply acting as 'eyes and ears' for them in a nonconfrontational manner (Laurence 2005). However, volunteers are 'out there' patrolling in vehicles and on foot, not merely observing activity as they go about their own daily activities. They have been known to engage in traffic direction (New Zealand Police Association 2005) and the pursuit of offenders (Hodge 2005).

Leach (2006) has traced a similar development in Canada: citizen patrols in Manitoba. The police or council initiate and support some of the 120 patrol organisations in the province but many others are purely citizen-initiated. Most, she says, "report regularly to police about their findings but not their practices", which may include being armed. The state may choose to 'turn a blind eye' or give only tacit consent to the existence of patrol groups of the latter kind, especially where there is some question over their methods. In the United States, the Minutemen Civil Defense Corps, comprised of civilians who patrol both the U.S./Mexican and the U.S./Canadian borders on the lookout for illegal immigrants and traffickers, denote themselves as a "National Citizens Neighborhood Watch". Despite the fact that when the Minutemen project was first set up, the president referred to its participants as "vigilantes" (see Dobbs, 2005), no move has been made to prevent the project from continuing its activities. In fact, provided the Minutemen cooperate with the U.S Border Patrol, their right to exist and to present their political agenda is recognized. The potential benefit to the nation as a whole from their activities has been acknowledged (Turnbull and Tu 2005).

There are many other similar examples of citizen-initiated patrols that initially attracted little or no state support. Some drew fervent criticism; for instance, the Guardian Angels, a citizen group first established in 1978 to patrol the New York subway that has since replicated itself in thirteen different countries, was at first suspected by police and bureaucrats of vigilante tendencies (Pennell et al. 1989: 379). Although the group has since won a number of high-level awards in the United States, it is still viewed by many with a degree of cynicism (CBS News 2006; Eames 2006). Other patrols have been lauded as effective and culturally appropriate mechanisms to deal with problems that have proved resistant to traditional police-centred strategies; for example, some Aboriginal communities in both remote outback and urban Australia operate volunteer night patrols to deal with problems associated with substance abuse and to defuse aggression before violence ensues (Curtis 1993; Lloyd and Rogers 1993: 162; Walker and Forrester 2002; Blagg and Valuri 2004).

In South Africa, Crime Watch patrols were created in fairly affluent suburbs in the Western Cape for the purposes of supplementing the police. Communities serviced by the Crime Watch patrols paid a monthly levy to fund their operations through the purchasing of police reservists to patrol. Off-duty police officers would also some-times moonlight for their local Crime Watches. Sometimes the community would donate a vehicle to its local precinct and then utilise the vehicle for its Crime Watch patrol with petrol consumption and vehicle maintenance at the expense of the tight police budget. However, following complaints by a private armed response company to the Minister of Safety and Security objecting to the Crime Watches' use of police resources and their lack of registration as private secu-rity companies with the Private Security Industry Regulatory Authority (PSIRA), the Western Cape Provincial Commissioner instructed the disbanding of the Crime Watches and dismissed the reservists under its employ. This incited a very emotional and angry response from the affected communities in the Western Cape. The Provincial Commissioner subsequently issued guidelines for the way in which the Crime Watches should operate – as ordinary neighbourhood watches, patrolling and reporting on suspicious activity to the local police station (Berg 2004b; Minnaar 2005).

The Watchers. Sometimes a person's gift to the police of their 'eyes and ears' is formalised in a 'watch' structure. The best known of these is Neighbourhood Watch (or its equivalents in the United States "Community Watch", "Home Watch", "Apartment Watch" and "Block Watch": Fleming, 2005: 1). It has existed in the United States since the 1960s and in the United Kingdom and Australia since the early 1980s, and now appears under different appellations around the globe, in places as diverse as Taiwan (Alarid and Wang 2000: 116), Israel (Israel Police 2005) and Jamaica (Ministry of National Security 2006). Originally set up with the aim of reducing burglary and property theft and damage, Neighbourhood Watch was conceived as a partnership between the community and police and as an early and essential strategy in implementing community policing (Fleming, 2005: 2–3). Community members take it upon themselves to stay alert to unusual activity and contact the authorities in the event they see or hear something suspicious. There is generally no requirement for patrol; the community is expected to be alert only within the bounds of its usual business. In return, the police are supposed to provide useful information to the community about crime in their area although the extent to which (and, it must be said, the enthusiasm with which) police undertake this role varies.

The concept of a community of watchers has been given flesh in a whole host of other 'watches', some of which require more dedication by its participants than others, and are run with varying degrees of police involvement. Some examples are provided in Table 6.1. A different type of 'watch' scheme, run without police involvement in many cities throughout both the United States and Canada, is called "Copwatch". Volunteers conduct foot and vehicle patrols and videotape police in their interactions with the public. The aim is to expose brutality and discrimination by police officers and, in so doing, make police more accountable. Although volunteer groups

TABLE 6.1 *Examples of 'Watch' programs.*

Watch	Jurisdiction	Target	Volunteers	Police Role	Source
Stop Watch	U.S.–Tampa Bay area of Florida	Suspicious activity (mainly that of sex offenders) near school bus stops	Citizens wearing t-shirts identifying them as Stop Watch volunteers	Vet and train volunteers; receive reports	Hillsborough County Sheriff's Office http://www.hcso.tampa.fl.us/Stop_Watch-o62005/Sheriff's_Letter.htm; *St Petersburg Times* 7 June 2005 "Sheriff to train bus stop sentries".
Bush Watch	Australia–Tasmania	Criminal activity (arson, theft of flora or fauna, growing marijuana etc.) in the state's forests	Forest users	Instigator, along with other government and private organisations; receive reports	Tasmania Police http://www.police.tas.gov.au/security_and_safety/bush-watch
Council Watch	Australia–Adelaide, S.A.	Suspicious/criminal activity around city	Council workers	Receive reports	South Australia Police *Annual Report 2003–2004:* 35
(Community or Neighborhood) Speed Watch	U.K., U.S., Canada	Speeding offences	Local residents	Advise residents; provide speed detection/display equipment and train volunteers in its use; receive reports	*The Sunday Times* 3 July 2005 "Village vigilantes go for their speed guns". Various council, community and police organizations, e.g., U.S. - http://www.saferoutesinfo.org/guide/enforcement/neighborhood_speed_watch_program.cfm;

(continued)

TABLE 6.1 (*continued*)

Watch	Jurisdiction	Target	Volunteers	Police Role	Source
					U.K. Cambridgeshire County Council http://www. cambridgeshire.gov.uk/ testnav2/around/speedwatch
Pubwatch	U.K.–London	Violence and criminal conduct by patrons of licensed premises	Licensees	Provide liaison officer, advice, material support (e.g. posters); host meetings; receive reports	The Metropolitan Police http://www.met.police.uk/ crimeprevention/pubwatch.htm
Shopwatch	U.K.	Theft, fraud, antisocial behaviour in retail outlets	Retail staff	Train and appoint retail staff as Special Constables; receive reports	Shopwatch http://www.shopwatch.info/ about/; Home Office "Shopwatch Launched at New Scotland Yard", press release 27 February 2004.
Highway Watch/ School Bus Watch	U.S.	Suspicious activity that may indicate terrorist activity (e.g., plans to use vehicles or cargoes as weapons)	Highway workers (truckers, tollbooth staff, construction crews, rest-stop employees, school bus drivers)	Respond to reports made by workers using toll-free hotlines	Highway Watch (administered by the American Trucking Associations in cooperation with the Department of Homeland Security, U.S.) http://www.highwaywatch.com/; http://www.yellowbuses.org/ sbw.html

Watch	Jurisdiction	Target	Volunteers	Police Role	Source
Farmwatch	South Africa	Attacks on farms and farmers	Farmers	Assist if called in by farmers	Minnaar, A. (2004) Private-public partnerships: private security, crime prevention and policing in South Africa. Inaugural lecture: Department of Security Risk Management, School of Criminal Justice, College of Law, University of South Africa.
eBlockwatch	South Africa	Criminal activity	Any person registered with eBlockwatch may receive crime alerts via SMS to network subscribers, or report crime online		http://www.eblockwatch.co.za/ Minnaar, A. (2005) 'Private-public partnerships: private security, crime prevention and policing in South Africa', *Acta Criminologica* 18(1): 85–114.

involved in monitoring police behaviour are not always popular with police, they are clearly performing a function that police themselves are expected to do and that police sometimes pay others to do for them.[8]

The Reporters. Law enforcement agencies sometimes provide other opportunities for members of the community to report crime or anti-social behaviour to them, outside the confines of formal 'watch' programs. Occasionally police will invite information on particular crimes as part of an ad hoc blitz. In Wellington, New Zealand, police recently offered $100 in petrol vouchers for information that would help find a stolen car, the theft of which was connected to an attempted robbery (Palmer 2006). In a similar move, Sussex Police in England offered rewards of £10 in mobile phone credits for people who used their phones to text useful information on criminal activity to a special 'Textme' number (AFP 2006).

Permanent 'hotlines', or telephone numbers on which citizens can provide information to police on crimes committed or suspected, are common in western jurisdictions, but also exist elsewhere (such as in China). In June–July 2005, passengers on buses in Edinburgh were encouraged to report crimes like vandalism, theft and assault, through the plastering of posters on the buses and the distribution of police business cards by bus drivers (McEwen, 2005b). The posters and cards for this "shop-a-lout" scheme carried the Crimestoppers number. Crimestoppers is an international scheme that began in the United States in 1976. A telephone number is provided, which is separate from the police emergency and general inquiries lines, for people to make anonymous reports about crime, criminals or suspicious activity. Rewards are only paid if the information provided leads to arrest and criminal prosecution – furthermore, in Australia at

---

[8] For example, the Police Assessment Resource Center, set up by the Vera Institute of Justice in the United States, charges fees to jurisdictions and agencies that employ it to assist police themselves to "set up lasting systems to identify problem officers and stations, document and investigate the use of force, detect racial profiling, review disciplinary decisions, measure community satisfaction, assess the risk of litigation, and track, analyze, and respond to citizen complaints", see http://www.vera.org/project/ project1_1.asp?section_id=2&project_id=7 (accessed 22 July 2008) and http://www. parc.info/questions/wherefunding.html (both accessed 14 November 2006).

least, many people do not claim their rewards. Crimestoppers is run in close cooperation with police by a not-for-profit company whose board is staffed by volunteers from a cross-section of the community. The idea behind Crimestoppers is that giving people the opportunity to assist police anonymously, and without speaking to them or having to testify in court, surmounts the main barriers to informing – apathy, fear of reprisals and reluctance to 'get involved'.

The Actors. Some citizen groups take action one stage further than merely watching and reporting. Perverted Justice, based in the United States, is a group of volunteers dedicated to exposing users of Internet chatrooms who have predatory tendencies towards children. Members pose as underage boys and girls and engage in conversations with other chatroom participants. If an adult person solicits sex with the underage persona, their photo and details are elicited and this information may be forwarded to police, or sometimes a 'sting' will be set up and the person will be filmed turning up at the house of the 'child' for sexual purposes. These videos may be given to police; alternatively, if no police agency expresses interest in prosecuting these adults, the group will make public personal details about them (photos, name, telephone number etc.). Perverted Justice once cooperated with NBC in the making of a television series, aired nationally in the United States, which filmed a number of such 'sting' operations. Police often appear to be unimpressed by Perverted Justice's tactics, warning that they risk making any collected evidence inadmissible by not complying with laws against entrapment (Associated Press 2004). However, police have also been known to work with them in some cases.[9] Perverted Justice is perhaps the most prominent and controversial of several citizen organisations dedicated to bringing to justice adults that use the Internet to solicit sex with children.[10]

---

[9]   See, for example, the report on the Perverted Justice Web site of its partnership, in a sting recorded for the Dateline NBC series *To Catch a Predator*, with Harris County Sheriff's Department in Georgia, the Metro Narcotic Drug Task Force, the U.S. Marshals Service, the United States Secret Service and the Georgia Bureau of Investigation.

[10] These include U.S. Cyberwatch, Jailbait Justice and Predator Hunter.

Various types of community-based policing systems exist in Africa, usually as a response to state police inefficiencies. They include, for instance, religious police, ethnic clan militias, civil defence forces and informal commercial security groups. Baker (2004a; 2004b; 2005a) provides many examples. In Nigeria, security groups called *hisba* were created in the absence of any meaningful state enforcement of Shari'a penal codes. *Hisba* ensure that Islamic principles are upheld, guiding Muslims in the practice of their religious duties. Similarly, in Ghana the *Isakaba*, a volunteer group, enforces Islamic law and order, punishing transgressors, as well as performing debt collector duties. In Uganda, UTODA – the Uganda Taxi Operators and Drivers Association – serves as a forum for taxi drivers. Consisting of about sixty thousand members and headed by a management committee, UTODA have over the years developed a good relationship with the police (Baker 2005a: 33). In its taxi park in Kampala, UTODA's traffic warden department enforces traffic regulations and directs traffic in peak hours and its Law Enforcement Department, trained by the police and Local Council, is able to arrest those suspected of engaging in criminal activities (Baker 2005a). In Angola, civil defence groups, composed of ordinary men and women and created jointly by the community and the authorities, conduct weapons checks at roads into towns (Baker 2004a). In Sierra Leone, work-based policing associations such as the Motor Drivers' and General Transport Workers' Union and the Bo Bike Rental Association check drivers' licenses, prevent the overloading of vehicles and enforce speeding regulations (Baker 2005b). In Lesotho, stock theft associations have been created to punish stock thieves as well as retrieve stolen stock (Baker 2004b).

Self-policing. An upsurge in the policing of personal and home security by citizens themselves, conducted either by those individuals or their agents, has been the topic of much discussion in academic literature on policing in the last few decades. The focus has mainly been on the growth in private security (Shearing and Stenning 1983; Stenning 2000; Forst 2000: 21; Law Commission of Canada 2002: 10; Sarre and Prenzler 2005; Law Commission of Canada 2006). The numbers of those engaged in the business of private security have for some time far outweighed the numbers engaged in public policing. While it is difficult to come up with accurate figures, Sarre and Prenzler (2005: 20–21) suggest that, Australia-wide, there is likely to be at least two persons employed in private security for every one police officer and that this growth in private security is a global phenomenon. A similar ratio (2:1) is posited by Bayley and Shearing (2001) for numbers of private security versus police worldwide. In South Africa the figure is as high as three private security officers for every one police officer (Berg 2007: 30). The current focus on private security expansion and modes of regulating it often obscures the impetus for this growth, the increasing voluntary assumption of responsibility by individuals and businesses themselves for ensuring their own security. They may choose to pay not only for services but also for hardware, such as home alarms, security lighting, security doors and windows, locks, vehicle immobilizers, vehicle tracking systems and personal alarms. In South Africa, specialist companies have concentrated their efforts on improving the protection of cash-in-transits and preventing bank robberies through a number of innovations, such as the provision of rear view video camera sur-veillance on armoured vehicles and the release of dye from opened cash boxes. People also often choose to act in ways that give them a sense of taking control of their own safety, such as removing vege-tation from around their premises, locking their doors or not walking alone at night. All actions designed to secure individuals or businesses and their possessions may be regarded as a gift to police when they bring about a reduction in crime and the fear of crime that puts pressure on police resources.

Benefits for Police and Others

The variety of personal gifts to police that now exists invites consid-eration of the reasons for this abundance at this time in history. If, as Little and Sheffield (1983) suggest, forms of organised self-help in the criminal justice field arise in times and places of substantial social change, one might conclude that this is such a time. Unease gener-ated by global problems such as terrorism, economic fluctuations and environmental destruction has culminated in increasing feelings of insecurity (Greenberg 2005: 17–18) and the recognition that new forms of crime may need new responses. At the same time police have come under increased pressure to be more fiscally efficient. Little wonder, then, that many citizens, beset by insecurity and recognizing that the police are not necessarily in a position to cope with ever-broadening responsibilities on an ever-tighter budget, take it upon themselves to remedy this either by assisting law enforcement or through independent moves to self-help.

Whatever the reason for the growth in gifts of the person to police, there are clear benefits.

Increase in police resources. The boon to police resources is the primary benefit. If citizens are willing to take responsibility for their own security, whether this is by hiring private security services or engaging in patrolling, watching and reporting, a burden on police has been eased. Similarly, those citizens who volunteer to help out the police organisation by becoming volunteer police officers, under-taking specialist assignments or simply lending a hand with day-to-day tasks, free paid police officers to concentrate on 'core' and more topical policing matters. Money, time and energy are saved. Along with resource savings for police, the result of voluntary citizen par-ticipation in law enforcement that is carried out in cooperation with police can be to broaden the reach of police – the 'force multiplier' effect. In addition, volunteers who provide a 'police presence' on the streets are fulfilling an identified need for reassurance for the public (Innes 2004; Millie and Herrington 2005; Crawford 2006b) by increasing the visibility of police.

More self-regulation. Furthermore, volunteers form a more widely socially integrated force for crime detection and prevention than the police alone – a kind of mass 'capable guardianship'. Like Bentham's Panopticon, the knowledge of the possibility that an unseen observer may be watching may well lead to a degree of self-regulation of behaviour that otherwise would not occur, a response known as "anticipatory conformity" (Zuboff 1988; Norris 2007). Who has not checked their speed when driving in an area renowned for hidden speed detection devices, just in case?

Improved public policing. There may also be wider beneficial effects
for public policing. Community participation in policing that
involves interchange between citizens and the police can open communication channels, bring an increased understanding to police of
community values, increase police responsiveness to community
concerns and provide new sources of information to police. It may
also increase police accountability for their actions (Greene 2000;
Fung 2001; Fleming 2005).

Better communities. Finally, the investment by a community in
policing is likely to build that community's social capital (Pino 2001:
202). Social capital is defined by Putnam (1995) as "features of social
organisation such as networks, norms, and social trust that facilitate
coordination and cooperation for mutual benefit". Social capital is a
similar concept to that of a society's collective efficacy, defined by
Sampson et al. (1997) as "social cohesion among neighbours combined with their willingness to intervene on behalf of the common
good" (see also Sampson 2004). The creation of social capital occurs
when relationships between people change in a way that facilitates
action (Pino 2001: 201). Social capital creation, per se, can be
regarded as a public benefit (Greenberg 2005: 19). Moreover, it has
been shown that higher levels of social control, cohesion and trust
within a community are associated with lower levels of violence and
property crime (Sampson et al. 1997: 923; Carcach and Huntley
2002). Lower levels of crime have the potential to reduce pressure on
police resources, benefiting both the police and the community.

Costs and Risks
As noted in Part 1 of this chapter, gifts are often accompanied by
obligations and expectations (Mauss 1950; Sahlins 1972) and these
may translate into costs and risks for the recipient. Some of the
inherent costs and risks to police and society in allowing citizens to
involve themselves in police organisations and to conduct policing
activities are discussed below. Grabosky (1992: 267, following
Braithwaite and Petit 1990), states that citizen participation should be
encouraged only so far as it intrudes no more than is necessary on the

freedom of other citizens. Within the scope of this general strategy, more detailed thought needs to be given to how, in practice, identified risks might be minimized. Some suggestions on risk minimization are given as a first step in this direction.

Costs. The gain in police resources from the contribution of citizens through the gift of their own labour must be offset against, and ideally should exceed, the costs of those gifts. Volunteers within police organisations generate additional work for police in terms of advertising, recruitment, training and supervision, as well as pure financial costs for uniforms, space and other overheads. Police organisations are required to consider the minutiae associated with employment of nonpaid workers, such as the complexities of scheduling shifts, whether volunteers might be required to undertake overtime and the conditions under which their services can be terminated. Furthermore, time and energy must be given to consideration of the proper allocation of tasks to volunteers, to consultation with unions and to ensuring job satisfaction for volunteers. Citizen participation in law enforcement in terms of formal police/community partnerships also generates additional demands on police.

Police concerns. The introduction of civilians into the police organisation is often seen by police as a threat. The Police Federation of Australia (PFA), in its policy on civilianisation and the use of unsworn officers, opposes outright any proposal to introduce volunteer/auxiliary police and states that the only positions that might be 'civilianised' would be those that do not require the use of police powers and authority or the application of specific police knowledge and training. There should be "clear lines of demarcation so as to properly defend any police positions". Clearly, police are concerned about possible loss of jobs and overtime, as well as the more intangible effect that an increase in civilians in police organisations might have on the recognition of police as a profession.[11]

---

[11]   As the PFA policy recognises, an increase in civilians in police organisations can come about not only by the presence of volunteers, but also through the growing use of unsworn officers to undertake jobs sworn officers might otherwise do. For example, in recent years a team of Crime Scene Attendants at burglaries in east

These concerns are nothing new. Bryett (1996: 28) refers to comparable concerns expressed by the New South Wales Police Association in 1991 when a government task force was considering the possibility of introducing volunteer police. Greenberg (2005: 11) reports on a similar reaction from police unions and individual police to volunteer programs introduced in the United States in the 1980s and 1990s. Gaston and Alexander (2001) suggest that relations between regular police officers and volunteers have historically been troubled, loaded with hostility and distrust. Although the continued recruitment of U.K. Special Constables and the popularity of volunteers-in-policing programs in many jurisdictions might suggest that police are perhaps becoming more accepting of civilians in their professional world, it is clear that this is not universally the case. There remains a significant potential for the use of volunteers to provoke police opposition and affect police morale.

Perhaps it is the 'gift' aspect of the volunteer contribution that is the underlying obstacle for police. Schwartz (1967: 2) suggests that gifts impose an identity on both the giver and the receiver. In giving a gift the giver reveals the idea that the receiver evokes in the mind of the giver. Gifts to a group therefore influence group boundaries by clarifying them (Schwartz 1967: 11). The gift of voluntary labour to police, as well as any official endorsement of it, may be seen by police as challenging their ability to handle their remit, and as suggesting that the boundaries of the police identity are fuzzy, mutable or porous. By accepting the gift, are they are accepting that they are in need of assistance, that they have a tenuous hold on their responsibilities, or that others can do their job as well as they can? Police may also consider that any suggestion that they are not in complete control of their area of expertise will raise questions in the public's mind

Auckland, New Zealand, has been exclusively constituted by unsworn officers, including a retired police officer and people with no policing background but with particular expertise (e.g., in forensics) (New Zealand Police 2007: 27). In the Australian Federal Police (AFP), unsworn personnel are involved in, amongst other things, records management, property advisory services, forensics and internal audit. According to an AFP manager to whom we spoke, embracing civilianisation is "a huge strength for the AFP" as sworn police are more productive when they have administrative support that frees them up for operational work.

over their value, professionalism and legitimacy, and by doing so ultimately make their job even more difficult.

There may also be questions over the liability of the police service for the actions of volunteers. With parts of policing becoming increasingly sophisticated, it is likely that many volunteers working in police organisations will be engaged on the more mundane tasks involving public interaction, such as patrol, and it is important that their actions are both legal and ethical and that the impression of the police that they give is appropriate (Worton 2003: 15). Attempts by volunteers to use their status to wield power over others, or expectations of favouritism or even immunity in circumstances where police intervention in their affairs is necessary or desirable, will endear volunteers to neither police nor the general public. Proper selection, training and supervision of volunteers may well head off any 'loose cannons', but accountability for the actions of volunteers may still pose an issue of concern for police, especially in situations where they may possibly endanger (physically or mentally) the public, or indeed regular police officers.

It is the job of police unions to protect their members' interests. It is doubtful that any strategy will completely allay their suspicions over the impact that the use of volunteers will have on their jobs and on the identity, perceived value and legitimacy of the police in the public's eye. However, consultation with unions over proposals involving use of volunteers, close police control over allocation of tasks between regular officers and volunteers, as well as supervision of volunteers' day-to-day activities, will go some way to assuaging their fears. Only when police officers work with volunteers and can perceive their value will they be properly accepted as co-workers rather than threats. This has already happened to a great extent with the Special Constabulary in the United Kingdom.

Confidentiality and privacy concerns. In her research on misuse of confidential police information, Davids (2006) identifies knowledge gleaned in the normal course of duties or acquired from police databases as information that has sometimes been misused by police for private purposes. Clearly, the potential that Davids identifies for confidential information held by police to be misused by officers or other staff may also exist in relation to citizens working in volunteer capacities within police organisations or even those working closely with police.

Most volunteers in police organisations work in areas where they do not have direct access to police databases.[12] However, their presence in the organisation may mean that they are privy to some kinds of private information held, or even simply discussed, by police. The kinds of controls that police organisations have over their employees (contracts of employment, codes of behaviour and the threat of wage loss) may not be applicable to volunteers. In addition, volunteers may not consider they owe accountability to the organisation to the same degree that employees do. There may be understandable questions over the amount of allegiance volunteers feel to an organisation that does not pay them (Bryett 1996: 29) and sometimes undervalues their contribution (Christmann 2003; Gaston and Alexander 2001). There is therefore some risk of volunteers misusing confidential information to which they have access in that capacity, compromising the privacy of other citizens or police themselves, and thereby threatening police legitimacy (Davids 2006: 38). A leaky boat is unlikely to engender trust.

Even in partnerships with the community, police need to be careful about those with whom they deal. The creation of the Community Police Forums (CPFs) in South Africa was meant to facilitate communication and cooperation between the community and the police. However, many CPFs have failed in their communities, one of the reasons being corruption. In one Western Cape suburb known for its gang problems, members of a gang became part of the executive committee of their local CPF, giving them access to information supplied by the police at the CPF meetings for their own purposes. Once the community became aware of the gang infiltration, the executive committee was re-elected (Kinnes 2000).

---

[12] In defending against claims of misusing information, police officers sometimes claim that they personally did not access personal information held on police databases, but may have inadvertently left the database open on their computer that must then have been accessed by another officer (Davids 2006: 8). If this has any truth to it, a volunteer may be in position to take advantage of such a lapse as easily as any police officer.

Controls over access by volunteers or other community contacts to sensitive materials are essential. These may be contained in police organisations' policies. Other tools already employed by many police organisations to deal with this risk are selection checks of those working closely with police and the inclusion of confidentiality provisions in volunteers' contracts.

Erosion of security. In moving beyond the engagement of volunteers by the police towards citizen-initiated policing gifts, a new raft of risks appear. The research by Leach (2006) into Manitoba citizen patrols notes that many patrols lack any accountability to the community. Most members are self-selected rather than elected. Furthermore there are often no requirements to report back to the larger community (Leach 2006: 4). Such patrols also tend to concentrate on keeping an eye on the activities of those who are in some way 'different' or in the minority: strangers, indigenous people, youths, sex trade workers and so on. The rights of such people "have little bearing on their work" (2006: 5). She suggests that, as a result, patrols effectively redefine the community they purport to represent to exclude certain groups that are undesirable in the opinion of patrol participants. Patrols of this nature may erode rather than strengthen security by deepening mistrust and inequalities in the community, engendering conflict as a result, and thereby increase the need for policing (Leach 2006: 7).

Crawford (2006a: 137) makes a similar point, saying that the kind of social capital that citizens provide when they band together to ensure their own security in what he terms "security clubs" is likely to be intra-club and parochial (or 'bonding' rather than 'bridging' capital: Putnam 2000), and so create strong antagonism towards nonclub members (see also Pino 2001: 213–4). Observations of a like nature to those about the Manitoba patrols could be and have been made about other citizen groups, such as the Minutemen and Perverted Justice.

So it seems that not all instances of policing by citizens will win approval from other citizens, the police or the state. Not all community policing initiatives will build social capital (Pino 2001: 203). Moreover, some citizen initiatives create more problems than they solve. Law enforcement officials, for example, have observed that Perverted Justice's 'stings' can compromise police investigations and that their evidence may be unreliable (Associated Press 2004).

Sometimes organisations of citizens dedicated to crime control take their actions so far that they are labelled vigilantes. The history and varying forms of vigilantism has been studied in depth by a number of scholars (e.g., Little and Sheffield 1983; Brown 1991; Johnston 1996; Bruce and Komane 1999; Garland 2005) and will not be examined here. Most scholars take the position that, in order to enforce the law, vigilantes act as if they are temporarily above the law (Little and Sheffield 1983: 804). Johnston (1996), however, defines vigilantism in such a way that illegal or extra-legal activities are not a necessary precondition. In his view, the activities of self-help groups (such as citizen patrols) that enjoy a potential to exercise or threaten force may be vigilantism (1996: 233).[13] Punishment is often a part of vigilante activities, but may not be (Johnston 1996: 233).

The risk is, then, that citizen groups that act without coordinating their activities with relevant law enforcement agencies, even with the best will in the world, may slide into vigilantism, for example by luring their targets to behave in ways they would not ordinarily do, or by engaging in acts or threats of violence or forms of punishment that amount to unacceptable or even criminal acts. In parts of Indonesia, it is not uncommon for people caught thieving by local residents to be beaten or even burned alive. Public lynchings and dismemberment of suspected witches also occur (USINDO 2003; Barker 2005). Mob violence is also a feature of self-policing in many parts of Africa (Baker 2004a, 2005a, 2005b; Dempster 2002). In Sierre Leone, mobs engage in beatings, stonings and machete attacks, and burn others alive (Baker 2005b). But vigilantism is not only apparent in less developed nations. Perverted Justice's strategies of naming and shaming offenders have been described as the technological equiv-alent of the historical mob justice actions of tarring and feathering an offender and running him out of town (Cotroneo 2004). Like the citizen groups that conducted public torture lynchings in the

---

[13] Johnston's precise criminological definition of vigilantism also has a number of other features not dealt with here: see Johnston (1996).

southern American states from the 1890s to the 1930s (Garland 2005: 814), some citizen groups appear to consider that 'regular' justice is too good for their targets.

Furthermore, while regular law enforcement is not immune to charges of discrimination against minorities, vigilantism is far more likely to result in this abuse (Little and Sheffield 1983: 807). The actions of vigilante taxi drivers in Durban, South Africa, for example, are not about "a generalised intolerance of criminality but rather a selective hostility to the criminality of 'outsiders'" (Bruce and Komane 1999). The public torture lynchings of which Garland writes were designed to, among other things, repress the black population, "increase the day-to-day effectiveness of more routine racial controls" (2005: 821) and illustrate white superiority. For police, the necessity of dealing with the activities of vigilantes, whether they be illegal, discriminatory or merely anti-social, only serves to increase the pressure on resources. Moreover, the existence of vigilante groups does nothing to help build or maintain social capital, instead creating distrust and fear, and so further eroding security.

State censuring of vigilantism in both rhetoric and practice (through legislation and the courts) is vital. When governments suggest, by positive affirmation or simply an absence of comment, that citizen behaviour that oversteps legal or moral boundaries is acceptable or even useful to them, an increase in such behaviour, with its concomitant challenge for police resources, can be expected. Garland (2005) observes that the outpouring of racist violence in the form of public torture lynchings was positively encouraged by the rhetoric, action and abstention from action of the authorities, at various levels (federal, state and local) and of various types (politicians, courts and law enforcement), in relation to the rights and interests of the American South's black population.

For police, the challenge is to properly distinguish between appropriate and inappropriate citizen law enforcement activity, welcoming the former and condemning the latter. This may involve having to refuse to use improperly gathered information for apprehensions and prosecutions, however tempting it is to 'nail' an offender, in order to avoid encouraging citizens from engaging in behaviour verging on the vigilante. Formally constituted crime prevention partnerships between police and citizens (as well as social-capacity building partnerships between citizens and other agencies), where roles and the limits of those roles are worked out in some detail, are the key to ensuring that such behaviour is kept in check and that the building of social capital within groups is not used to marginalize or actively discriminate against less powerful citizens.

Surveillance society. While many have applauded the growth in citizen involvement in policing the community, others have warned of the potential for this extension of the policing 'family' to bear fruit in the form of a society increasingly focused on surveillance.

In 2002, when the U.S. government proposed its Terrorist Information and Prevention System (TIPS), which was effectively an expansion of the Highway Watch program to include not only transportation workers but also postal and utility workers, it drew trenchant criticism from civil liberties groups and others for promoting spying by Americans on Americans (CBS News 2002; Healy 2002). The scheme was eventually abandoned. Pfuhl (1992) describes how anonymous informing, or as he calls it, "snitching", which was once regarded as morally repulsive because of its connotations of betrayal, became legitimated in Crimestoppers. He notes that Crimestoppers was in fact initially opposed by police because they believed it smacked of vigilantism (1992: 515 n.13).

Even a climate of acceptance by authorities of surveillance activities by citizens, perhaps signalled by increasing numbers of government hotlines for reporting crimes or suspicious activities, might result in those activities being undertaken with excessive zeal. An example of this phenomenon is found in the cases of *United States v. Steiger* 318 F.3d 1039 (11th Cir. 2003) and *United States v. Jarrett* 338 F.3d 339 (4th Cir.2003). In both those cases, convictions of child pornographers were secured on the basis of information provided by 'Unknownuser', a (possibly foreign) person who illegally hacked into the computers of the offenders using a Trojan Horse program, copied files from those computers and anonymously forwarded the files to law enforcement officers in America. Both offenders were sentenced to imprisonment. Although one might perceive the outcome of these cases as positive, the message they give to other citizens may well be that illegal acts are acceptable for the purpose of engaging in surveillance.

Do we really want a society of spies and snitches? As many scholars have noted, interpersonal trust and the social bond would thereby be put at risk (Marx 1989: 516; Grabosky 1992: 26; Pfuhl 1992: 525). Sampson (2004: 112) warns of the danger that community social control may result in unwanted and unjust scrutiny, particularly of racial minorities. Arguments about whether security can be defended by waiving or infringing rights, such as rights to privacy and freedom of expression, now familiar in relation to the 'War on Terror', have appeared in academic discourse on citizen policing of crime for some time (see, for example, Marx 1989: 508). It is clear then that the risk of damaging society by allowing a degree of snitching and spying must be weighed against the benefits of growing social capital through participation by community members in ensuring their own security. "One should strive for a balance," says Grabosky (1992: 26) "where an active citizenry serves as a bulwark against the abuse of power by governments, and a vigilant government stands as a safeguard against an overzealous and potentially tyrannous citizenry."

Careful thought needs to be given to the appropriateness and wider societal impact of asking people to inform on others. Perhaps some consideration could be given to developing a set of criteria for the circumstances in which such a request might be appropriate. These could take into account, for example, the severity of the crime or possible crime on which people are being asked to report (for instance, detection of potential terrorist acts might be a cause for informing, whereas an observed parking infringement may not); whether detecting the information would require the informer to actively intrude into a person's private space or otherwise infringe their privacy; whether the informer themselves could be put in jeopardy by informing; and so on. It might also be appropriate, when the use of information is considered, for police to speculate about the motive of the informer and consider whether its publication or other use might have a divisive impact or bring a particular minority into disrepute. A cautious and carefully structured approach to the use of rewards and incentives to encourage the provision of information may need to be adopted (for more on this, see Chapter 4).

Implications for Police and Conclusions

What are the implications for the future of policing of the increasingly diverse ways in which people are bestowing on the police the gift of their person? The extra resources that police volunteers provide, and the relief from policing duties that citizen crime prevention groups and citizen self-regulation can afford police, may well allow police to achieve better results in their own policing responsibilities. This is in fact a basic premise of the community policing strategy (Skogan and Hartnett 1997: 5).

However, this simple equation of more resources equals increased productivity, and its related equation, that increased productivity equals better policing, may not hold consistently true, for a variety of reasons. One of these, as has been discussed, is that the gift of people can produce additional work for police that may soak up some or all of these savings in resources, for example in training and supervision of volunteers, dealing with increases in information provided by citizens and even dealing with tendencies to vigilantism. Extra resources, be they people or police time, need thoughtful and time-consuming shepherding.

Moreover, if citizens undertake these roles well and effectively, it is possible that the future that police unions fear will indeed come to pass. Perhaps police will find they *are* regarded as increasingly irrelevant; that citizens think they can undertake what is presently regarded as within the police domain just as effectively as police. The growth in policing by groups other than police (volunteers, private security, municipally funded agents etc.) may challenge the very identity of the police and leave for them only the policing that remains after others have taken care of their own interests – what Crawford (2006a: 112) calls the "residualization of policing", result-ing in a situation in which the public police become a last resort for policing the really bad risks (Crawford 2006a: 136–37). The bound-aries of public policing may indeed be proved to be fuzzy, mutable or porous. And if all this does occur, what then will happen to police recruitment? If police come to be seen as powerless (or only equally as powerful as others), irrelevant or unappreciated, this is bound to present difficulties for attracting new staff.

These possibilities are, however, some way down a track that may still have other destinations. For the moment, public policing remains distinctive and "of a qualitatively different order to other forms of policing" (Crawford 2006a: 137). The key to minimizing the risks that have been identified is, for the present at least, for the state to take the lead in defining the nature and limits of personal gifts to police that are appropriate and desirable, and for the police to carefully oversee those gifts of people that are within their purview and monitor those that are not. Along with risk minimization strategies, ongoing evaluation of the value of citizen participation in law enforcement in its various forms is also crucial, something that has not been given much priority to date (Rogers and Robinson 2004: 18; Beckman et al. 2005: 298). And in the meantime, it is also worthwhile to consider the potential for the growth in the policing 'family' and the increasingly nodal form it inhabits to lead to a future that perhaps few intend. The gift of human labour to law enforcement presents a real and present challenge to police in terms of oversight and management, but also raises issues that need further consideration concerning the future compass of the public police role in community and national security provision.

CHAPTER SEVEN

AMBIGUOUS EXCHANGES AND THE POLICE

INTRODUCTION

As previous chapters have shown, police departments engage in all manner of exchanges with institutions and individuals outside their ranks. They command assistance from common citizens. They buy and sell goods and services. They receive donations in cash and in kind from business and from ordinary individuals.

At times, these exchanges have been inherently criminal transactions. Coerced confessions and 'third degree' methods were common practice a century ago in English-speaking democracies (Skolnick and Fyfe, 1993: 43–48),[1] and still take place in many countries.[2] Although rare as a matter of official policy, police have sold all varieties of contraband, and have traded dispensation in return for cash or favours. And gifts to police in implicit anticipation of special consideration have long been commonplace in urban society.

But today, at least in advanced democracies, most of the exchange along the three dimensions of coercion, sale, and gift is completely legitimate. Requiring assistance to law enforcement by mandating record-keeping and disclosure of transactions by second-hand goods dealers makes the fencing of stolen goods more difficult to accomplish. Fee-for-service or user-pays policing helps defray the cost of

---

[1] As an example, see the discussion by Chief Justice Hughes of the lower court decisions leading up to this Supreme Court Decision: *Brown v. Mississippi*, 297 US 278, 56 S.Ct. 461, 80 L.Ed. 682 (1936)

[2] See Rudoren 2006 for a report about the brutalisation of suspects by police officers in Chicago in the 1970s and 1980s.

deploying public police to secure special events of a commercial or private nature such as concerts and professional sporting events. In addition to uniforms, firearms and motor vehicles, police purchase products as diverse as kitchen and bathroom fittings and equipment, specialised apparel photographic equipment, musical instruments and livestock in the form of dogs and horses (see Chapter 4). And, as discussed in Chapter 6, they receive gifts in cash and in kind, including petrol, pushbikes, office space, and communications equipment (Pilant 1998; New South Wales Police Service 2000: 61–2; Singh 2005).

Anthropologists and historians of exchange relationships remind us that such relationships rarely exist in their 'pure' form. In the past, considerable ambiguity has surrounded forms of exchange. The transition from prehistoric societies of hunters and gatherers to contemporary market economies was an evolutionary one (Polanyi 1944). Davis (2000) described how the exchange of gifts in sixteenth-century France was in some respects a prelude to buying and selling. In addition, she observed how the giving of some gifts was in fact compulsory, dictated by strict customs. Mauss (1950) discussed how lavish gifts bestowed by the indigenous peoples of what is now British Columbia and the Pacific Northwest of the United States were really demonstrations of power. He went on to refer to some gifts as a blend of the voluntary and the obligatory. Hyde (1979: 70) favours defining gifts to minimise the recipient's sense of debt. He observes that whenever the donor or the recipient begins to treat a gift as an obligation, it ceases to be a gift. Sahlins (1972) refers to exchange relations as a 'spectrum of reciprocities' ranging from pure altruism at one pole, to outright theft at the other. Sponsorship, as a form of gift involving some explicit obligations on the part of the recipient, is part way along the continuum towards commercial exchange which, with its explicit weighing of value, is situated at the centre.

This chapter explores some of the ambiguities inherent in exchange relationships involving public police organisations, look- ing in greater detail at the trio coercion, gift and sale explored in previous chapters. We look first at various pairs of relational types (Sale/Coercion; Coercion/Gift; Gift/Sale), and identify basic patterns of overlap. We then identify circumstances in which the types of exchange relations may be sequentially linked. The chapter concludes with a discussion of the implications of these ambiguities and linkages for police administration.

THE INTERFACE OF COMMERCE AND DURESS (SALE/ COERCION)

Commercial exchange is not entirely without its coercive elements (Barnhizer 2006: 3, 41). The structure of markets may make for ruthless outcomes. A monopolistic provider can charge all the market will bear for its products. A monopsonistic purchaser may reduce the profit margins of its suppliers to negligible levels. A large retailer such as Wal-Mart can prescribe not only price to its suppliers, but can also specify details of packaging and content. If one wishes to sell to Wal-Mart, one follows its dictates. As has been said of another powerful consumer, 'When McDonald's says "Jump", 500 suppliers ask "How high?"' (Earle 1996).

Coercion in Sales by Police

Police are not without market power of their own, which in some instances may be reinforced by the coercive power conferred upon them. Some commercial arrangements are inherently coercive. Consider, for example, the institution of user-pays policing that we considered in Chapter 5. In some jurisdictions, promoters of public events for profit, such as rock concerts or sporting events, are *required* to engage police services for the delivery of traffic control or event security, to a specified extent and at a specified fee. In Australia, for example, both New South Wales and Victoria Police make it quite clear in their user-pays policing policies that the ultimate responsibility for assessment of policing needs for events lies with the police. Organisers are 'expected to accept police advice' on this matter (New South Wales Police Service 2000: Policy Guideline 9). Under these circumstances, if the event is to take place, the promoter has no choice but to purchase the service. No fee, no event.

This is a variation on an old theme of hypothecated licence fees, discussed more than two centuries ago by Colquhoun (1795 [1969]). He recommended that various "suspicious trades" such as second-hand goods dealers, "Persons keeping Slaughtering-houses for Horses," and "Wholesale purchasers of Rags, and unserviceable Cordage" be licensed, with the revenue derived from licence fees dedicated to policing with the object of ensuring the integrity of the respective markets (Colquhoun 1795 [1969]: 541–51).

Coercion in Sales to Police

Police as coercive consumers. Police may also be coercive consumers of goods and services. The larger police agencies, with staff numbering in the thousands if not tens of thousands, wield substantial buying power. While a police service may not enjoy the clout of Wal-Mart, they, too, can dictate to suppliers, particularly when the product or service in question is of a specialised nature having few other potential buyers.

The relationship between police and informants provides another example of the overlap of coercion and sale. The exchange of money for information is often a feature of the police–informant relationship. Police can offer sticks as well as carrots, sometimes simultaneously. As suggested in Chapter 4, it is not unknown for police to use threats, such as the threat of prosecution, to secure informants' cooperation. The presence of threat introduces an element of coercion into what might otherwise be a commercial relationship. Similarly, police may request information in return for a nominal payment and protection of an informant's illegal activities, with the clear implication that if the information is not forthcoming, not only will the protection be withheld, but there may be police intervention to prevent those activities continuing (Marx 1988: 156–57).

Police as coerced consumers. Police themselves may be vulnerable to coercion in their capacity as consumers. When faced with a monopoly supplier, or with circumstances in which a change in suppliers would entail prohibitive transaction costs (for instance, the acquisition of certain IT hardware or software or of certain counterterrorism related items), police may simply have to accept the terms dictated to them. Under these circumstances, the police are at the mercy of the market.

COMPULSION AND BENEVOLENCE (COERCION/GIFT)

Gifts that Compel

In some cultures, norms of reciprocity are powerfully binding. Social obligations may include both an obligation to give and an obligation to reciprocate (Mauss 1950: 16, 17).

Lavish gift giving in some pre-industrial societies was an ostentatious demonstration of power. Similarly, today if gifts are given publicly, they may result in prestige for the giver and a diminution of status and even stigmatization for the recipient, which only the ability and opportunity to reciprocate can ease (Pinker, 1971: 135–75). "Most of us," says Pinker (1971: 153), "prefer a measure of equivalency in our social relationships." While few if any police executives will admit to feeling indebted to a benefactor, the risk of unconscious favouritism, or the potential for perception of favouritism, can exist. So it is that gifts can be subtly coercive.[3] One former police executive told us that he would find it very difficult "to accept a gift from [company X] and then have to go in and conduct an investigation" if allegations of wrongdoing, even unrelated to the gift, should arise. For this reason, many jurisdictions prohibit their police organisations from accepting gifts altogether. In other jurisdictions, personal gifts to police officers are unacceptable but gifts to the organisation may be allowed, as long as they do not involve the police in giving anyone special consideration.[4]

Conditional gifts, such as a gift of cash given with the proviso that it is spent on a particular activity, can compel police to spend more time on that activity than they might otherwise choose to do. In addition, some gifts, by their nature, can lock a recipient into a course of action that might otherwise not be taken. Gifts of particular equipment or premises could mean that police agendas are reshaped in new directions. Assistance in the form of computers, software and technical support given by Alberta Energy Corporation to the Royal

---

[3] The drug marketing practices of pharmaceutical industry representatives provide some interesting illustrative examples. See Elliott 2006.

[4] See, for example, New Zealand Police 'General Instructions dealing with Sponsorship' S582(1)(c).

Canadian Mounted Police in the late 1990s appears to have proved catalytic in getting an investigation into 'oilpatch vandalism' in Northern Alberta off the ground and to the point of prosecution (Blatchford 2000; Nikiforuk 2000), although as mentioned in Chapter 6, the court ultimately concluded that the integrity of the investigation was not compromised by the donation.

A donor's questionable motives may be invoked to justify declining a gift. The issue of police 'wannabees' was noted in previous chapters. A gift may also be declined where the gift is offered by a donor with whom the police do not wish to be associated because of a perceived conflict of interest. The association between alcohol and violence may lead some police services not to accept gifts from the alcohol industry. Some police services will not accept gifts from industries such as cigarette manufacturers, whose interests may conflict with more general government policy (such as health promotion). The New South Wales Police Service Sponsorship and Endorsement Policy of 2001, for example, makes this explicit in s. 5.3 dealing with 'Government and Police Service Sponsorship Limitations'.[5]

Gifts that Are Compelled

The act of extortion may be represented by joining the polar opposites of Sahlins' continuum of reciprocities, so that it becomes a *circle* of reciprocities. Extortion involves a person's *demand for something of value, accompanied by the threat of harm* in the event of non-compliance. Extortion threats may be implicit (Chin 1996: 35–36, 44–45). When a group of rough-looking youths enter a shop and ask the shopkeeper if he or she would like to contribute to their social club, the shopkeeper will usually understand the consequences of turning them down.

Mild forms of extortion are deeply embedded in some cultures. Davis (2000: 27) reminds us of the tradition of Charivari, where young childless couples were visited by boisterous villagers demanding payment in return for ceasing their revelries. This, after

---

[5] See also Victoria Police (2005) 'Donations and Sponsorship', VPM 205–5 Section 4.1.

all, is the logic of the time-honoured Halloween custom of 'Trick or Treat'.

The line between bribery and extortion is not a bright one (Noonan 1984: 584–88). Bribery is the offering of some consideration in return for favourable treatment. I pay you $50 with the understanding that you will not write me a speeding ticket. Extortion is the demand for some consideration in return for favourable treatment. You threaten to write me a speeding ticket unless I pay you $50. However, reality is rarely that simple. In both bribery and extortion, key elements may be implicit.

It may be unstated, but understood, that companies awarded government contracts kick back 10 percent to a designated official. It may be unstated, yet understood, that payment for work performed pursuant to the contract will not be made unless the kickback is forthcoming. The quid pro quo is rarely articulated, probably to provide for plausible deniability in the event that the criminal law is mobilised. Yet it may be well understood by both parties. Where either practice becomes routinised, no threats need be made, nor favours requested. The distinction between bribery and extortion disappears.

Legitimate Requests of a Quasi-coercive Nature

In many jurisdictions, because of their power and legitimacy, police command a great deal of respect (Loader 1997; Tyler 2004: 86–87). While some citizens might ignore or refuse a police request (other than a request pursuant to the compulsory powers that police might have), other citizens may be more instinctively obedient. When the Japanese police 'request' assistance from the private sector to combat phishing (National Police Agency 2004) or 'persuade' citizens to lease anticrime cameras to mount outside their houses and shops (Hoffman 2006), it may be unclear what it is that drives a person's decision to cooperate. Where an individual perceives a degree of asymmetry of power relations, that person may feel unable to decline a request by the more powerful party. Some police agencies, such as the Baton Rouge Police Department in Louisiana, will not solicit contributions from the public for precisely this reason. The risk of damage to their legitimacy is just too great.

Of course, those police agencies that *lack* legitimacy often do so for a reason. This may include a reputation for heavy-handedness in dealing with the public. Citizens who ignore a request from such agencies often do so at their peril.

COMMERCE AND BENEVOLENCE (SALE/GIFT)

Gifts with Strings Attached: Commerce Masquerading as Gift

The earliest forms of exchange in human societies, before the advent of money, were gifts. The evolution of exchange relationships from gifts to modern commerce has not been absolute, nor is it yet complete. Hyde (1979: 139) observes of gift and commodity that "Neither is ever seen in its pure state, for each needs at least a touch of the other". As we have noted in Chapter 5, Mauss (1950) used the term "contractual gifts" to refer to emerging obligations of exchange.

Ambiguities may be explicit or implicit. The requirement that a private citizen engage police on a user-pays basis is straightforward. The distinction between fee-for-service and corporate sponsorship may be less so. Consider relationships between police and the private sector in relation to sale and gift, where differentiating between sponsorship and user-pays policing is sometimes difficult. Such circumstances may arise where the managers of a shopping mall offer to underwrite the cost of police presence on site during opening hours and to provide complimentary office space for the police. Depending on the eye of the beholder, the shopping centre manager's donation of office space to police may appear to be a gift, or an example of user-pays policing.

A similar perspective may be taken on the relationship between the New York City Police Foundation (NYCPF), Major League Baseball, and the Motion Picture Association of America. The latter two organisations' contributions to the NYCPF support the NYPD trademark infringement unit by providing funds for the undercover purchases of pirated clothes, CDs and DVDs (Weissenstein 2003).

The sponsorship of police patrols by local authorities and others in many parts of the United Kingdom is another example of a gift arrangement which might just as easily be characterised as user-pays policing. In Cornwall, for instance, the Polzeath Council, businesses and residents have paid for the police overtime needed so that officers can patrol their popular beach in summer (Gibbons 1996: 23).

In the United States during the first decades of the twentieth century, police often intervened in labour disputes on behalf of management. The interventions in question tended to involve protection of strikebreakers and/or of employers' property (Ray 1995: 425). It was not uncommon for local employers to provide in-kind support (such as temporary lodging) to police in these situations. Employers also supplemented the costs of local law enforcement (Fishback 1995: 436).

Perhaps the difference between a gift and a commercial arrangement lies in who controls the activity: under a sponsorship arrangement, the police; with user-pays policing, the client (Grabosky 2004: 73). But sometimes, as the above examples illustrate, this is not entirely clear. Both sides may have a say over the nature and limits of police involvement in the activity. The crucial factor may be the presence or absence of a formal agreement that would specify the role of the police on site.

The term 'loss leader' refers to a commercial arrangement whereby a seller offers a product at a greatly reduced price in order to pave the way for continuing commercial relationships at more typical market rates. A seller may be happy to wear the short-term loss if it will contribute to the development of a long-term, and more lucrative, commercial relationship.

Consider the offer of a software manufacturer who proposes, free of charge, to develop a personnel administration system for a police agency. Depending on the architecture of the product, the recipient may be captured, in a commercial sense. When the time comes to update the system, the recipient may be faced with a stark choice: engage a new provider to replace the system, or purchase a new system from a new provider, or pay the existing provider whatever it wishes to charge for updates. The transaction costs involved in a change of supplier may see the police locked into a commercial relationship (Dehoog and Salamon 2002: 326).

One of the authors recalls a shopping experience in Indonesia where he thought he had driven a particularly hard bargain. Toward the close of the transaction, the apparently reluctant merchant gave the impression that he was giving the item away at cost. Feeling somewhat guilty about his meanness, the shopper took the goods and turned from the counter. Before he reached the door of the shop, the shopkeeper caught up with him and gave him a small gift. Even in western cultures, regular customers may be rewarded by a grateful vendor. And the practice of extending extra hospitality to clients (or potential clients) is not uncommon.

Gift Masquerading as Commerce

The term 'sweetheart deal' refers to a commercial exchange in which one of the parties does the other a favour. Where gifts outright are prohibited by law, laundering mechanisms may be used to portray a gift as a sale, at a peppercorn price.

In Chapter 6, we mentioned the arrangements for corporate sponsorship of police vehicles that the U.S. company, Government Acquisitions (GA), enters into with police organisations. A company pays for a vehicle which GA buys, and GA then 'sells' it to a public police organisation for $1. In return for the gift of the vehicle, police allow carefully vetted company advertisements on the vehicle's hood, boot and quarter panels for three years. At the end of that period the vehicle is 'sold' back to GA for $1 (Mollenkamp 2003: 80).

POLICE AS MANAGERS OF AMBIGUITY: CONCLUSIONS AND IMPLICATIONS

As the eminent economic historian Karl Polanyi (1944) demonstrates, the emergence of market economies did not occur overnight. The evolution of exchange relationships has left us with some interesting ambiguities.

The earliest forms of commerce took the form of an exchange of gifts. Commercial exchange was later to become more routinised. Gifts to the leader became obligatory, and then evolved into taxes. The two existed in parallel, but hardly voluntary, form during part of this trajectory. Today there are a few generous souls who make bequests to the Tax Office, but not many.

Mixed Motives

More often than not, the motives that underlie exchange are mixed. Police 'wannabees' may be driven by both egotistical and altruistic impulses. Behind the proffer of a gift may be the desire for celebrity, or the expectation of some form of reciprocity. Hyde (1979) refers to "the 'tyranny of gift' which uses the bonding power of generosity to manipulate people". The Hindu epic the *Mahabharata* cites a number of motives underlying gifts: pity, free choice, desire of merit, desire of profit, and fear (Ganguli 1883–1896).

Linked Exchanges

Exchanges, of course, do not occur in a vacuum. Any given police agency exists in a web of relationships, some coercive, some commercial, some charitable, and some hybrid. One form of exchange may follow another, or give rise to it.

As we have already noted, using foundations or charitable trusts to receive donations on behalf of police organisations, while it may serve to protect against an appearance of impropriety that might arise from a direct donor–recipient relationship, does not guarantee this and may indeed have just the opposite effect. Circumvention of procurement safeguards by channelling funds for police organisations through police foundations is not unknown, leaving those organisations vulnerable to allegations of misconduct.

Arguably less controversial is the use of gifts to foster subsequent sales. Donations to the New York City Police Foundation enabled it to engage an agency to license the NYPD logo for use on action figures, stuffed toys, bicycles, and children's sleepwear (New York City Police Foundation 2004).

Cost-Effectiveness, Equity and Legitimacy

It matters how police–private arrangements are characterised, and that these ambiguities are recognised, because this affects the kinds of considerations the police bring to bear in assessing the benefits and dangers of entering into those exchanges, as well as the types of controls needed over the relationships generated by them. More thought is required on the conditions under which 'gift' should be encouraged. For instance, if sponsorship is seen purely as a gift, police may not recognise that they have something the sponsor wants and with which they can bargain. And if the relationship between informants and police is seen as a purely commercial exchange, there is a danger that appropriate safeguards against the improper use of coercion will not be considered.

When is a gift equivalent to a commercial transaction? One of our respondents, in the course of discussing corporate sponsorship of policing activities, suggested that the two may be normatively indistinguishable. When a police force solicits sponsorship, the sponsor benefits to some extent, if only in terms of acknowledgment and association with a prestigious agency of government. However, competitors of a successful sponsor could be forgiven for feeling left out, especially if the sponsorship engagement arose from bilateral negotiations. For the police to confer a promotional opportunity upon a favoured entity without allowing for competitive bidding may strike some as both unfair and inefficient. As noted in Chapter 6, it has been suggested that sponsorship arrangements should flow from a process that mimics that of procurement tendering (Independent Commission Against Corruption 2006: 11, 29).

Police in many, if not most, contemporary industrial societies are firmly in the political spotlight. Accountability measures are stringent, media scrutiny exacting, and political oversight unrelenting. It is not surprising, therefore, that police engage in a significant degree of self-regulation with regard to their exchange relationships. Indeed, it would not be inappropriate to refer to some police as 'super-cautious' in their management of exchange relations. Hyde (1979: 73) reminds us that folktales rarely if ever relate examples of gifts proffered by witches having been accepted by their intended recipients. Gifts of evil people must be refused, lest the recipient be bound to that evil. This is a lesson that sophisticated police organisations learn early on: they are unlikely to accept gifts from businesses, industries or individuals with an unsavoury public image.

The *raison d'être* of some gifts is to establish a bond between donor and recipient. As Douglas (1990) reminds us, "[a] gift that does nothing to enhance solidarity is a contradiction." By contrast, the sale of a commodity leaves little connection between buyer and seller. A degree of bonding between the police organisation and the community it serves (or significant institutions within that community) is entirely appropriate. What matters, however, is that interests other than the donor's are not excluded. And the exchange must not leave a feeling of obligation within the recipient.

The environment of political sensitivity in which contemporary police agencies operate cannot be understated (Fleming 2004). The maintenance of a positive image has itself become part of policing's core business. Indeed, one of the senior executives to whom we spoke expressed discomfort with the mere use of the term 'coercion'.

Managing ambiguity in exchange relations has become a challenge of twenty-first-century policing. Just as the *Mahabharata* contains long lists of what kinds of things may accepted, from what kind of people, under what circumstances, so too do many police organisations have elaborate guidelines governing their exchange relations. And for good reason.

CHAPTER EIGHT

CONCLUSIONS

Contemporary policing is a reflection of both continuity and change. At the outset of this book, we said that police management at the beginning of the twenty-first century is undergoing a dramatic transformation. This change is a response to the pressure on police to 'do more with less' resulting from the revolution in public management that began in the latter half of the last century and ushered in an era of chronic and enduring financial restraint for public institutions. In the chapters that followed, we sought to give flesh to the bones of this transformation, exploring in some detail the techniques police are using today to enhance their resources. These techniques involve police in exchanges with the 'outside' world: with other government agencies, with community organisations, with the business community and with individuals in various capacities. Some of these arrangements we have examined have been wholly new and even quite startling; others have proved to be 'old friends'. Through this examination, the complexity of what Bayley and Shearing (2001) termed the multilateral character of policing, and what Shearing and others have since referred to as the governance of security has revealed itself (Burris, Drahos and Shearing 2005).

In this concluding chapter, we look first at how we have gone about the task of unpacking this transformation in public policing. We then examine some of the implications of our findings. Finally, we look at some possible models of how different types of exchange relationships might interrelate and consider the scope for further research.

METHOD

A Focus on State Police

We very consciously made our focus in the book primarily the state or public police as an institution, rather than any of the other actors that contribute to public safety in this world of plural policing. By so doing we have challenged three ideas that seem to be implicit in much contemporary policing scholarship:

- First, that multilateralism in policing is primarily concerned with the emergence of nonstate policing institutions rather than with state police and state policing.
- Second, that state police are an autonomous and more or less self-contained institution with firm rather than permeable boundaries with other institutions.
- Third, that state police engagement in multilateral policing is a new idea, and one that is limited to a small set of programs, developed under signs such as "partnerships" and more recently "third-party policing" (Mazerolle and Ransley 2005). Examples of these programs include community policing and neighbourhood watch.

In place of these pervasive, and largely implicit, ideas, we have developed a picture of multilateral policing as something that is essential to the way police have always gone about their work and the way they continue to police today. This is not to minimise the very significant changes that are taking place in the way that police do their business.

A Typology of Exchange

In exploring this 'multilateralism', we have used Natalie Zemon Davis' (Davis 2000) typology of three modes of exchange – coercion, sale and gift – to conceive of policing as exchanges of knowledge, capacity and resources. Recognizing the long history of such policing exchanges, as well as the contemporary manifestations of coercion, sale and gift in policing, we have drawn our examples from across space and time to demonstrate that, while the shape of exchange is very often context-specific, multilateral policing is an extraordinarily widespread phenomenon. Our objective here has been to contribute

towards   Wood and Kempa's (2005: 300) 'comprehensive
mapping' of public security and its engagement with external
institutions.

A Focus on the Everyday

In developing our map we have, as suggested earlier, taken a
somewhat unconventional tack of focusing our attention, not on the
fashions of pluralistic policing that occupy current scholarly attention, but on the everyday partnerships that are, and for some time
have been, central to the policing enterprise. Thus, while we touch
on the partnerships that are highlighted in such current fashions as
community policing initiatives – what might be thought of as the
'front stage' of policing (law enforcement, prevention and so on) –
our focus is much more on the routine business of policing, the 'back
stage' forms that provide the organisational infrastructure and
support to frontline policing. Such everyday tasks as shopping for
products like computer hardware and selling police services for a fee
comprise the chief substance of this book. It is not simply that police
engage with other entities in a variety of ways, but that doing so is an
essential part of policing, whether police seek to monopolize
policing or share it with others. It is only when one looks across the
front and the back stages of policing that one appreciates just how
firmly embedded and widespread multilateralism is *within* state
police institutions. Both partnerships and third party arrangements
have a much wider ambit than has been recognized in more conventional, front stage focused analyses. Indeed, the emblematic idea
that police are the people and the people are the police builds
multilateralism into state policing at its symbolic roots. Whether the
police are seen as monopolizing policing or as only one provider of
policing services amongst many, the police institution itself is
thoroughly pluralistic.

Exploring Normative Questions – The Balance of Advantage

We also explore normative questions around the multilateral
character of state policing. The distinction between, on the one hand,
the "symbolic ordering" that the police are engaged in as representatives of the state, "the symbolic repository of societal values"

(Marx 1992b: 13), and, on the other, the "behavioural ordering" that they undertake in seeking to promote the behavioural conditions for safe and secure places within which people can work and play (Stenning et al. 1990) is relevant here. It is at the symbolic level that police present themselves as a unified state organisation that stands for, and represents, a unified society. They are, quite literally, the living embodiment of law and order. It is at the behavioural level that we see the police as a multilateral organisation within a very complex set of institutional assemblages. Perhaps this distinction, and the importance for the police of retaining their symbolic stature as an emblem of what Lipsitz (1968) thinks of as the "primordial" religious meanings associated with modern states, accounts for the historical reluctance of policing scholars to move beyond the symbolic presentation of police as autonomous and explore their multilateral features. But this is changing, as more recent works of Crawford, Loader, Zedner, Wood and many others illustrate.

The questions we raise at the normative level are questions about the right balance to be achieved by police organisations in mobilizing the resources of others. Just what should be the trade-offs between realizing behavioural and symbolic advantages in any particular exchange arrangement? The issue comes down to how far the particular mode of exchange can be taken before certain core values of liberal democratic societies – equity, cost-effectiveness and legitimacy – are threatened. In using these values as touchstones, we have adopted the position of Marx (1992b: 20–21) that general values should be seen not as prescriptive but as providing guidance that must be interpreted in context-specific ways. There can be no single set of rules, no recipes for addressing the many normative issues raised by multilateral policing. Values, in our analysis, constitute criteria that guide, but do not determine, decisions about specific courses of action.

For example, in the case of informants we acknowledge that the police could hardly operate if they were to refuse to receive information from others. Further, if police were always to seek to gain information themselves directly this would mean either ineffectiveness or a degree of police intrusion into the daily lives of citizens that would be completely unacceptable within a liberal democratic society.

The question, therefore, is not whether police should gather information in this way, but rather when, how and under what sets of
restraints it should be gathered. Advantages at the behavioural level
need to be considered in the context of the symbolic implications of
realizing these advantages.

Sometimes these value criteria cannot easily be reconciled, and in
such cases, difficult choices have to be made between equity, cost-
effectiveness and legitimacy. The thorny question that police face is
the pragmatic question of where, or with whom, the 'balance of
advantage' should lie. In thinking about this balance, three categories
of interest have to be reconciled – the interests of private actors, of
police as an institution, and of the public. Our principle has been that
there should be a strong presumption against allowing either of the
first two interests to trump the third.

Identifying and Reconciling Patterns
It is helpful, when thinking about these issues, to think not of normative recipes in both designing and enacting multilateral institutional arrangements, but rather of what Christopher Alexander and
his collaborators (Alexander et al. 1977), in considering landscape
and architectural design, call "patterns" and "pattern language". A
pattern for Alexander refers to a set of design elements that have
been shown empirically to work to promote a particular set of
desirable outcomes. A set of such patterns constitutes a pattern language. Inevitably, hard choices have to be made in creating any actual
design, as patterns will often compete with each other – one pattern's
requirements may be incompatible, in a specific setting, with those of
another pattern. The art of good design is the art of compromise and
of mitigation where a desirable outcome cannot easily be achieved.

What we have sought to identify in our normative analyses in each
chapter are a series of patterns that seem to us, on the basis of our
reviews of the literature and evidence, to be good ways of promoting
equity, cost-effectiveness and legitimacy. Together they constitute what
we see as an emerging pattern language. The art of regulating multilateral state policing is the art of reconciling these patterns, recognizing
their conflicts and finding ways of mitigating the effects of the inevitable
compromises. In looking to how this art might be realized, we have

throughout argued for pragmatism informed by the three value criteria we have outlined, coupled with an insistence on transparency so that the patterns put in place can be examined and reviewed with a view to improving the regulation of multilateral policing.

Articulating Design Principles – Promoting Desirable Outcomes

The issue, then, is essentially one of how best to configure governing arrangements for exchanges so as to protect core values and promote the public interest, while at the same time recognizing the importance within liberal democracies of creating spaces for the realization of legitimate private enterprises and their associated interests. In exploring the contours of coercion, sale and gift, we have attempted to articulate guidelines that can be applied by police in making that judgment in the case of any particular exchange relationship. These guidelines might also be thought of, following Ostrom (1990: 137–58), as 'design principles' for constructing and regulating collaborative forms of state/nonstate governance, and especially those forms that are deeply entwined with state governance institutions.

In developing these principles in each of our chapters, we have made clear what we believe are the biases that should inform decisions. We have constructed these in terms of a set of strong presumptions that should normally determine the way in which normative tensions should resolved. Where these presumptions are not considered applicable, there should be good reason.

Just what we consider these presumptions should be has varied somewhat across the empirical domains we have considered – but in all cases they have been constructed in terms of the three value criteria that have guided our normative analyses. In Chapter 2, in which we explored budgeting issues, we considered several principles that are taken into consideration in making budgetary decisions, including transparency, accountability and effectiveness. In looking at the interactions between these principles, we made some suggestions about how they may relate to one another empirically. For example, we noted that as accountability increases, effectiveness may decrease. In considering these empirical tendencies we drew attention to the importance of designing processes in ways that recognize these relationships. In each case we stressed the necessity of balancing advantage. An appropriate balance between efficiency and effectiveness, for instance, may require design changes such as enhancing skills sets that would (for example) enable a police officer "to think like an accountant".

Similarly, in thinking about coercion and its use as a way of bringing resources together to pluralise policing, we developed the strong presumption from Braithwaite and Pettit (1990) that coercion should ideally be used "only when it enhances overall freedom". We then explored how this design principle might play out in different specific contexts. In doing so, we proposed a set of normative questions that should be asked by decision makers who are considering coercive measures. For example, questions requiring that proportionality should be considered, such as "are the policy objectives in question of sufficient importance to justify the coercive measures employed?" and "are they of sufficient importance to justify the risk of collateral damage to innocent third parties?"

In the case of sale, we identified a series of risks to be avoided and then considered possible safeguards that might be put in place to guard against these risks. Again, the objective was to find ways of balancing advantage. In the light of the particular nature of the policing environment, we asked whether broad principles to do with outsourcing that had been developed for government agencies in general should simply be transferred into a police arena. Here we drew upon the strong presumption of the public interest by suggesting the following:

> Decisions about what to outsource and to what degree a contractor should be granted discretion will perhaps be ones where police should give particular thought to how the public will be affected.

Again, the central question was the 'balance of advantage' against the backdrop of considerations of equity, cost-effectiveness and legitimacy. Where we considered the use of informants, we have encouraged a 'balance of advantage' by outlining a set of presumptions, for example, "that informants should be used as a last resort", thereby requiring justification for their use.

To reiterate, our normative proposals are designed, not as hard and fast rules, but as a way of encouraging an identification of "patterns" and the formation of a "pattern language" from which it is understood, at the very outset, that departures will be necessary. However, at the core of this recognition is the understanding that pattern departures should be justifiable in terms of values. The inevitable risks of police/private collaborative arrangements need to be identified and consideration given to their mitigation. To this end, design principles have been articulated with a view to providing guidance to police in dealing with risk and attaining a desirable balance of interests.

IMPLICATIONS

Below we consider six conclusions that we believe can be drawn from our research.

Multilateralism Is Embedded in Police Organisations

The contemporary focus on state police partnerships does not constitute a radical break from more autonomous forms of state policing but should rather be understood as the most recent stage in a long history of state involvement in pluralistic policing arrangements (Zedner 2006). Contemporary initiatives have received considerable attention. They have been prompted by changes in public administration that emphasize the value of multilateral forms of governance as well as by budgetary constraints that are encouraging police to explore new forms of pluralistic policing. These contemporary forms are, however, a continuation of a history of state police involvement in, and encouragement of, multilateral policing arrangements.

Furthermore, multilateralism as a strategy of security governance is embedded in virtually every sphere of the state police as an institution. This is true whether one looks at how state police procure the equipment they need as an institution or how they acquire the information they need in order to undertake their role as police. State police work with, and rely upon, a host of other institutions when doing their work. They are not an island and they never have been. Whatever the desirability and whatever the reality of the Hobbesian inspired dream of a state police that monopolizes policing, in fact state police have engaged and always will engage with a wide range of other institutions and individuals, and rely upon their resources in order to achieve their goals.

State Security Governance is a Collaborative Affair

Our analyses across several areas of police activity leads to a conclusion that the public interest cannot be, and most certainly should not be, equated with a public sector that is somehow divorced from other sectors. Such an isolated sector, as our analysis of the police institution makes clear, does not really exist. It is only an analytic creation that at best functions as a Weberian ideal type, but it should not be understood as describing an empirical reality. Policing is, we believe, by definition a matter of networks and institutional assemblages, no matter where the centre of gravity lies.

One might argue, as does Johnston (1999), that the public and private spheres are becoming increasingly blurred so that all institutions of governance are better thought of as having a hybrid character that mixes elements of public and private. This hybrid character is most certainly the case with respect to state police. We have clearly shown how state police agencies are supported by, and embedded within, complex arrangements of public and private auspices and providers of governance services.

So far as state security governance is concerned, the public and private spheres, have been, and continue to be, intersecting and finely integrated spheres. Indeed, while it may makes sense to think of public and private knowledge, capacity and resources as spheres at an analytic level, it makes no sense to think of them as forming discrete empirical spheres. The idea that public and private spheres have *become* blurred arises from a reification of analytic categories that has resulted in a very misleading empirical account of the nature of state governance, and governance more generally. State governance is not governance by state agencies but rather governance by state-directed arrangements (that include state agencies) established in furtherance of state objectives. While this resonates with the metaphor of state steering and non-state rowing that is associated with modern conceptions of governance (Osborne and Gaebler 1992), it is important to recognize that this is by no means a product of recent neo-liberal values (although this has done much to bring this into focus and to encourage it). The fact of the matter is that, in relation to security, the rowing of state governance, and very often the steering, is a collaborative affair that involves both state and nonstate entities working together through a variety of arrangements that involve coercion, sale and gift at both the front and back stages of policing.

To take 'sale' as an example, it is clear that police are avid consumers. While they may not be quite 'born to shop', they certainly engage in considerable shopping – both conventional as in the case of purchasing equipment and less conventional in the case of purchasing information – and they do so for very good reasons. Shopping enables them to create governance assemblages that bring together resources from a wide variety of actors within, and even across, societies. The trade in goods and services for governance is, as we have seen, a two-way street. It is not simply that states shop for nonstate products. Nonstate actors shop for, and are encouraged by state agencies like the police to shop for, state products. While it might be argued that, within democratic states at least, nonstate actors by definition buy state services through the payment of taxes, what we have shown is that the purchase of state governance takes other more clearly commercial forms. Nonstate actors can and do directly buy state services for a fee over and above the taxes that they pay.

Furthermore, this is something that states actively encourage and sometimes insist upon. As we have shown in the field of security governance, there are governance 'products' that can only be acquired through commercial transactions with state agents. This includes the sale of police officers themselves as security service providers. It is not just private security that has commercialized and commodified the governance of security; so has the state. The police have, in many ways, in the words of the senior Singaporean police officer cited in Chapter 1, "become a business" run by business men and women.

Like coercion and gift as means for mobilizing resources, sale involves the engagement of state and nonstate resources in the provision of public governance in ways that create complex governing arrangements made up of state and nonstate resources. Unlike coercion, which uses the threat of punishment to persuade reluctant "partners" to comply, the collaborations that sale and gift make possible are consensual and occur within a market place.

With coercion, the steering of governance resides clearly and firmly with state actors. With sale (and indeed also with gift), steering can shift between state and nonstate actors. When state actors are using tax monies to purchase goods and services (including security services like guarding) from nonstate actors, steering also remains relatively firmly with state auspices. When, however, nonstate actors are the purchasers and state actors are the sellers, the situation may be more complex.

The Task of Shaping Governance Directions Is Shared
Sale in particular raises questions that concern tensions between representative and participatory conceptions of democracy (Fung 2003). With the purchase of security governance as a commodity, consumers are very often enabled to participate more fully than they would otherwise be able to in shaping the nature of the governance service they receive. In doing so, however, they are at an advantage over others whose primary means of shaping governance is through representative processes. Again, normative issues arise: should policing be driven, for example, by plutocracy, or by a tyrannous majority? These are not questions that can be settled in a simple manner but require a pragmatic consideration of the "balance of advantage" within particular contexts.

The sharing of direction within governance is also a feature of gifts by private entities to governing entities. Gifts frequently come with constraints as to how they can be used. Unless they are cash gifts with no limitations attached, they often have implications for the steering of governance. A gift of a police work station, as we have seen, creates an architectural form of regulation (Lessig 1999) that locates police 'here' rather than 'there'. Similarly, other forms of gift can have practical effects on police priorities and agendas. Gifts often build dependencies, just as market relationships do, and such dependencies may well imply a sharing of direction. Quite apart from what gifts mean for the distinction between public and private assets, they can and do create shifts in the locus of governance.

All of this, as we have already suggested, presents profound normative questions that are hidden from view if we think of the public and private spheres as empirically distinct. But looking at public governance differently, as a public-private business, brings these normative questions to centre stage.

Pluralism Has Had Profound Effects on Police Organisations

Although no police organisation is an island, sea levels have risen and fallen at different times throughout history. Despite the fact that policing by institutions of the state has always been, in varying degrees, a pluralistic endeavour, at present the level of interchange with outside entities for the purpose of enhancing resources appears to be at an all time high. As a result, one sees some novel developments which constitute the 'dramatic transformation' to which we alluded in our introduction.

The degree of scrutiny accorded state police, in western democracies at least, appears unprecedented. Political oversight of, and media attention to, state institutions is unrelenting. While not many members of the public, or public officials themselves, would have been bold enough publicly to criticise J. Edgar Hoover's FBI, few such inhibitions exist today. As a result of this scrutiny, the quasi-judicial autonomy previously enjoyed by police chiefs in some jurisdictions has been replaced by a more strict accountability to their political masters.

This development is perhaps most vividly reflected in the increasingly risk-averse nature of contemporary police management. Police executives have had to become risk managers. We see this clearly, for example, when we look at the entry of police into the commercial marketplace. In Chapters 4 and 5, we explored the kinds of risks that police could expect to encounter in buying and selling goods and services. We also considered the mechanisms they currently use to manage the risks they do identify, such as the promulgation of guidelines and policies, the formal sharing of decision making (such as in relation to the management of paid informants), the use of written templates that force police officers to consider risks and costs and weigh them against the benefits, the use of graduated fees and waivers, and so on. Risk management is also exercised, we see, in the acceptance or rejection of certain gifts and sponsorship offers, and in the deals negotiated around them.

A second and related development that characterises contemporary state policing, is what one might call the growth of a business mentality. This change has many practical ramifications for the ways in which police approach their work and spend their resources, many of which we have noted in the preceding chapters. Today in many police organisations, initiatives of any significance, whether they entail crime prevention programs or major criminal investigations, require a business case to be made.

These changes have impacts not only within the police organisation but also on the exchange relationships between state police organisations and other entities. No police chief wants to rely excessively on coercive practices; to "get into bed with fleas" (even if they are potential donors); or to squander scarce resources on the procurement of inferior materiel. Partnerships that involve accepting resources from a private business or community organisation, or contributing a police organisation's own resources, be they funds or labour, often set in train a complex process of approval that involves cost-benefit analyses of the proposal as part of the business case.

Contractualisation Is Occurring, but Status Is Still Important
What we are seeing in police organizations today is perhaps an expression of what the Victorian legal historian Sir Henry Maine called "a movement from Status to Contract" that he believed typifies progressive societies (Maine 1861 [1920]: 174). As we have seen, where once police relied heavily on their status as the embodiment of the State's monopoly on coercive force to obtain the assistance they needed to do their job, now police are relying more and more on formalized arrangements of reciprocity. Crawford's work on the management of (anti)social behaviour in the United Kingdom through what he terms 'contractual governance' makes this clear in relation to the front stage of policing (Crawford 2003). And in relation to the back stage, the contractualisation of policing is certainly evident, and to an astonishing extent. We see it, for instance, in the complex procedures surrounding the acquisition of necessary

equipment and services, in arrangements for citizens in both paid and voluntary capacities to assist with policing tasks, in the adoption of standardized arrangements for the contribution of funds from businesses and other organizations in return for acknowledgement or more (including registers of donations and sponsorships), and in the offer of police services, merchandise and intellectual property for an agreed fee and subject to agreed conditions. We see it too in informal or unwritten forms – informants may not always be subject to any 'contract' so-called, but their obligations and entitlements are certainly the subject of verbal agreement. A gift to police may be accepted without putting pen to paper, but nevertheless its acceptance may be subject to expectations of reciprocity or to conditions about its use.

But whether this increased contractualisation signifies a move away from reliance on status at the same time as it demonstrates a move towards contract is another question. The grant of coercive power remains contingent on the police's status. And the fact that the police are the police is very often the reason that other entities want to enter contractual arrangements with them, whether for profit or not. Furthermore, the legitimacy of police, their symbolic authority which enables them to obtain compliance, remains an issue for the police themselves. The flipside of the increased scrutiny to which police are subject today is a police preoccupation with image. It is at the forefront of anything they do. The question is always asked: how will this arrangement make us look? Will it detract from our authority and therefore make it more difficult for us to do our job? The contractualisation of police relationships with 'outsiders' only increases the risks to police legitimacy. Police know this. So one finds that 'mystique management' constitutes a large part of the risk management undertaken in relation to these formal arrangements. And legitimacy is also, of course, a real concern when there are no formal agreements in place to govern relationships, such as when police seek to obtain cooperation from citizens in lieu of exercising coercive powers. We are not yet (and perhaps never will be) in a place where the status of police is irrelevant to the routine business of policing, even though contractualisation is increasingly important.

Lengthening the Arm of the Law Creates Dangers

One should harbour no illusions about the risks entailed in the increasing reliance on exchange relationships discussed in this book. Each of the relational forms we have discussed is fraught with danger. The risks to equity and to cost effectiveness in the delivery of policing services, and to the legitimacy of the police organization, should by now be self-evident.

A fundamental assumption that underlies our suggestion that police use exchange relationships to enhance their capacity is that the police organization possesses a degree of competence and integrity. Unfortunately, one cannot assume that every police organization is endowed with the qualities that would allow it to manage these relational forms without creating substantial harm, intentionally or inadvertently. We are writing not only for police in advanced industrial democracies, but for police services where political and economic development, and sensitivities to standards of human rights that we take for granted, may not exist. By way of illustration, one of us attended a seminar some years ago where the speaker, a distinguished area studies specialist, was describing conditions in an emerging democracy. We naively inquired if organized crime existed in that country. "Yes," the speaker replied. "It's called the police."

We have noted the important symbolic role that police play in democratic societies as the embodiment of safety and order, conditions that are fundamental to any civilized society. Of course, in more autocratic places, police are often negative symbols, the embodiment of repression. Where equity, cost-effectiveness and legitimacy are not attributes that police have or are expected to have in abundance, there may be little risk for police themselves in engaging in exchange relationships. But the risks to the public of poor handling of those relationships by police may be multiplied.

It is sobering to recall that the examples of adverse unintended consequences that we have observed are mostly taken from policing in those English-speaking democracies that hold themselves out as paragons of best practice. There is a bitter irony in the fact that the common law tradition of policing in the United Kingdom and the United States, which evolved in self-conscious contrast to the policing arrangements developed by the autocrats of pre-World War II continental Europe, has come to embrace some solutions of which the latter would be proud. The mandatory reporting that transforms professional-client relations into state surveillance, the confiscation of assets that can leave perfectly innocent people without a roof over their head, the reliance on informants who use their engagement as a platform for personal enrichment from further criminal activity may have become part of the law enforcement toolkit in the United States, but they contain an unpleasant echo of the tools of governance employed in some of the more notorious totalitarian dictatorships of the twentieth century.

Nevertheless, ironies abound in criminal justice. While some police agencies that have developed guidelines for managing informants keep these procedures a closely guarded secret, others, such as the United States, post them on the Internet.

The institutions that exist (or could exist) to ensure that policing is conducted appropriately are familiar to most of us. A vibrant democracy with a robust opposition is perhaps the *sine qua non*, necessary but not sufficient. Also essential is a free and inquisitive media. Although the press may at time appear to police executives as troublesome and vexatious, it exists to ask difficult questions. Modern public administration has also seen the evolution of institutions of financial oversight such as the Australian National Audit Office, the (U.S.) Government Accountability Office and the (U.K.) Audit Commission. Institutions of operational oversight such as ombudsmen and police complaints authorities also play an important role in monitoring the integrity of policing practices (Goldsmith 1991; Lewis and Prenzler 1999).

A crucial question, then, is whether the developments that we have discussed in this book will, if taken too far, weaken the symbolic value of the police and whether this in turn will detract from police performance. If police cars are seen as mobile billboards, if citizens come to believe that safety is a purchasable commodity, if coercive measures proliferate to create the perception of a society of informers, the police institution, the private actor, and the general public all lose. For these reasons, the extreme caution with which many police now go about their business is both warranted and laudable.

THREE THEORIES OF EXCHANGE
RELATIONSHIPS

One might ask how the three modes of public/private exchange coexist in practice. Is it possible to predict or to explain just what the configuration of relational modes will look like at a given time or place? Do they behave systemically or independently?

We offer three alternative theoretical models to explain a given institutional configuration. The first two envisage a systemic relationship between coercion, sale and gift, while the third would reflect a degree of cultural idiosyncrasy.

The Hydraulic or Zero-Sum Model

Here, the relative prominence of one mode of exchange will depend on the others. Where coercion is high, one might expect sale and gift to be low. Where user-pays policing predominates (that is, to the extent that policing becomes a purchasable service) one would expect less coercion and less donation. A dynamic illustration of the hydraulic model may be seen in the rise of the state during the seventeenth century, when gift evolved into coercion. As Davis (2000) observed, offerings to nobles became routinised, then *de rigeur*, and ultimately developed into systems of taxation. Another illustration is evident in the transition from welfarism to what has been termed "the new public management" in some European democracies (most notably the United Kingdom), where the primary mode of police-public exchange has begun to shift from coercion to gift and sale. Damaska (1984: 91) observes that state activity tends to vary inversely with the strength of markets.

The Resource Constraint Model

Under the resource constraint model, the driving factor behind institutional relationships is fiscal constraint. All forms of public/private interface will vary together, reflecting the relative intensity of fiscal pressure. In other words, where the fiscal crisis is most acute, coercion, sale and gift will all be great. Conversely, in societies with fewer resource constraints, the state will be less inclined to foster or invent mechanisms of co-production, whether based on command, commercial exchange, or donation. The fiscal pressures prevailing in contemporary South Africa appear to be manifested in the strong reliance on all three dimensions of exchange. The resource constraint model would seem to reflect circumstances in which the state has (a) a small revenue base, borne of either poverty or a reluctance to impose taxes; and (b) significant security problems, either objective or perceived.

The Cultural Salience Model

Here, the institutional configuration of public/private interface will depend upon the relative salience of the three forms of exchange within a culture. Monetary gifts to public institutions will be greater in those societies where charitable giving in general is greater. Volunteers in policing will be more common in those cultures characterized by a spirit of voluntarism. User-pays policing will be more prominent in those jurisdictions where public services in general are more commercialized. Coercion will be greatest in strong authoritarian states. The cultural salience model does not purport to predict whether the three forms of exchange will converge or diverge within a society, merely that the strength of each will mirror the strength of the general form of exchange within the society. This model is most consistent with the thinking of David Bayley (1985: 154), who notes the enduring importance of culture in explaining the configuration of police systems. It is also resonant with Damaska's (1984) thinking on the relationship between structures of legal procedure and state power.

There are, of course, global influences at work that will affect all but the most isolated nations. The increasing acceptance of business thinking and risk management, born of the new managerialism, seems unlikely to reverse. Global markets will further constrain public expenditure. And the concerted actions of some states, or groups of states, will continue to lead to the adoption of particular policies. The global diffusion of cash transaction reporting regimes, inspired by the United States and its friends, is illustrative (Nadelmann 1993; Andreas and Nadelmann 2006).

One can see that these three theories are not necessarily mutually exclusive. There may be elements of cultural salience that are consistent with a hydraulic or zero-sum configuration. Each of the models lends itself to empirical testing both cross-jurisdictionally or within a single jurisdiction over time.

If it is possible to generalize across the United States, one might suggest that elements of each model are visible. The United States is perhaps unique in the very strong salience of coercion, sale, *and* gift. Despite priding itself as a beacon of liberty, many U.S. jurisdictions, federal as well as subordinate, self-consciously embrace coercive solutions. One need only recall some of the draconian outcomes of assets confiscation policy, and the widespread popularity of mandatory reporting legislation, to see that coercion is, if not ubiquitous in American criminal justice, certainly very common.

At the state and municipal level at least, the strong American tradition of philanthropy has begun to impact on policing. Cash-strapped cities no doubt welcome the emergence of police foundations. Unrestricted gifts or bequests by individuals may not be unique to U.S. state and municipal law enforcement agencies, but they do appear more common than elsewhere. And, in the United States, where "Commerce is King," the convergence of gift and commerce, visible in such institutions as "Adopt-a-car", has few counterparts elsewhere.

Postwar Japan has a market economy, a tradition of gift-giving, and an authoritarian flavour in social relations. Nevertheless, it relies almost exclusively on state funding to resource law enforcement (although there is some degree of citizen involvement in crime prevention activity). Japan's institutional configuration would seem best explained by the resource constraint model. Because of its relative affluence (and the strength of its informal institutions of social control), it has not had occasion to rely on coercion, sale or gift to resource law enforcement.

China, traditionally a strong authoritarian state that has encouraged co-production of public security through in-kind contributions by the public, has begun to experience a pluralization of policing. The move to a market economy has been accompanied by the advent of fee-for-service policing, in the form of a government business enterprise that markets policing services, primarily to selected communities and to commercial clients (Zhong 2002; Zhong and

Broadhurst 2007). This suggests that the cultural salience model may have explanatory power in contemporary China. It remains to be seen whether the same patterns are emerging in the transitional states of Eastern Europe.

Nations of continental Europe, especially France, have tended to exemplify the hydraulic model. Well-resourced, strong states have traditionally seen little need to rely on commerce and philanthropy to support the delivery of public safety (Dupont 2008). Whether this configuration will persist in the face of globalization and the looming spectre of the new managerialism remains to be seen. These developments may herald the ascendancy of the resource constraint model.

THE SCOPE FOR FURTHER RESEARCH

These superficial illustrations merely hint at the kind of theory testing that is possible, using cross-sectional or time-series analysis. The concepts of sale and gift are easily operationalised, indeed, easily quantified. Coercion may be less amenable to quantification, but can lend itself to nominal or ordinal measurement. So, too, are such plausible rival explanatory variables such as centralization/decentralization of police organization, and accountability structures. Clearly, there is scope for much additional research in this area.

A FINAL WORD

It can be seen that the pervasive pluralism of contemporary policing is pregnant with problems, possibilities and prospects for further research. It seems likely that policing will become increasingly pluralistic in the years ahead. One hopes that exchange relationships between state police and other organisations will be managed carefully. Whether communities will be safer as a result, and whether state police retain their mystique and their symbolic authority, remain to be seen.

References

ABC News (2008) "Teen may have to pay bill for rowdy party", 14 January. Available at http://www.abc.net.au/news/stories/2008/01/14/2137920.htm (accessed 16 May 2008)

Abrahamsen, R. and Williams, M. C. (2005a) *The Globalisation of Private Security Country Report: Kenya*. Aberystwyth: Department of International Politics, University of Wales.

(2005b) *The Globalisation of Private Security Country Report: Sierra Leone*. Aberystwyth: Department of International Politics, University of Wales.

(2005c) *The Globalisation of Private Security Country Report: Nigeria*. Aberystwyth: Department of International Politics, University of Wales.

AFP (2006) "Crime pays for texting informants", *ABC Online*, 29 April. Available at http://www.abc.net.au/news/newsitems/200604/s1626650.htm (accessed 16 May 2008).

Alarid, L. F. and Wang, H-M. (2000) "Cultural Influences on Taiwanese Police Management and Patrol Practices: An Explanatory Investigation of Ouchi's Theory", *International Journal of the Sociology of Law* 28: 113–27.

Alberta Government (2008) "Municipal Policing Assistance Grant Program". Available at http://www.solgps.alberta.ca/programs-and-services/public-security/policing/Pages/municipal-policing-assistance-grant-program.aspx (accessed 16 May 2008).

Alexander, C., Ishikawa, S. and Silverstein, M. (1977) *A Pattern Language: Towns, Buildings, Construction*. New York: Oxford University Press.

Allstate Insurance (2001) "Los Angeles Community Safety". Available at http://allstate.com/community/sha/safety/safela.html (accessed 17 January 2001).

Amar, Akhil Reed (1997) *The Constitution and Criminal Procedure: First Principles*. New Haven and London: Yale University Press.

American Civil Liberties Union, Break the Chains: Communities of Color and the War on Drugs and The Brennan Center at NYU School of Law (2005) "Caught in the Net: The impact of drug policies on women and families". Available at http://fair-laws4families.com/final-caught-in-the-net-report.pdf (accessed 16 May 2008).

American Police Beat (nda) "Can't Cope with Costs: Smaller agencies are dropping like flies". Available at http://www.apbweb.com/articles-z89.htm (accessed 9 January 2007).

Andreas, P. and Nadelmann, E. (2006) *Policing the Globe: Criminalization and Crime Control in International Relations*. New York: Oxford University Press.

Anechiarico, F. and Jacobs, J. B. (1996) *The Pursuit of Absolute Integrity: How Corruption Control Makes Government Ineffective*. Chicago and London: The University of Chicago Press.

Anon. (2004a) "Moonlighting common among police officers", *The Jakarta Post*, 29 November. Available at http://news.indahnesia.com/item/200411292/moonlighting_common_among_police_offic ers.php (accessed 16 May 2008).

(2004b) *Social Concern*, Cheng Loong Corporation. Available at http://www.clc.com.tw/community/eng_community_events.asp (accessed 16 May 2008).

(2006) *Overview-Public Welfare Activities*, Shuanghor. Available at http://www.shuanghor.com/Display.php?ID=kingdom_overview (accessed 16 May 2008).

Archbold, C. A. (2005) "Managing the bottom line: risk management in policing", *Policing: An International Journal of Police Strategies and Management* 28(1): 30–48.

Armas, Genaro C. (2007) "FBI Chief: Patriot Act ruling misguided", *Associated Press*, 8 November.

Arnold, C. (2006) "Big gains from weight loss program", *Police Life*, December, pp. 18–19.

Arnold, H. (1989) "Sanctions and Rewards, An Organizational Perspective". In M. Friedland (ed.) *Sanctions and Rewards in the Legal System*. Toronto: University of Toronto Press, pp. 137–55.

Associated Press (2004) "Vigilante group, TV News Channels draw fire for underage sex stings", 8 March. Available at http://www.rickross.com/reference/perverted_justice/perverted_justice8.html (accessed 16 May 2008).

(2005) "Utah, other states mulls how to handle search-and-rescue costs", *USA Today*, 20 June 2004. Available at http://www.usatoday.

com/news/nation/2004–06-20-funding-searches_x.htm (accessed 16 May 2008).

Audit Commission (1993) *Helping With Enquiries: Tackling Crime Effectively*. London: HMS.

Australasian Police Ministers' Council (2005) *Directions in Australasian Policing 2005–2008*. Available at http://www.acpr.gov.au/pdf/Directions05–08.pdf (accessed 16 May 2008).

Australian Associated Press (1999) "Company Calls on NSW Government to reverse tender process", *Sydney Morning Herald*, 6 February.
  (2005) "Customs 'knew port system had errors'", *The Age*, 22 November. Available at http://www.theage.com.au/news/National/Customs-knew-port-system-had-errors/2005/11/22/1132421625359.html (accessed 16 May 2008).

Australian Bureau of Statistics (2003) "Australian Social Trends – Family and Community – Services: Child protection". Available at http://www.abs.gov.au/Ausstats/abs@.nsf/0/7d95127fb3bfd9caca256d39001bc33f?OpenDocument#Links (accessed 12 October 2005).

Australian Council for Safety and Quality in Health Care (2004) "Sentinel Events Fact Sheet". Available at http://www.safetyandquality.org/internet/safety/publishing.nsf/Content/former-pubs-archive-factshe ets (accessed 16 May 2008).

Australian Federal Police (2001) "Investigating Procurement Fraud", *Comfraud Bulletin*, April.
  (2003) *ACT Policing Annual Report 2002–2003*. Canberra: Australian Federal Police.
  (2005) "Consultancy Services". Available at http://www.afp.gov.au/afp/page/GovCorporate/GovtReporting/consultants.htm (accessed 13 September 2005).
  (2006a) "Consultancy Services for 2005–2006", Appendix to the *Annual Report 2005–2006*. Available at http://www.afp.gov.au/__data/assets/pdf_file/25007/AFP_Consultancy_services_05_-_06.pdf (acce ssed 9 January 2008).
  (2006b) "Security Services and Training". Available at http://www.afp.gov.au/services/protective/information_security (accessed 29 September 2006)

Australian Federal Police Association (2001) "The Australian Federal Police and Community Policing", Submission to A.C.T Legislative Assembly. Available at http://www.afpa.org.au/get/13 (accessed 19 January 2006).
  (2008) "AFPA Merchandise Policy". Available at https://secure.afpa.org.au/shopping/index.html (accessed 16 May 2008).

Avant, Deborah D. (2005) *The Market for Force: The Consequences of Privatizing Security*. Cambridge: Cambridge University Press.

(2006) *The Marketization of Security: Adventurous Defense, Institutional Malformation, and Conflict.* In Jonathan Kirshner (ed.) *Globalization and National Security.* New York: Routledge, pp. 105–42.

Bagby, Jennifer (2000) "Justifications for State Bystander Intervention Statutes: Why crime witnesses should be required to call for help", *Indiana Law Review* 33: 571–97.

Baicker, Katherine and Jacobson, Mireille (2004) "Finders Keepers: Forfeiture Laws, Policing Incentives, and Local Budgets", *NBER Working Papers* 10484, National Bureau of Economic Research. Available at http://ideas.repec.org/p/nbr/nberwo/10484.html (accessed 16 May 2008).

Bajkowski, J. (2005) "Australian Customs portal exposes data", *Computerworld Australia*, 20 October. Available at http://www.computer world.com/printthis/2005/0,4814,105581,00.html (accessed 16 May 2008).

Baker, B. (2004a) "Protection from crime: what is on offer for Africans?", *Journal of Contemporary African Studies* 22(2): 165–88.

(2004b) "Multi-choice policing in Africa: is the continent following the South African pattern?" *Society in Transition* 35(2): 204–23.

(2005a) "Multi-choice policing in Uganda", *Policing & Society* 15(1): 19–41.

(2005b) "Who do people turn to for policing in Sierra Leone", *Journal of Contemporary African Studies* 23(3): 371–90.

Barger, J., Bucy, P., Eubanks, M. and Raspanti, M. (2005) "States, Statutes, and Fraud: An Empirical Study of Emerging State False Claims Acts", *Tulane Law Review* 80: 465–488.

Barker, Joshua (2006) "Vigilantes and the state", *Social Analysis* 50(1): 203–7.

Barnhizer, Daniel (2006) "Bargaining Power in Contract Theory". In L. DiMatteo, D. Barnhizer, B. Morant and R. Preston (eds.) *Visions of Contract Theory: Rationality, Bargaining, and Interpretation.* Durham: Carolina Academic Press.

Bayley, David (1985) *Patterns of Policing.* New Brunswick, NJ: Rutgers University Press.

(2006) *Changing the Guard: Developing Democratic Police Abroad.* New York: Oxford University Press.

Bayley, D. and Shearing, C. (2001) *The New Structure of Policing: Description, Conceptualization, and Research Agenda.* Washington, DC: National Institute of Justice.

BBC News (2003) 'Met to sell crime footage", 27 March. Available at http://news.bbc.co.uk/2/hi/uk_news/england/2893477.stm (accessed 16 May 2008).

(2007) "Police condemn 'target culture' ", 15 May. Available at http:// news.bbc.co.uk/1/hi/uk/6656411.stm (accessed 16 May 2008).

Bean, P. (1996) "Informers and the Police: Drug Dealers as Informers," in online archive of the Foundation for Drug Policy and Human Rights, Amsterdam. Available at www.drugtext.org/library/articles/index.html (accessed 16 May 2008).

Beckman, K., Gibbs, J., Beatty, P. and Canigiani, M. (2005) "Trends in Police Research: A Cross-Sectional Analysis of the 2002 Literature", *Police Practice and Research* 6(3): 295–320.

Bell, Stephen (2003) "Police face Xmas shopping disruption", *Computerworld*, 15 December.

Benson, Bruce L. (1994) "Are Public Goods really Common Pools? Considerations of the Evolution of Policing and Highways in England", *Economic Inquiry* 32(2): 249–71.

Berg, J. (2004a) 'Private policing in South Africa: The Cape Town city improvement district – pluralisation in practice', *Society in Transition* 35(2): 224–50.

(2004b) 'Suspension of Crime Watch patrols in Cape Town areas', *Police Accountability Newsletter*, August. Available at http://www.policeaccountability.co.za.

(2007) "The Accountability of South Africa's Private Security Industry: Mechanisms of Control and Challenges to Effective Oversight", Newlands: Open Society Foundation for South Africa Criminal Justice Initiative Occasional Paper Series, 2.

Bernstein, Elizabeth (2005) "Gift of the Week: Crime Stopper", *Wall Street Journal*, 19 August, p. W2.

Berwick, D. (1988) *The Application of the User-Pays Principle to the Policing of Sporting and Entertainment Events: Principal Considerations.* Interim Report, October, National Police Research Unit.

Bhanu, C. and Stone, C. (2004) "Public-private partnerships for police reform", Vera Institute of Justice. Available at http://www.vera.org/publications/publications_5.asp?publication_id=230 (accessed 4 April 2007).

Billingsley, R., Nemitz, T. and Bean, P. (eds) (2000) *Informers: Policing, Policy, Practice.* Cullompton: Willan Publishing.

Bittner, Egon (1970) *The Functions of Police in Modern Society.* Washington, DC: National Institute of Mental Health.

Blagg, Harry and Valuri, Giulietta (2004) "Aboriginal Community Patrols in Australia: Self-policing, self-determination and security", *Policing & Society* 14(4): 313–28.

Blair, I. (1998) 'The Governance of Security: Where do the police fit into policing?', Paper presented at the Association of Chief Police Officers Annual Conference (July), Birmingham, U.K.

Blair, Mark (1992) "The Debate over Mandatory Corporate Disclosure Rules", *UNSW Law Journal* 15(1): 177–95.

Blair, Tony (2001) *Reform of Public Services*, Speech at the Royal Free Hospital London, 16 July. Available at http://www.pm.gov.uk/news. asp?NewsId=2305 (accessed 20 August 2001).

Blaskett, Beverley and Taylor, S. Caroline (2003) "Facilitators and inhibitors of mandatory reporting of suspected child abuse: a research study", prepared for The Criminology Research Council, at http://www.aic.gov.au/crc/reports/200102–09.html (accessed 16 May 2008).

Blatchford, Christie (2000) "AEC gave RCMP computers and software: Deployed to track 'people of interest'", *National Post*, 23 February, p. A1.

Blue, Jon (1992) "High Noon Revisited: Commands of Assistance by Peace Officers in the Age of the Fourth Amendment", *Yale Law Journal* 101: 1475–90.

Blumenson, Eric and Nilsen, Eva (1998) "Policing for Profit: The Drug War's Hidden Economic Agenda", *University of Chicago Law Review* 65: 35–114.

Bobbitt, Philip (2002) *The Shield of Achilles*. New York: Knopf.

Boni, Nadia and Packer, Jeanette (1998) *The Police Role Survey: A Tool for Comparing Public and Police Perceptions of the Police Role*, Report Series No 126.1, Australasian Centre for Policing Research. Available at http://www.acpr.gov.au/publications2.asp?Report_ID= 11 (accessed 16 May 2008).

Bordua, D. J. and Haurek, E. W. (1970) "The Police Budget's Lot: Components of the Increase in Local Police Expenditures, 1902–1960", *The American Behavioral Scientist*, 13 (5/6): 667–80.

Borland, Ben (2005) "Pub tycoons offer to pay for extra policing", *The Scotsman Evening News*, 16 February. Available at http://news.scotsman.com/topics.cfm?tid=585&id=178362005 (accessed 16 May 2008).

Boudon, Raymond (1982) *The Unintended Consequences of Social Action*. London: Macmillan.

Bourne, M. (1989) "Finance – the ultimate control" in J. Vernon and D. Bracey (eds.) *Police Resources and Effectiveness*, proceedings of a seminar held 31 May–2 June 1988, No. 27. Canberra: Australian Institute of Criminology, pp. 115–31.

Bowling, Ben (2006) "Sovereignty vs Security: Transnational Policing in the Contemporary Caribbean", *Caribbean Journal of Criminology and Social Psychology* 2006: 1–21. Available at https://www.kcl.ac.uk/content/1/c6/01/84/31/sovereigntyvssecurity.pdf (accessed 16 May 2008).

Boyer, B. and Meidinger, E. (1985) "Privatizing Regulatory Enforcement", *Buffalo Law Review* 34: 833–964.

Braithwaite, J. (2002) "Rewards and Regulation", *Journal of Law and Society* 29(1): 12–26.

Braithwaite, J. and Drahos, P. (2000) *Global Business Regulation*. Cambridge: Cambridge University Press.

Braithwaite, John and Pettit, Philip (1990) *Not Just Deserts: A Republican Theory of Criminal Justice*. New York: Oxford University Press.

Branigan, Tania (2005) "Blair extends anti-social behaviour crackdown", *The Guardian* 2 September.

Bratton, William, (2006) Unpublished remarks, Session 250: Policing Urban America: Challenges and Successes, American Society of Criminology Annual Meeting in Los Angeles, California, 2 November.

Brodeur, J-P. and Dupont, B. (2006) : "Knowledge Workers or "Knowledge" Workers?", *Policing & Society*, 16(1): 7–26.

Brown, Richard Maxwell (1991) "Vigilante Policing". In C. B. Klockars and S. D. Mastrofski (eds.) *Thinking about Police: Contemporary Readings*. Boston: McGraw-Hill, pp. 58–72.

Bruce, David and Komane, Joe (1999) "Taxis, Cops and Vigilantes: Police attitudes towards street justice", *Crime and Conflict* 17: 39–44. Available at http://www.csvr.org.za/papers/papdbjk.htm (accessed 14 November 2006).

Bryett, Keith (1996) "Privatisation – Variation on a theme", *Policing and Society* 6: 23–35.

Bumgarner, M. and Sjoquist, D. L. (1998) "The impact of crack enforcement on police budgets", *Journal of Drug Issues* 28(3): 701–24.

Burris, S., Drahos, P. and Shearing, C. (2005) "Nodal Governance as an Approach to Regulation", *Australian Journal of Legal Philosophy* 30: 30–58.

Bush, George W. (2001) *Rallying the Armies of Compassion*, 23 July. Available at http://www.whitehouse.gov/news/reports/faithbased.html (accessed 16 May 2008).

Business Against Crime (2006) "Another Successful SPPS Leadership Development Programme", 19 July. Available at http://www.bac.co.za/MS_Anot_Succ_SPPS_LS_Dev_Prog.pdf (accessed 16 May 2008).

Business Against Crime – Western Cape, and the City of Cape Town (1998) at http://www.rotary9300.org.za/bac/bac_ct%20surv.html (accessed 17 January 2001).

Business in the Community (2004) "PSNI partners with business leaders for community benefit", 19 May. Available at http://www.bitc.org.uk/news/news_directory/psni.html (accessed 18 November 2004).

Butterfield, Mr Justice N. (2003) *Review of Criminal Investigations and Prosecutions conducted by HM Customs and Excise*. Available at http://

www.hm-treasury.gov.uk./newsroom_and_speeches/speeches/state
ment/butterfield03_report_index.cfm (accessed 7 December 2007).

Butterfield, R., Edwards, C. and Woodall, J. (2004) "The New Public
Management and the UK Police Service", *Public Management Review*
6(3): 395–415.

Callahan, E. and Dworkin, T. (1992) "Do Good and Get Rich: Financial
Incentives for Whistleblowing and the False Claims Act", *Villanova
Law Review* 37: 273–336.

Caminker, E. (1989) "The Constitutionality of Qui Tam Actions", *Yale
Law Journal* 99: 341–88.

Carcach, Carlos and Huntley, Cathie (2002) "Community participation
and regional crime", *Trends and Issues in Crime and Criminal Justice*,
No. 222, April. Canberra: Australian Institute of Criminology.

Carr, Patrick J. (2005) *Clean Streets: Controlling Crime, Maintaining Order,
and Building Community Activism*. New York: NYU Press.

Casey, Cathy and Collinson, Cathie (2005) *Citizen Police? Civilian
Reservists in New Zealand*. Auckland: Institute of Public Policy,
Auckland University of Technology.

CBC News (2005) "Experts rap private hiring of Ontario police officers",
19 March. Available at http://www.cbc.ca/canada/story/2005/03/18/
police-hire-050318.html (accessed 16 May 2008).

(2002) "Operation TIPS Trips Up?", 8 August. Available at http://www.
cbsnews.com/stories/2002/08/10/national/main518273.shtml (accessed 16 May 2008).

(2006) "Guardian Angels get lukewarm welcome from Ottawa police",
31 July. Available at http://www.cbc.ca/canada/ottawa/story/2006/07/
31/angels-mon.html (accessed 16 May 2008).

Chamber of Minerals and Energy (2005) *Annual Report 2005*. Perth:
Chamber of Minerals and Energy.

Cheh, Mary M. (1998) "Civil Remedies to Control Crime: Legal Issues
and Constitutional Challenges". In L. G. Mazerolle and J. Roehl
(eds.) *Civil Remedies and Crime Prevention*. Monsey, NY: Criminal
Justice Press.

Cheng, Edward K. (2006) "Structural Laws and the Puzzle of Regulating
Behavior", *Northwestern University Law Review* 100(2): 655–717.

Chin, Ko-Lin (1996) *Chinatown Gangs*. New York: Oxford University
Press.

Christmann, K. (2003) *Evaluation of West Yorkshire Police's Volunteers in
Policing Project*, Abstract. University of Huddersfield. Available at
http://www.hud.ac.uk/hhs/dbs/acc/research/abstracts/complete/0200
vip.htm (accessed 16 May 2008).

City of London Police (2008) "Automatic Number Plate Recognition
System (ANPR)". Available at http://www.cityoflondon.police.uk/

CityPolice/Advice/TrafficTravel/numberplate.htm (accessed 16 May 2008).

Clark, R. (2000) "Informers and Corruption". In R. Billingsley, T. Nemitz, P. Bean (eds) *Informers: policing, policy, practice*. Cullompton, Devon: Willan Publishing, pp. 38–49.

Clark, L. (2007) "Pito goes as Police IT 'streamlined'," Computer Weekly, 3 April.

Coe, C. K. and Wiesel, D. L. (2001) "Police budgeting: Winning strategies", *Public Administration Review* 61(6): 718–727.

Collier, P. M. (2001a) "The power of accounting: a field study of local financial management in a police force", *Management Accounting Research* 12: 465–86.

(2001b) "Police Performance Measurement and Human Rights", *Public Money and Management* 21(3): 35–39.

Colquhoun, Patrick (1795 [1969]). *A Treatise on the Police of the Metropolis*. Reprinted from the seventh London edition 1806. Montclair, NJ: Patterson Smith.

Commercial Activities Panel (2002) *Final Report: Improving the Sourcing Decisions of the Government*, U.S. Government Accountability Office. Available at http://archive.gao.gov/f0502/a03209.pdf (accessed 16 May 2008).

Commercial Alert (2002) "Criminal Justice Experts Ask Companies Not to Put Ads on Police Cars". Available at http://www.commercialalert. org/issues/government/police-cars/criminal-justice-experts-ask-com panies-not-to-put-ads-on-police-cars (accessed 16 May 2008).

Cope, S., Leishman, F. and Starie, P. (1997) "Globalization, new public management and the enabling State", *International Journal of Public Sector Management* 10(6): 444–60.

Cotroneo, Christian (2004) "Vigilantes versus pedophiles", *Toronto Star*, 8 August. Available at http://www.c-a-t-c-h.ca/vigilante2.htm (accessed 16 May 2008).

Council of Australian Governments (2004) "Principles for the Regulation of Ammonium Nitrate", Meeting 25 June 2004. Available at http://www. coag.gov.au/meetings/250604/attachments_d.pdf (accessed 16 May 2008).

Crawford, Adam (2003) "'Contractual Governance' of Deviant Behaviour", *Journal of Law and Society* 30(4): 479–505.

(2006a) "Policing and security as 'club goods': the new enclosures?". In J. Wood and B. Dupont (eds.) *Democracy, Society and the Governance of Security*. Cambridge: Cambridge University Press, pp. 111–38.

(2006b) "Fixing Broken Promises? Neighbourhood Wardens and Social Capital", *Urban Studies* 43(5–6): 957–76.

(2006c) "Networked governance and the post-regulatory state?: Steering, rowing and anchoring the provision of policing and security", *Theoretical Criminology* 10(4): 449–79.

Crawford, A. and Lister, S. (2004) "The patchwork shape of reassurance policing in England and Wales: Integrated local security quilts or frayed, fragmented and fragile tangled webs?", *Policing: An International Journal of Police Strategies and Management* 27(3): 413–30.

— (2006) "Additional Security Patrols in Residential Areas: Notes from the Marketplace", *Policing and Society* 16(2): 164–88.

Crawford, A., Lister, S., Blackburn, S. and Burnett, J. (2005) *Plural Policing: The mixed economy of visible patrol in England and Wales*. Bristol: The Policy Press.

Critchley, T. A. (1972) *A History of Police in England and Wales*, 2nd ed. Montclair, NJ: Patterson Smith.

Curtis, Dave (1993) "Julalikari Council's Community Night Patrol". In S. McKillop (ed) *Aboriginal justice issues: proceedings of a conference held 23–25 June 1992*, AIC Conference Proceedings no. 21. Canberra: Australian Institute of Criminology. Available at http://www.aic.gov.au/publications/proceedings/21/Curtis.html (accessed 16 May 2008).

Dalton, S. and Sellars, P. (2005) "Boys in blue send events into the red", *The Weekly Times*, 2 March.

Damaska, Mirjan (1984) *The Faces of Justice and State Authority*. New Haven: Yale University Press.

Davids, Cindy (2006) "(Mis)use of confidential police information: Delineating the problem and its effect on integrity and public trust in policing". Paper delivered at *Australian and New Zealand Society of Criminology Conference*, Hobart, Tasmania, 7–9 February.

Davids, Cindy and Hancock, Linda (1998) "Policing, Accountability, and Citizenship in the Market State", *The Australian and New Zealand Journal of Criminology* 31(1): 38–68.

Davies, Martin (2003) "Obligations and implications for ships encountering persons in need of assistance at sea", *Pacific Rim Law and Policy Journal* 12: 109–41.

Davis, Natalie Zemon (2000) *The Gift in 16th Century France*. Madison: University of Wisconsin Press.

Dearne, Karen (2004) "Spy law to curb hot cash roasted", *The Australian*, 15 June.

Deci, E. and Ryan, R. (1985) *Intrinsic Motivation and Self-Determination in Human Behavior*. New York: Plenum Press.

DeHoog, Ruth Hoogland and Salamon, Lester M. (2002) "Purchase of Service Contracting". In L. M. Salamon (ed.) *The Tools of Government: A Guide to the New Governance*. Oxford: Oxford University Press, pp. 319–339.

Delahunty, H. (2005) "Delahunty calls on Minister to give guarantees", 24 March. Available at http://vicnats.com/news/default.asp?action= article&ID=2269&WorkDate=1/03/2005&Archived=true (accessed 16 May 2008).

Dempster, Carolyn (2002) "SA vigilantes fill police gap", *BBC News*, 15 April. Available at http://news.bbc.co.uk/1/hi/world/africa/1924142. stm (accessed 16 May 2008).

Department of Information Resources (1998) "Lease vs. Purchase: Guidelines for Lease vs. Purchase of Information Technologies", Austin, Texas. Available at http://www.dir.state.tx.us/oversight/lvp/ leasepur.pdf (accessed 16 May 2008).

Department of Safety and Security, South Africa (1998) *In Service of Safety 1999–2004*, White Paper on Safety and Security. Available at http:// www.info.gov.za/whitepapers/1998/safety.html (accessed 16 May 2008).

Department of Treasury and Finance (nda) "Best Practice Advice – EC4P: Ensuring Open And Fair Competition In Government Procurement", at http://www.vgpb.vic.gov.au/CA256C450016850B/ WebObj/BestPracticeAdvice-EC4P/$File/Best%20Practice% 20Advice%20-%20EC4P.pdf (accessed 16 May 2008).

Derrida, Jacques (1991) *Donner le Temps*. Paris: Éditions Galilée.

Dillon, Wilton S. (2003) *Gifts and Nations*. London: Transaction Publishers.

Dobbs, Lou (2005) "Feds' border action not nearly enough", *CNN*, 5 July. Available at http://www.cnn.com/2005/US/03/31/border.agents/ index.html (accessed 16 May 2008).

Doherty, Ben and March, Stephanie (2005) "Bad Govt buying costing us millions", *Canberra Times*, 15 November.

Dore, Christopher (1999) "NZ sues IBM over Police", *The Australian*, 24 August.

Douglas, Mary (1990) "Foreword: No Free Gifts". In: Mauss, Marcel (1950). *Le Don*. Presses Universitaires de France, Paris. Translation by Halls, W. D., 1990. *The Gift: The Form and Reason For Exchange in Archaic Societies*. Routledge, London, pp. ix–xxiii.

Drug Enforcement Administration (2005) "Drugs of Abuse". Available at http://www.usdoj.gov/dea/pubs/abuse/doa-p.pdf (accessed 16 May 2008).

Dunne, S. (1990) "Attorneys' Fees for Citizen Enforcement of Environmental Statutes: The Obstacles for Public Interest Law Firms", *Stanford Environmental Law Journal* (9): 1–45.

Dunningham, C. and Norris, C. (1999) "The Detective, the Snout and the Audit Commission: The Real Costs in Using Informants", *The Howard Journal* 38(1): 67–86.

Dupont, B. (2008) "The French Police System Caught Between a Rock and a Hard Place: The Tension of Serving both the State and the Public". In M. Haberfield, Y. Cerrah and H. Grant (eds) *Democratic Policing: Global Change from a Comparative Perspective*. Thousand Oaks, CA: Sage Publications.

Eames, David (2006) "Crimefighting group looks to set up in West Auckland", *The New Zealand Herald*, 11 January. Available at http://www.nzherald.co.nz/section/story.cfm?c_id=1&objectid=10363178 (accessed 16 May 2008).

Earle, Jr., Ralph (1996) Personal Communication. Alliance for Environmental Innovation, Boston, November.

Eggen, Dan (2007) "Judge invalidates Patriot Act provisions", *Washington Post*, 7 September.

Eggers, W. D. and Goldsmith, S. (2003) "Networked Government", *Government Executive* 35(8): 28–33.

EGS (2007) "Bluelight Marketplace". Available at http://www.egsgroup.com/exchanges/bluelight.php (accessed 16 May 2008).

El Cajon City Council (1998) "Minutes", 27 October. Available at http://www.ci.el-cajon.ca.us/council/minutes_archive.asp (accessed 16 May 2008)

Elliott, Carl (2006) "The Drug Pushers", *Atlantic Monthly* 297(3) (April).

Enoch, B. (2006) "Joint anti-crime action hits Joburg", *SAPA*, 18 March.

Ericson, R. and Haggerty, K. (1997) *Policing the Risk Society*. Oxford University Press, New York.

Etter, Barbara (2001) "Computer Crime", Paper presented at the *4th National Outlook Symposium on Crime in Australia*, New Crimes or New Responses, Australian Institute of Criminology, Canberra 21–22 June 2001.

Feldbrugge, F.J.M. (1966) "Good and Bad Samaritans: A comparative survey of criminal law provisions concerning failure to rescue", *The American Journal of Comparative Law* 14: 630–57.

Finnimore, P. (1982) "How should the effectiveness of Police be assessed?", *The Police Journal* LV: 56–66.

Fischhoff, B. (1975) "Hindsight ≠ foresight: The effect of outcome knowledge on judgment under uncertainty", *Journal of Experimental Psychology: Human Perception and Performance* 1: 288–99.

Fishback, Price W. (1995) "An Alternative View of Violence in Labor Disputes in the Early 1900s: The Bituminous Coal Industry, 1890–1930", *Labor History* 36(3) (Summer): 426–56.

Fisse, Brent and Braithwaite, John (1993) *Corporations, Crime and Accountability*. Cambridge: Cambridge University Press.

Fitzpatrick, Cara (2005a) "Police Criticize Patrol Car Software", *Knight Ridder Tribune Business News*, 28 January.

(2005b) "Dispatch Software Pains Flaring Up", *Knight Ridder Tribune Business News*, 14 April.

(2005c) "Group Says Intergraph Should Stay", *Knight Ridder Tribune Business News*, 25 May.

Fixler, Philip E. Jr. and Poole, Robert W. Jr. (1988) "Can Police Services Be Privatized?", *The Annals of the American Academy of Political and Social Sciences* 498 (July): 108–18.

Fleming, J. (2004) "Les liaisons dangereuses: Relations between police commissioners and their political masters", *Australian Journal of Public Administration* 63 (3): 60–74.

(2005) " 'Working Together': Neighbourhood Watch, Reassurance Policing and the Potential of Partnerships", *Trends and Issues in Crime and Criminal Justice* No. 303, September. Canberra: Australian Institute of Criminology.

Fleming, J. and Lafferty, G. (2000) "New management techniques and restructuring for accountability in Australian police organisations", *Policing: An International Journal of Police Strategies & Management* 23 (2): 154–68.

Fleming, J. and Wood, J. (2006) "Introduction: Networked Policing". In J. Fleming and J. Wood, (eds.) *Fighting Crime Together: The Challenges of Policing & Security Networks*. Sydney: University of New South Wales Press, pp. 1–14.

Fleury-Steiner, B. and Wiles, K. (2003) "The use of commercial advertisements on public police cars in the United States, post-9/11" *Policing and Society* 13(4): 441–50.

Forst, Brian (2000) "Privatization and Civilianization of Policing". In C. M. Friel (ed.) *Criminal Justice 2000, Volume 2: Boundary Changes in Criminal Justice Organizations*. Washington, DC: National Institute of Justice/NCJRS, pp. 19–79.

Freiberg, A. (1986) "Reward, Law and Power: Toward A Jurisprudence of the Carrot", *Australian and New Zealand Journal of Criminology* 19(2): 91–113.

(2005) "Managerialism in Australian Criminal Justice: RIP for KPIs?", *Monash University Law Review* 31: 12–36.

Fujitsu (2005) "Fujitsu Services Plus – Helping Western Australia Police Service close the net on crime", *Interaction*, March. Available at http://www.fujitsu.com/au/casestudies/wa_police.print.html (accessed 31 August 2005).

Fung, Archon (2001) "Accountable Autonomy: Toward Empowered Deliberation in Chicago Schools and Policing", *Politics & Society* 29 (1): 73–103.

Fung, A. (2003) "Associations and Democracy: Between Theories, Hopes and Realities", *Annual Review of Sociology* 29: 515–39.

Gallagher's Beat (1994) "Justice for sale?", *Police Review* 102 (13 May): 26–27.

Ganguli, K. M. (tr.) (1883–1896) *The Mahabharata*, Book 13: Anusasana Parva: Sec. CXXXVIII p. 282. Available at http://www.sacred-texts.com/hin/m13/m13b103.htm (accessed 16 May 2008).

Gans, Jeremy (2000) "Privately Paid Public Policing: Law and Practice", *Policing and Society* 10: 183–206.

Garland, David (1996) "The Limits of the Sovereign State: Strategies of Crime Control in Contemporary Society", *British Journal of Criminology* 36: 445–71.

(2002) *The Culture of Control: Crime and Social Order in Contemporary Society*. Chicago: University of Chicago Press.

(2005) "Penal Excess and Surplus Meaning: Public Torture Lynchings in Twentieth-Century America", *Law & Society Review* 39(4): 793–833.

Gaston, Kevin and Alexander, Jackie A. (2001) "Effective organisation and management of public sector volunteer workers: Police Special Constables", *The International Journal of Public Sector Management* 14 (1): 59–74.

Geason, Susan and Wilson, Paul R (1992) "Administrative and security systems". In S Geason and P R Wilson *Preventing retail crime*. Canberra: Australian Institute of Criminology, pp. 61–72. Available at http://www.aic.gov.au/publications/crimprev/retail/ass-t.html (accessed 16 May 2008).

Geis, G., Huston, T. and Wells, J. (1991) "Rewards by Businesses for Crime Information: The Views of Law Enforcement" *American Journal of Police* 10(3): 69–81.

Gibbons, Sarah (1996) "Sponsored Beats", *Police Review* 104 (26 July): 22–24.

Gilboy, Janet (1998) "Compelled Third-Party Participation in the Regulatory Process: Legal Duties, Culture and Noncompliance", *Law and Policy* 20: 135–55.

Gladwell, Malcolm (2005) *Blink*. New York: Little Brown.

Glazer, Myron and Glazer, Penina (1989) *The Whistle Blowers: Exposing Corruption in Government and Industry*. New York: Basic Books.

Global Road Safety Partnership (nda) *Corporate Sponsorship of Road Safety*. Available at http://www.grsproadsafety.org/themes/default/pdfs/sponsorShip.pdf (accessed 16 May 2008).

Goldsmith A. (ed.) (1991) *Complaints Against the Police: The Trend to External Review*. Oxford: Clarendon Press.

Goldsmith, S. and Eggers, W. D. (2004) *Governing by Network*. Washington, DC: Brookings Institute Press.

Goodin, Robert (1976) *The Politics of Rational Man*. London: John Wiley.

(1980) "Making Moral Incentives Pay", *Policy Sciences* 12: 131–45.

Government Accountability Office (2005) "Information Technology: FBI Is Taking Steps to Develop an Enterprise Architecture, but Much Remains to Be Accomplished", Report to Congressional Committees, September. Available at http://www.gao.gov/new.items/d05363.pdf (accessed 16 May 2008).

Government Acquisitions (2004) "Program Guidelines", Vehicle Procurement Division. Available at http://www.govad.com/gov.asp (accessed 16 May 2008).

Grabosky, P. (1988) "Efficiency and effectiveness in Australian Policing", *Trends and Issues in Crime and Criminal Justice* No.16 (December), Canberra: Australian Institute of Criminology.

—— (1992) "Law Enforcement and the Citizen: Non-Governmental Participants in Crime Prevention and Control", *Policing and Society* 2: 249–71.

—— (1995) "Counterproductive Regulation", *International Journal of the Sociology of Law* 23: 347–69.

—— (1995) "Using Non-governmental Resources to Foster Regulatory Compliance", *Governance* 8 (4): 527–50.

—— (2004) "Towards a Theory of Public/Private Interaction in Policing". In J. McCord (ed.) *Beyond Empiricism: Institutions and Intentions in the Study of Crime: Advances in Criminological Theory*. Piscataway, NJ: Transaction Publishers, Vol. 13: 69–82.

Greenberg, Martin A. (2005) *Citizens defending America: from colonial times to the age of terrorism*. Pittsburgh, PA: University of Pittsburgh Press.

Greene, Jack R. (2000) "Community Policing in America: Changing the Nature, Structure, and Function of the Police", *Criminal Justice 2000 Vol. 3: 299–370. Policies, Processes, and Decisions of the Criminal Justice System*, Washington, DC: U.S. Department of Justice, National Institute of Justice.

Guangdong Provincial Public Security Department (2005) *Shaoguan City Begin to Use Funds from Police Foundations to Assist the Bereaved Families of Officers who Died on Duty*. Available at http://www.gdga.gov.cn/xwtd/gdgaxw/t20050205_35142.htm (accessed 3 March 2006).

Gusfield, Joseph R. (1969) *Symbolic Crusade: Status Politics and the American Temperance Movement*. Urbana: University of Illinois Press.

Hale, C.M., Uglow, S.P. and Heaton, R. (2005) "Uniform Styles II: Police Families and Policing Styles", *Policing and Society* 15(1): 1–18.

Hall, Rod (2004) "Police sign 3 year e-procurement deal with Tranzsoft", *iStart*, March. Available at http://www.istart.co.nz/index/HM20/PCo/PV21874/EX253/CS25623 (accessed 16 May 2008).

Hamilton, Jane (2003) "Rent-a-cop plan for city gets go-ahead", *The Scotsman Evening News*, 11 February. Available at http://news.

scotsman.com/topics.cfm?tid=580&id=170332003 (accessed 16 May 2008).

Hancock, Linda (1998) "Contractualism, Privatisation and Justice: Citizenship, the State and Managing Risk", *Australian Journal of Public Administration* 57(4): 118–127.

Handler, J. F. and Hasenfeld, Y. (1991) *The Moral Construction of Poverty: Welfare Reform in America*. Newbury Park, CA: Sage Publications.

Hansard (2002) "Supplementary Policing", Questions Without Notice, NSW Legislative Council, 14 March. Available at http://www.parlia ment.nsw.gov.au/prod/parlment/hansart.nsf/V3Key/ LC20020314017 (accessed 16 May 2008).

Harrison, W., Heuston, G., Mocas, S., Morrissey, M. and Richardson, J. (2004) "High-Tech Forensics", *Communications of the ACM* (July) 47 (7): 49–52.

Hayes, S. (2005) "Legal guns take aim at Customs", *Australian IT*, 22 November. Available at http://australianit.news.com.au/articles/ 0,7204,17323543%5E15341%5E%5Enbv%5E15306%2D15317,00. html (accessed 16 December 2005).

Healy, Gene (2002) "Volunteer Voyeurs?", 29 July. Available at http:// www.cato.org/dailys/07–29–02.html (accessed 16 May 2008).

Healy, J. and McKee, M. (2004) "Delivering Health Services in Diverse Societies". In J. Healy and M. McKee (eds.) *Accessing Health Care*. Oxford: Oxford University Press, pp. 351–69.

Herber, Bernard P. (1960) "The Use of Informers' Rewards in Federal Tax Administration". Unpublished Ph.D. Dissertation, University of Washington.

Hernandez Jr., E. (1981) "The Influence of Tight Budgets on Proactive Law Enforcement". In James J Fyfe (ed.) *Contemporary Issues in Law Enforcement*, Sage Research Progress Series in Criminology, Vol. 20, Beverly Hills, CA: Sage Publications, pp. 59–81.

Hight, James (2000) "Working with Informants: Operational Recommendations", *FBI Law Enforcement Bulletin* 69, 5, 6–9.

Hill, Deborah (1997) "Secret Inquiry Probes Police Tender Process", *National Business Review*, 16 May.

Hills, Ben (1999a) "ICAC Asks Why Police Paid Extra for 'flawed' Radio Desk", *Sydney Morning Herald*, 6 February.

(1999b) "It's A Cover-up, Says Man Who Missed Out On Police Contract", *Sydney Morning Herald*, 9 February.

(1999c) "Radio Giant Courted Our Police", *Sydney Morning Herald*, 8 September.

(1999d) "To Curry Favour", *Sydney Morning Herald*, 8 September.

Hindess, B. (1996) *Discourses of Power*. Oxford: Blackwell.

Hinds, Stephen (1994) "Private Policy and Policing – Does Private Enterprise have a Role in Delivering the Output of Public Safety and Security?" In David Biles and Julia Vernon (eds.) *Private Sector and Community Involvement in the Criminal Justice System: proceedings of a conference held 30 November – 2 December 1992, Wellington, New Zealand*. AIC Conference Proceedings No. 23. Canberra: Australian Institute of Criminology. Available at http://www.aic.gov. au/publications/proceedings/23/Hinds.pdf (accessed 16 May 2008).

Hodge, Karen (2005) "Patrol nabs youths on first night", *The Dominion Post* 8 November. Available at http://www.communitypatrols.org.nz/ news-dompost.html (accessed 16 May 2008).

Hoffman, M. (2006) "Surveillance cameras at stations: your face could soon become just another 'bar code'", *The Japan Times*, 25 April.

Home Office (2006) "Good Practice: Reassurance – Using Specials for Reassurance". Available at http://specials.homeoffice.gov.uk/Good-practice/reassurance/ (accessed 14 November 2006).

Homel, P. (2004) "The Whole-of-Government Approach to Crime Prevention", *Trends and Issues in Crime and Criminal Justice*, Canberra: Australian Institute of Criminology.

Hood, C. and Lodge, M. (2006) *The Politics of Public Service Bargains*. Oxford: Oxford University Press.

Hoofnagle, Chris Jay (2004) "Big Brother's Little Helpers: How Choice Point and Other Commercial Data Brokers Collect, Process, and Package Your Data for Law Enforcement", *N.C.J. Int'l L. & Com. Reg.* 29: 595.

Hope, Tim (2000) "Inequality and the clubbing of private security". In Tim Hope and Richard Sparks (eds.) *Crime, Risk and Insecurity*. London and New York: Routledge, pp. 83–106.

Hoque, Z., Arends, S. and Alexander, R. (2004) "Policing the Police Service: A case study of the rise of 'new public management' within an Australian police service", *Accounting, Auditing & Accountability Journal* 17(1): 59–84.

Houghton, Ian (2007) Personal Communication, Federal Agent Ian Houghton, National Coordinator Covert Policing, Australian Federal Police, 2 May 2007.

Howard, John (1999) *Building a Stronger and Fairer Australia: Liberalisation in Economic Policy and Modern Conservatism in Social Policy*, Address to the Australia Unlimited Roundtable, 4 May, at http://pandora.nla. gov.au/pan/10052/20040521_0000/www.pm.gov.au/news/speeches/ 1999/AustraliaUnlimitedRoundtable.htm (accessed 16 May 2008).

(2000) Address to the Learning for Life Access for Rural Youth in partnership with the Westpac Foundation, The Smith Family,

Melbourne, 23 June, at http://www.pandora.nla.gov.au/nph-arch/
2000/Z2000-Nov-9/http://www.pm.gov.au/news/speeches/2000/speech
2306.htm (accessed 16 May 2008).

Howson, Gerald (1970) "Thief-Taker General: The Rise and Fall of
Jonathan Wild", London: Hutchinson.

Hudzik, J. (1988) *Managing Police Budgets in Australia*. Canberra:
Australian Institute of Criminology.

(1994) "Comprehensive criminal justice planning: successes, failures
and lessons from the American experience", *Criminal Justice Planning and Coordination*: proceedings of a conference held 19–21 April
1993, Canberra.

Hudzik, J., Bynum, T. S., Greene, J. R., Cordner, G. W., Christian, K. F.
and Edwards, S. M. (1981) "The Environment of Manpower Decision Making". In J Hudzik (ed.) *Criminal Justice Manpower Planning:
an overview*, Washington, DC: US Law Enforcement Assistance
Administration, pp. 180–208.

Hunter, Jeff (2001) "The case for mandatory reporting of medical negligence", *Healthcover* February-March: 58–60.

Hyde, Lewis (1979). *The Gift: Imagination and the Erotic Life of Property*.
Vintage Books, New York.

Independent Commission Against Corruption (2006). *Sponsorship in the
public sector*. Independent Commission Against Corruption, Sydney.

Innes, Martin (2000) "'Professionalizing' the Role of the Police Informant: The British Experience", *Policing and Society* 9(4): 357–83.

(2004) "Reinventing tradition?: Reassurance, neighbourhood security
and policing", *Criminal Justice* 4(2): 151–71.

International Crisis Group (2001) *Indonesia: National Police Reform*. ICG
Asia Report No.10. Jakarta/Brussels: ICG.

Ishihara, Shintaro (2005) "Tokyo Takes the Lead in New Policy Development", Policy Speech by the Governor of Tokyo at the Fourth
Regular Session of the Metropolitan Assembly. Available at http://
www.metro.tokyo.jp/ENGLISH/GOVERNOR/SPEECH/2005/fgg1c
102.htm (accessed 16 May 2008).

Israel Police (2005) "Civil Guard Volunteer Fields". Available at http://
www.police.gov.il/English/News/CivilGuard/04_volunteer_fields.asp
(accessed 16 May 2008).

Jackson, Russell (2005) "Reliance wins longer deal to monitor tagged
criminals", *The Scotsman*, 11 January.

Janetta, Jesse (2006) "Compstat for Corrections", p. 7. Available at http://
ucicorrections.seweb.uci.edu/pdf/COMPSTATforCorrectionsWork
ingPaper.pdf (accessed 16 May 2008).

Johnston, L. (1992) *The Rebirth of Private Policing*. London: Routledge.

(1996) "What is Vigilantism?". *British Journal of Criminology* 36(2): 220–36.

(1999) *Policing Britain: Risk, Security and Governance*. Harlow, England: Longman.

(2003) "From 'pluralisation' to 'the police extended family': Discourses on the governance of community policing in Britain". *International Journal of the Sociology of Law* 31: 185–204.

(2006) "Diversifying police recruitment? The deployment of police community services officers in London", *Howard Journal of Criminal Justice* 45(4): 388–402.

Jones, C. (1993) "Auditing Criminal Justice", *British Journal of Criminology* 33(2): 187–202.

Jones, T. (2003) "The governance and accountability of policing". In T. Newburn (ed.) *Handbook of Policing*. Cullompton: Willan Publishing.

Jones, T. and Newburn, T. (2002) "The Transformation of Policing?: Understanding Current Trends in Policing Systems", *British Journal of Criminology* 42: 129–46.

(2006) "Understanding Plural Policing". In T. Jones and T. Newburn (eds.) *Plural Policing; A comparative perspective*, Abingdon, UK: Routledge, pp. 1–11.

Kane, Kanoelani. M. (2002) "Driving into the Sunset: A Proposal for Mandatory Reporting to the DMV by Physicians Treating Unsafe Elderly Drivers", *University of Hawaii Law Review* 25: 59–83.

Kash, Douglas. E. (2002) "Hunting Terrorists Using Confidential Informant Reward Programs," *FBI Law Enforcement Bulletin* 71(4): 26–31.

Keech, Anthony C., Wonders, Susan M., Cook, David I. and Gebski, Val. J. (2004) "Balancing the outcomes: reporting adverse events", *Medical Journal of Australia* 181: 215–18.

Keelty, Mick. (2006) "Security and Fraud". Address to the Mastercard International Consumer Credit Card Summit. Available at http://www.afp.gov.au/media/national_media/national_speeches/2006/mastercar d_international_consumer_credit_card_summit_2006 (accessed 16 May 2008).

Kelman, Steven. J. (2002) "Contracting". In L. M. Salamon (ed.) *The Tools of Government: A Guide to the New Governance*. Oxford: Oxford University Press.

Kempa, M., Stenning, P. and Wood, J. (2004) "Policing Communal Spaces: A Reconfiguration of the 'Mass Private Property' Hypothesis", *British Journal of Criminology* 44: 562–81.

Kentucky Government (2006) "Governor Fletcher Approves Body Armor Funding for Various Law Enforcement Groups", Governor's Office for Local Development, 29 September. Available at http://www.kentucky.gov/Newsroom/gold/bodyarmor.htm (accessed 16 May 2008).

Kettl, Donald (1993) *Sharing Power: Public Governance and Private Markets*, Washington, DC: The Brookings Institution.

Kingsley, T-A (2005) "Police charge fishing competition", 10 March at http://www.abc.net.au/centralvic/stories/s1320515.htm (accessed 20 September 2006).

Kinnes, I. (2000) "From urban street gangs to criminal empires: The changing face of gangs in the Western Cape", *ISS Monograph* No. 48.

Kopic, Jaroslav (2006) "Pirátství kolem poč ítačové techniky bez morálních zábran", *Časopis Policista*, February. Available at http://www.mvcr.cz/casopisy/policista/2006/02/malro206.html (accessed 16 May 2008).

Kraakman, R. H. (1986) "Gatekeepers: The Anatomy of a Third-Party Enforcement Strategy", *Journal of Law Economics and Organization* 2: 53–104.

Laurence, Dave (2005) "Community patrols is about crime prevention, not policing, meeting told", *Wanganui Chronicle*, 11 November. Available at http://www.communitypatrols.org.nz/news-wanganui.html (accessed 16 May 2008).

Lauro, P. W. (2002) "New York police and firefighter merchandise tests the market at the 2002 licensing exposition", *New York Times*, 10 June.

Law Commission of Canada (2002) *In Search of Security: The Role of Public Police and Private Agencies – Discussion Paper*. Ottawa: Law Commission of Canada.

(2006) *In Search Of Security: The Future of Policing In Canada*. Ottawa: Law Commission of Canada.

Leach, Pamela (2006) "Regimes of Insecurity? Citizen Security Initiatives as Regulatory", paper delivered at Australian and New Zealand Society of Criminology Conference, Hobart, Tasmania, 7–9 February.

Leggett, T. (2002) "Performance measure for the South African Police Service: setting the benchmarks for service delivery", *Transformation* 49: 55–85. Available at http://muse.jhu.edu/journals/transformation/v049/49.1leggett.pdf (accessed 16 May 2008).

Leingang, M. (2004) "Psychic to help in Oxford case", *The Enquirer*, 23 October. Available at http://www.enquirer.com/editions/2004/10/23/loc_missing23.html (accessed 16 May 2008).

Leishman, Frank, Cope, Stephen and Starie, Peter (1995) "Reforming the police in Britain: New public management, policy networks and a tough 'old bill' ", *International Journal of Public Sector Management* 8 (4): 26–37.

Lessig, L. (1999) *Code and other Laws of Cyberspace*. New York: Basic Books.

Levi, Michael (1996) "Money-Laundering: Risks and Countermeasures". In A. Graycar and P. Grabosky *Money Laundering in the 21st century: risks and countermeasures*, Australian Institute of Criminology Research and Public Policy Series No 2, Seminar held on 7 February

1996, Canberra, pp. 1–11. Available at http://www.aic.gov.au/publi cations/rpp/02/RPP02.pdf (accessed 13 July 2008).

Levmore, Saul (1986) "Waiting for Rescue: An Essay on the Evolution and Incentive Structure of the Law of Affirmative Obligations", *Virginia Law Review* 72(5): 879–941.

Lewis, L. (2004) "Kimono cops to take on muggers", *The Australian* 23 November.

Lewis, C. and Prenzler, T. (1999) "Civilian oversight of police in Australia", *Trends and Issues in Crime and Criminal Justice* No. 141, Canberra: Australian Institute of Criminology.

Lichtblau, Eric (2005) "FBI may scrap vital overhaul for computers", *New York Times*, 14 January.

Lipsitz, L. (1968) "If, as Verba says, the state functions as a religion, what are we to do then to save our souls?", *The American Political Science Review* 62(2): 527–35.

Liptak, Adam (2007) "Judge voids F.B.I. tool granted by Patriot Act", *New York Times*, 7 September.

Little, Craig. B. and Sheffield, Christopher. P. (1983) "Frontiers and Criminal Justice: English Prosecution Societies and American Vigi- lantism in the Eighteenth and Nineteenth Centuries", *American Sociological Review* 48: 796–808.

Lloyd, Jane and Rogers, Nanette (1993) "Crossing the last frontier: problems facing Aboriginal women victims of rape in central Australia". In P. Weiser Easteal (ed.) *Without consent: confronting adult sexual violence: proceedings of a conference held 27–29 October 1992*, AIC Conference Proceedings no. 20. Canberra: Australian Institute of Criminology.

Loader, Ian (1997) "Policing and the social: Questions of symbolic power", *British Journal of Sociology* 48 (1): 1–18.

(1999) "Consumer Culture and the Commodification of Policing and Security", *Sociology* 33(2): 373–92.

(2000) "Plural Policing and Democratic Governance", *Social and Legal Studies* 9(3): 323–45.

Loader, Ian and Walker, Neil (2001) "Policing as a Public Good: Reconstituting the Connections Between Policing and the State", *Theoretical Criminology* 5(1): 9–35.

(2006) "Necessary virtues: the legitimate place of the state in the production of security". In J. Wood and B. Dupont (eds.) *Democracy, Society and the Governance of Security*. Cambridge: Cambridge Uni- versity Press, pp. 165–95.

London Safety Camera Partnership (2005) "FAQs". Available at http:// www.lscp.org.uk/faqs.asp?id=14 (accessed 15 November 2005).

Los Angeles County Sheriff's Department (2007) "Contract Transit Policing Services". Available at http://www.lasd.org/lasd_services/ contract_law/transit_srv1.html (accessed 16 May 2008).

Los Angeles Police Department (2004) "Returning the Alvarado Corridor/MacArthur Park to the Community", 11 March. Available at http://www.lapdonline.org/march_2004/news_view/20300 (accessed 16 May 2008).

(2007) "Quarterly Reports of the Independent Monitor". Available at http://www.lapdonline.org/consent_decree/content_basic_view/90 10 (accessed 16 May 2008).

Loveday, B. (2005) "The Challenge of Police Reform in England and Wales", *Public Money and Management* (October): 275–81.

Luo, Michael (2004) "Now a Message From a Sponsor of the Subway?", *The New York Times*, 27 July, available at http://www.nytimes.com/2004/ 07/27/nyregion/27branding.html?ex=1248580800&en=04074690a fca5399&ei=5090&partner=rssuserland (accessed 16 May 2008).

Lusty, David (2002) "Civil Forfeiture of Proceeds of Crime in Australia", *Journal of Money Laundering Control* 5: 345–59.

Maguire, M. and John, T. (2006) "Intelligence Led Policing, Managerialism and Community Engagement: Competing Priorities and the Role of the National Intelligence Model in the UK", *Policing and Society* 16(1): 67–85.

Maine, Sir Henry Sumner (1861 [1920]) *Ancient Law: Its Connection With the Early History of Society, and Its Relation to Modern Ideas*, 10th ed. London: John Murray.

Mallard, Trevor (2003) "Government e-procurement trial concludes", 9 December. Available at http://www.beehive.govt.nz/ViewDocument. aspx?DocumentID=18574 (accessed 16 May 2008).

Manning, Peter. K. (2003) *Policing Contingencies*. Chicago: University of Chicago Press.

Marx, Gary (1981) "Ironies of Social Control: Authorities as Contributors to Deviance Through Escalation, Nonenforcement and Covert Facilitation", *Social Problems* 28 (3): 221–246.

(1987) "The Interweaving of Public and Private Police in Undercover Work". In C. Shearing and P. Stenning (eds.) *Private Policing*, Newbury Park, CA: Sage Publications, pp. 172–93.

(1988) *Undercover: Police Surveillance in America*. Berkeley: University of California Press.

(1989) "Commentary: Some Trends and Issues in Citizen Involvement in the Law Enforcement Process", *Crime and Delinquency* 35(3): 500–19.

(1992a) "Some Reflections on Undercover: Recent Developments and Enduring Issues", *Crime, Law and Social Change* 18: 193–217.

(1992b) "Under-the-covers undercover investigations: Some reflections on the state's use of sex and deception in law enforcement", *Criminal Justice Ethics* 11(1): 13–24.

(1995) "Undercover in Comparative Perspective: Some implications for knowledge and social research". In C. Fijnaut and G. Marx (eds.) *Undercover: Police Surveillance in Comparative Perspective.* The Hague: Kluwer, pp. 322–37.

Mauss, Marcel (1950). *Le Don.* Paris: Presses Universitaires de France [1990] WD Halls (Tr) *The Gift: The Form and Reason For Exchange in Archaic Societies.* London: Routledge.

Mazerolle, Lorraine and Ransley, Janet (2005) *Third Party Policing.* Cambridge: Cambridge University Press.

Mbeki, Thabo (2002) Address at the Business Trust Dinner, Hilton Hotel, Johannesburg, 1 September.

McCue, Andy (2004) "Met Police in £750m outsourcing 'megadeal': Force will hand its entire IT to one supplier for next 10 years", *Silicon.com*, 17 February. Available at http://management.silicon.com/itdirector/0,39024673,39118460,00.htm (accessed 16 May 2008).

McDowell, Gerald. E. (1988) "The Use of the Undercover Technique in Corruption Investigations", in U.S. Department of Justice (ed), *Prosecution of Public Corruption Cases.* Washington, DC: U.S. Department of Justice, pp. 101–14.

McElhatton, Jim (2005) "Traffic camera system will expand", *The Washington Times*, 25 May.

McEwen, Alan (2005a) "Capital CCTV network focuses in on 20 offenders every day", *Edinburgh Evening News*, 5 September.

(2005b) "Two crimes every day spotted on city buses", *Edinburgh Evening News*, 4 October.

McLaughlin, E., Muncie, J. and Hughes, G. (2001) "The permanent revolution: New Labour, new public management and the modernization of criminal justice", *Criminal Justice* 1(3): 301–18.

McLeod, Ian (2000) "Police Got $100,000 for Private Wiretaps, Lawyer Alleges: Cornwall Businessman Fighting Arson, Fraud Charges in Court", *The Ottawa Citizen* 1 April, p.A1.

McMullan, J. L. (1996) "The New Improved Monied Police: Reform, Crime Control, and the Commodification of Policing in London", *British Journal of Criminology* 36(1): 85–108.

McNeill, David (2004) "Watching the Detectives", *The Japan Times*, 28 November.

McPhee, M. (2005) "Fingerprint Gaffe Spurs Costly Outsourcing", *Boston Herald*, 4 April. Available at http://www.scafo.org/The_Print/The_PRINT_VOL_21_ISSUE_03.pdf (accessed 16 May 2008).

McSherry, Bernadette (2004) "Risk assessment by mental health professionals and the prevention of future violent behaviour", *Trends & issues in crime and criminal justice* No. 281. Canberra: Australian Institute of Criminology.

Merton, Robert. K. (1936) "The Unanticipated Consequences of Purposive Social Action", *American Sociological Review* 1(6): 894–904.

Metropolitan Police Service (nda)"Metropolitan Police Service Film Unit: Intellectual Property Frequently Asked Questions". Available at http://met.police.uk/filmunit/intellectualfaq.htm#000004 (accessed 16 May 2008).

Meyer, G. (2006) "Chicago seeking trademarks on city assets: Licensing fire and police dept. insignias for apparel could be money maker", *Crain's Chicago Business*, 5 July. Available at http://www.chicagobusiness.com/cgi-bin/news.pl?id=21210 (accessed 16 May 2008).

Microsoft (2003) "Microsoft Security Antivirus Information". Available at http://www.microsoft.com/security/antivirus/default.mspx (accessed 10 January 2008).

Miller, M. (1999) "Police and media: Spirit of co-operation", *Police Life*, September: 24–25.

Millie, Andrew and Herrington, Victoria (2005) "Bridging the gap: Understanding Reassurance Policing", *The Howard Journal* 44 (1): 41–56.

Ministry of National Security (2006) "Neighbourhood Watch Groups Successful in Reducing Crime", *Jamaica Information Service*, 12 December. Available at http://www.jis.gov.jm/security/html/20061211 t120000–0500_10837_jis_neighbourhood_watch_groups_successful _in_reducing_crime.asp (accessed 16 May 2008).

Ministry of Safety and Security (2006) "Business and Government agree on step change priorities in the fight against crime", 4 October. Available at http://www.info.gov.za/speeches/2006/06100508151001.htm (accessed 16 May 2008).

Minnaar, A. (2004) *Private-public partnerships: private security, crime prevention and policing in South Africa*. Inaugural lecture: Department of Security Risk Management, School of Criminal Justice, College of Law, University of South Africa.

(2005) "Private-public partnerships: private security, crime prevention and policing in South Africa", *Acta Criminologica* 18(1): 85–114.

Minnaar, A. and Mistry, D. (2004) "Outsourcing and the South African Police Service". In M. Schönteich, A. Minnaar, D. Mistry, and K. C. Goyer *Private Muscle: Outsourcing the Provision of Criminal Justice Services*. Institute for Security Studies, Monograph No. 93. Available at http://www.iss.org.za/AF/profiles/southafrica/crime.htm (accessed 16 May 2008).

Mollenkamp, Becky (2003) "Corporate Sponsorship for Law Enforcement", *Law & Order* 51(1): 80–82.

Mooney, Chris and Mather, Adrian (2005) "Scheme finds the way to beat crime", *The Scotsman Evening News*, 20 January.

Moore, M. H. and Braga, A. A. (2003) "Measuring and improving police performance: the lessons of Compstat and its progeny", *Policing: An International Journal of Police Strategies and Management* 26(3): 439–53.

Mulgan, R. (2001) "Accountability the key to successful outsourcing", *The Canberra Times*, 20 January.

Mulgan, R. and Uhr, J. (2000) "Accountability and Governance", Discussion Paper No. 71, ANU Public Policy Program. Available at http://hdl.handle.net/1885/41946 (accessed 16 May 2008).

Murphy, Christopher (2002) *The Rationalization of Public Policing In Canada: A study of the impact and implications of resource limits and market strategies in public policing*. The Police Future Group, CACP, Electronic Series No 1. Posted September 2000 at http://policefutures.org/docs/murphy_e.pdf.

Nadelmann, Ethan (1993) *Cops Across Borders: The Internationalization of U.S. Criminal Law Enforcement*. University Park: Pennsylvania State University Press.

Natapoff, Alexandra (2006) "Beyond Unreliable: How snitches contribute to wrongful convictions", *Golden Gate University Law Review* 37: 107–130.

National Business Review (1997) "Conflict of Interest Denied", *National Business Review*, 23 May.

National Center on Addiction and Substance Abuse at Columbia University (2005) *Under the Counter: The Diversion and Abuse of Controlled Prescription Drugs in the U.S.* New York: CASA.

National Immigration Law Center (2000) "New Rule Explains Limits of INS Reporting Requirements Under the 1996 Welfare Law", *Immigrants Rights Update* 14(6). Available at *http://www.nilc.org/imspbs/vr/verifreptg004.htm* (accessed 16 May 2008).

National Information Clearinghouse (2004) "Clergy as Mandatory Reporters of Child Abuse and Neglect: Full Text Excerpts of State Laws", *State Statutes Series*. Available at http://nccanch.acf.hhs.gov/general/legal/statutes/clergymandatedall.pdf (accessed 2 October 2005).

National Police Agency (2004) "Countermeasures against Phishing", 24 December. Available at http://www.npa.go.jp/cyber/english/policy/002.htm (accessed 16 May 2008).

Neiman, Max (1980) "The Virtues of Heavy-Handed Government". In John Brigham and Don Brown (eds.) *Policy Implementation: Penalties or Incentives*. Beverly Hills, CA: Sage Publications, pp. 19–42.

New South Wales Independent Commission Against Corruption (2006) *Sponsorship in the Public Sector: A guide to developing policies and procedures for both receiving and granting sponsorship*. Sydney: ICAC.

New South Wales Police (2004) *Cost Recovery and User Charges Policy*, December. Available at http://www.police.nsw.gov.au/__data/assets/pdf_file/0003/9066/cost_recovery_and_user_charges_policy.pdf (accessed 16 May 2008).

  (2005) *Annual Report 2004–2005*. Available at http://www.police.nsw.gov.au/__data/assets/pdf_file/0015/42171/nswp_annual_report_2004–2005.pdf (accessed 16 May 2008).

New South Wales Police Force (2001) "About: the Police Shop". Available at http://www.policeshop.com.au/about.htm (accessed 16 May 2008).

New South Wales Police Service (1992) *Sponsorship and Endorsement*. Sydney: New South Wales Police Service.

  (2000). *Annual Report*. Sydney: New South Wales Police Service.

  (2001) *Sponsorship and Endorsement Policy*. Sydney: New South Wales Police Service.

New York City Police Foundation (2004) "Licensing Program". Available at http://www.nycpolicefoundation.org/ontheboard.asp?categoryId=6 (accessed 16 May 2008).

New Zealand Independent Reviewer (1998) *Review of Police Administration and Management Structures*, August. Available at http://www.police.govt.nz/resources/1998/review-of-police-admin/review-of-police-admin-and-management.pdf (accessed 16 May 2008).

New Zealand Police (2007) *Policing Directions in New Zealand for the 21st Century*. Available at http://www.policeact.govt.nz/consultation.html (accessed 16 May 2008).

New Zealand Police Association (2005) "CPNZ continues to grow", *Police News*, November. Available at http://www.communitypatrols.org.nz/news-police.html (accessed 16 May 2008).

New Zealand Review Team (1998) *Report On Police Submissions On The Review Of Police Administration & Management Structures, Preliminary Draft Report*, July. Available at http://www.police.govt.nz/resources/1998/review-of-police-admin–report-on-police-submissions/review-of-police-admin–report-on-police-submissions.pdf (accessed 16 May 2008).

Newburn, Tim (2001) "The Commodification of Policing: Security Networks in the Late Modern City", *Urban Studies* 38(5–6): 829–48.

Nikiforuk, Andrew (2000) "RCMP ignored early oil vandalism in Northern Alberta", *The Globe and Mail*, 17 March.

Noonan, Jr., J. T. (1984) *Bribes*. New York: Macmillan.

Norris, Clive (2007) "The Intensification and Bifurcation of Surveillance in British Criminal Justice Policy", *European Journal on Criminal Policy and Research* 13: 139–58.

Northern Territory Police (2006) "Aboriginal Community Police Officers". Available at http://www.pfes.nt.gov.au/index.cfm?fuseaction=page&p=75&m=23&sm=51 (accessed 16 May 2008).

Northumbria Police (2006) "Selling Services". Available at http://ww1.northumbria.police.uk/ePolicing/web/wms.nsf/PolicyContentDocs/POL008061?OpenDocument (accessed 29 September 2006).

N.R.M.A. (2007) "New Police Recruit', *Open Road* (May/June): p. 12.

O'Connor, James R. (1973) *The Fiscal Crisis of the State*. New York: St Martin's Press.

O'Connor, T. (2006) "Informants, Surveillance, and Other Sources of Information," North Carolina Wesleyan College Faculty Web page. Available at http://faculty.ncwc.edu/TOConnor/315/315lect09.htm (accessed 14 June 2007).

OIG Audit Division (2005) "The Drug Enforcement Administration's Payments to Confidential Sources", Audit Report (Executive Summary Only), July. Washington, DC: Office of the Inspector General, Department of Justice. Available at http://www.usdoj.gov/oig/reports/DEA/index.htm (accessed 16 May 2008).

Oliveri, R. (2000) "Statutory rape law and enforcement in the wake of welfare reform", *Stanford Law Review* 52: 463–508.

O'Malley, Pat and Hutchinson, Steven (2006) *Converging Corporatisation? Police Management, Police Unionism, and the Transfer of Business Principles*. Ottawa: Department of Sociology and Anthropology, Carleton University.

O'Malley, P. and Palmer, D. (1996) "Post-Keynesian policing", *Economy and Society* 25(2): 137–55.

Osborne, D. and Gaebler, T. (1992) *Reinventing Government: How the entrepreneurial spirit is transforming the public sector*. Reading, MA: Addison-Wesley.

Ostrom, E. (1990) *Governing the Commons*. Cambridge: Cambridge University Press.

Palmer, R. (2006) "Dob in thief and win $100 of petrol", *The Dominion Post*, 11 April.

Patience, M. (2005) "Community halves crime by hiring police force", *The Scotsman*, 25 April.

Patten, C. (1999) *A New Beginning for Policing in Northern Ireland: The Report of the Independent Commission on Policing for Northern Ireland*. Belfast: HMSO.

Pennell, S., Curtis, C., Henderson, J. and Tayman, J. (1989) "Guardian Angels: A Unique Approach to Crime Prevention", *Crime and Delinquency* 35(3): 378–400.

Pennington, Bill (2004) "Reading, Writing and Corporate Sponsorship", *The New York Times*, 18 October, p. A1.

Pfuhl, Erdwin. H. (1992) "Crimestoppers: The legitimation of snitching", *Justice Quarterly* 9(3): 505–28.

Phillips, John (1992) *Testimony before the Subcommittee on Administrative Law and Governmental Relations*, Committee on the Judiciary, U.S. House of Representatives, 1 April. Washington, DC: U.S. Government Printing Office.

Phillips, Richard (2002) "Australia: Labor trials 'rent-a-cop' plan", 26 February. Available at http://www.wsws.org/articles/2002/feb2002/carr-f26.shtml (accessed 16 May 2008).

Pilant, L. (1998) "Creative funding", *Police Chief*, LXV(3): 42–46.

Pinker, Robert (1971) *Social Theory and Social Policy*. London: Heinemann Educational Books.

Pino, Nathan. W. (2001) "Community policing and social capital", *Policing: An International Journal of Police Strategies & Management* 24 (2): 200–15.

Polanyi, Karl (1944) *The Great Transformation: The Political and Economic Origins of Our Time*. New York: Rinehart & Company, Inc.

Police Commissioners' Conference Electronic Crime Steering Committee (2001) *Electronic Crime Strategy 2001– 2003*. Available at http://www.police.govt.nz/resources/2001/e-crime-strategy/e-crime-strategy.pdf (accessed 16 May 2008).

Police Forum for Income Generation (2003/2005) *A Guide to Income Generation for the Police Service in England Wales and Northern Ireland*, London: Association of Chief Police Officers of England, Wales and Northern Ireland.

  (2003/2006) *Guide to Income Generation for the Police Service in England, Wales and Northern Ireland*. London: Association of Chief Police Officers of England, Wales and Northern Ireland. Available at http://www.acpo.police.uk/asp/policies/Data/guide_to_income_generation_aug06_website_08x11x06.doc (accessed 18 May 2008).

Pollitt, C. (2003) "Joined-up Government: a Survey", *Political Studies Review* 1: 34–49.

Potter, Keith (1997) "Financing the Future", *Policing Today*, 28–31.

Productivity Commission (2006) *Report on Government Services 2006: Part C Justice*. Available at http://www.pc.gov.au/gsp/reports/rogs/2006/justice (accessed 16 May 2008).

Pudelski, Christopher (2004) "The Constitutional Fate of Mandatory Reporting Statutes and the Clergy-Communicant Privilege in a Post-Smith World", *Northwestern University Law Review* 98: 703–38.

Putnam, Robert (1995) "Bowling Alone: America's Declining Social Capital", *Journal of Democracy* 6(1): 65–78.

(2000) *Bowling Alone: The Collapse and Revival of American community*. New York: Simon and Schuster.

Queensland Police Service (2006) "General Conditions of Offering". Available at http://www.police.qld.gov.au/Resources/Internet/services/documents/GENERAL%20COO%20081206%20Uncontrolled.pdf (accessed 16 May 2008).

Radzinowicz, Leon (1956a) *A History of English Criminal Law and its Administration From 1750: The clash between private initiative and public interest in the enforcement of the law*, Vol II. London: Stevens and Sons Ltd.

(1956b) *A History of English Criminal Law and its Administration from 1750: Cross-currents in the Movement for the Reform of the Police*, Vol III. London: Stevens and Sons Ltd.

Ransley, J., Anderson J. and Prenzler, T. (2007) "Civil Litigation against Police in Australia: Exploring its Extent, Nature and Implications for Accountability", *Australian and New Zealand Journal of Criminology* 40(2): 143–160.

Ratcliffe, J. H. (2002) "Intelligence-led policing and the problems of turning rhetoric into practice", *Policing and Society* 12(1): 53–66.

Rauch, J. (1991) "The limits of police reform", *Indicator SA* 8(4): 17–20.

Ray, Gerda. W. (1995)"'We Can Stay Until Hell Freezes Over': Strike Control and the State Police in New York, 1919–1923", *Labor History* 36(3)(Summer): 403–25.

Reiss, A. J. (1988) *Private Employment of Public Police*. Washington, DC: National Institute of Justice.

Reuter, Peter and Truman, Edwin (2004) *Chasing Dirty Money: The Fight Against Money Laundering*. Washington, DC: Institute for International Economics.

Rhodes, R.A.W. (1997) *Understanding Governance*. Buckingham: Open University Press.

Riding, Alan (2007) "The Louvre's Art: Priceless. The Louvre's Name: Expensive", *The New York Times*, 7 March, p. E1.

Robinson, J. (1989) "Police Effectiveness: Old dilemmas, new directions". In J. Vernon, and D. Bracey (eds.) *Police Resources and Effectiveness*, Proceedings of a seminar held 31 May-2 June 1988, No. 27. Canberra: Australian Institute of Criminology, pp. 21–32.

Roden, Alan (2005) "Police squads to blitz street yob culture", *The Scotsman Evening News*, 17 August.

Rogers, Ben and Robinson, Emily (2004) *The Benefits of Community Engagement: A review of the evidence*. London: Active Citizenship Centre.

Romans, J. (1966) "Moral Suasion as an Instrument of Economic Policy", *American Economic Review* 56: 1220–1226.

Rood, David and Schneiders, Ben (2008) "Parents not happy, son not repentant" *The Age*, 15 January. Available at http://www.theage.com.au/news/national/parents-not-happy-son-not-repentant/2008/01/14/1 200159362714.html (accessed 16 May 2008)

Royal Canadian Mounted Police (2006) "Contract Policing". Available at http://www.rcmp-grc.gc.ca/ccaps/contract_e.htm (accessed 16 May 2008)

Rudoren, Jodi (2006) "Inquiry finds police abuse, but says law bars trials", *The New York Times*, 19 July.

Rudzinski, Aleksander (1966) "The Duty to Rescue: A Comparative Analysis". In J. Ratcliffe (ed.) *The Good Samaritan and the Law*. New York: Anchor Books, pp. 91–124.

Sahlins, Marshall (1972) *Stone Age Economics*. Chicago: Aldine Publishing Company.

Salmi, Satu, Voeten, Marinus and Keskinen, Esko (2005) "What citizens think about the police: Assessing actual and wished-for frequency of police activities in one's neighbourhood", *Journal of Community & Applied Social Psychology* 15(3): 188–202.

Saltman, R. B. and Figueras, J. (1997) *European Health Care Reform: Analysis of Current Strategies*, WHO Regional Publications, European Series, No. 72. Copenhagen: World Health Organization Regional Office for Europe.

Saltonstall, Polly and Rising, David (1999) "Drug loot fuels drug war", *Southcoast Today*, 8 August. Available at http://www.s-t.com/daily/08–99/08-08-99/a01loo10.htm (accessed 16 May 2008).

Sampson, Robert (2004) "Neighbourhood and Community: Collective efficacy and community safety", *New Economy* 11(2): 106–113.

Sampson, Robert J., Raudenbush, Stephen W. and Earls, Felton (1997) "Neighborhoods and Violent Crime: A Multilevel Study of Collective Efficacy", *Science* 277: 918–924.

Sarre, Rick and Prenzler, Tim (2005) *The Law of Private Security in Australia*. Sydney: Lawbook Co.

Schmitt, Eric (2001) "Helms Wants Religious Groups to Funnel Foreign Aid", *The New York Times on the Web*, 11 January. Available at http://www.nytimes.com/2001/01/11/politics/11CND-HELMS.html (accessed 16 May 2008).

Schmitt, Steve. J. (1997) "Fighting crime with data", *Communications News*, December. Available at http://www.comnews.com/ (accessed 8 June 2006).

Schönteich, M. (2004a) "Introduction". In M. Schönteich, A. Minnaar, D. Mistry, and K. C. Goyer *Private Muscle: Outsourcing the Provision of Criminal Justice Services*. Institute for Security Studies, Monograph No. 93. Available at http://www.issafrica.org/pubs/Monographs/N093/Contents.html (accessed 16 May 2008).

—— (2004b) "Outsourcing Risks and Benefits". In M. Schönteich, A. Minnaar, D. Mistry, and K. C. Goyer Private Muscle: Outsourcing the Provision of Criminal Justice Services. Institute for Security Studies, Monograph No. 93. Available at http://www.iss africa.org/pubs/Monographs/N093/Contents.html (accessed 16 May 2008).

—— (2004c) "Government Outsourcing Policy: Public Private Partnerships". In M. Schönteich, A. Minnaar, D. Mistry, and K. C. Goyer (eds.) *Private Muscle: Outsourcing the Provision of Criminal Justice Services*. Institute for Security Studies, Monograph No. 93. Available at http://www.issafrica.org/pubs/Monographs/N093/Con tents.html (accessed 16 May 2008).

Schultz, LeRoy. G. (1990) "Confidentiality, Privilege, and Child Abuse Reporting", Issues In Child Abuse Accusations, *Journal of the Institute for Psychological Therapies* 2(4). Available at http://www.ipt-forensics. com/journal/volume2/j2_4_5.htm (accessed 16 May 2008).

Schwartz, Barry (1967) "The Social Psychology of the Gift", *The American Journal of Sociology* 73 (1): 1–11.

Schwartz, Richard and Orleans, Sonya (1967) "On Legal Sanctions", *University of Chicago Law Review* 34: 274–300.

Scott, Michael. S. (2005) "Shifting and Sharing police responsibility to address public safety problems". In Nick Tilley (ed.) *Handbook of Crime Prevention and Community Safety*. Cullompton: Willan Publishing, pp. 385–409.

Scott, Michael. S. and Goldstein, Herman (2005) "Shifting and Sharing Responsibility for Public Safety Problems", *Problem-Oriented Guides for Police, Response Guide Series No. 3*. Washington, DC: Office of Community Oriented Policing Services, U.S. Department of Justice.

Scottish Prison Service (2004) "Non-Core Rollout Phase of Reliance in Strathclyde, Central Scotland & Dumfries & Galloway" 16 December. Available at http://www.sps.gov.uk/newsroom/newsindex.asp?NewsId=217 (accessed 1 September 2005).

Seligman, Joel (1983) "The Historical Need for a Mandatory Corporate Disclosure System", *Journal of Corporation Law* 9: 1–61.

Sellars, P. (2005) "Reprieve on police bill", *The Weekly Times*, 16 March.

Selznick, Philip (1949) *TVA and the Grassroots: A Study in the Sociology of Formal Organization*. Berkeley: University of California Press.

Settle, Rod (1995) *Police Informers: Negotiation and Power*. Sydney: The Federation Press.

Shane, J. M. (2004) "Compstat Process", The FBI Law Enforcement Bulletin, April.

Shearing, C. D. (1984) *Dial-a-Cop: A Study of Police Mobilization*. Toronto: Centre of Criminolgy, University of Toronto.

   (1992) "The Relation between Public and Private Policing". In M. Tonry and N. Morris (eds.) *Crime and Justice: An Annual Review of Research* Vol. 17. Chicago: University of Chicago, pp. 399–434.

   (2006) "Who should the police be in an age of plural governance?", paper presented at *Securing the future: Networked policing in New Zealand*, 22 November 2006, Wellington, New Zealand. Available at http://www.vuw.ac.nz/sog/events/stf_speakers/STF%20Shearing%20paper.pdf (accessed 16 May 2008).

Shearing, C D and Stenning, P C (1983) 'Private Security and its Implications: A North American Perspective'. In A. Rees (ed.) *Policing and Private Security*. Canberra: Australian Institute of Criminology, pp. 16–44.

Shearing, C. D. and Wood, J. (2003) "Governing Security for Common Goods", *International Journal of the Sociology of Law* 31(3): 205–25.

   (2005) "Nodal governance, denizenship and communal space: challenging the Westphalian Ideal". In Steven L. Robins (ed.) *Limits to liberation after Apartheid: Citizenship, governance and culture*. Oxford: James Currey Publishers, pp. 97–112.

Shiel, Fergus (2003) "Report into IBM's police deal shelved", *The Age*, 16 March.

Sieber, Sam (1981) *Fatal Remedies: The Ironies of Social Intervention*. New York: Plenum Press.

Sikwane, B. (2006) "SAPS gets tech-savvy", *ITWEB*, 7 December.

Silver, Jay (1985) "The Duty to Rescue: a reexamination and proposal", *William and Mary Law Review* 26: 423.

Singer, P. W. (2003) *Corporate Warriors: The Rise of the Privatized Military Industry*. Ithaca, NY: Cornell University Press.

   (2005) "Outsourcing war", *Foreign Affairs* 84(2): 119–32.

Singh, A-M. (2005) "Some critical reflections on the governance of crime in post-apartheid South Africa". In J. Sheptycki and A. Wardak (eds.) *Transnational and Comparative Criminology*. London: GlassHouse Press.

Skogan, W. and Hartnett, S. (1997) *Community Policing: Chicago Style*. New York: Oxford University Press.

Skolnick, J. H. and Fyfe, J. J. (1993) *Above the Law: Police and the Excessive Use of Force*. New York: The Free Press.

Smith, D. (1989) "Aligning Police Productivity to Organisational Goals". In Vernon, J. and Bracey D. (eds.) *Police Resources and Effectiveness*, proceedings of a seminar held 31 May–2 June 1988, No. 27. Canberra: Australian Institute of Criminology, pp. 147–52.

Smith, K. and Stalans, L. (1991) "Encouraging Tax Compliance with Positive Incentives: A Conceptual Framework and Research Directions", *Law and Policy* 13(1): 35–53.

Smith, P. S. (1995) "An argument against mandatory reporting of undocumented immigrants by state officials", *Columbia Journal of Law and Social Problems* 29: 147–74.

Soto, Javier (1998) "Informant Operations: Direction and Control of Human Sources of Information," *Law and Order* 46(10): 93–100.

South African Police Service (2006) "Launch of a drug reduction programme to enhance crime prevention", 25 May. Available at http://www.info.gov.za/speeches/2006/06052513451003.htm (accessed 16 May 2008).

South African Press Association (2001) "Pagad breakout: no foul play?", *24.com news*, 30 October. Available at http://www.news24.com/News24/Archive/0,,2-1659_1101458,00.html (accessed 16 May 2008).

    (2006a) "South Africa: R74m boost for crime fighters", *24.com news*, 18 October.

    (2006b) "Business joins state to fight crime in SA", *Independent Online*, 3 November.

Southern City News (2005) "Police Foundation Receives 500000RMB Donation from Foxconn Technologies Group". Available at http://city.sz.net.cn/city/2005–01/28/content_61652.htm (accessed 3 May 2006).

Steinhauer, Jennifer (2003) "City, Deep in Hole, Seeks Private Sector Help", *The New York Times*, April 30, p. A1.

Stellwagen, L. D. and Wylie. K. A. (1985) "Strategies for Supplementing the Police Budget", *Issues and Practices in Criminal Justice*. Washington, DC: National Institute of Justice.

Stenning, P. (2000) "Powers and Accountability of Private Police", *European Journal on Criminal Policy and Research* 8: 325–52.

Stenning, P. and Shearing, C. D. (1979) "Search and Seizure: Powers of Private Security Personnel", Study Paper prepared for the Law Commission of Canada. Ottawa: Minister of Supply and Services Canada.

Stenning, P., Shearing, C. D., Addario, S. M. and Condon, M. G. (1990). "Controlling Interests: Two Conceptions of Order in Regulating a Financial Market." In M. L. Friedland (ed.) *Securing Compliance*. Toronto: University of Toronto Press, pp. 88–119.

Stone, Christopher (2002) "Philanthropy and Criminal Justice Programs: Time for a Return?", *Souls* 4(1): 73–78.

Sunday Mail (Brisbane) (2004) "Police on the Cheap", *Sunday Mail*, 6 June, p. 85.

Sunshine, Jason and Tyler, Tom (2003) "The Role of Procedural Justice and Legitimacy in Shaping Public Support for Policing", *Law and Society Review* 37(3): 513–48.

Swanton, Bruce (1993) "Police & Private Security: Possible Directions", *Trends and issues in crime and criminal justice*, No. 42. Canberra: Australian Institute of Criminology.

Thagard, Elizabeth (1992) "The Rule That Clean Water Act Civil Penalties Must Go to the Treasury and How to Avoid It", *Harvard Environmental Law Review* 16(2): 507–34.

Thames Valley Police (nda) "Risk Management Policy". Available at http://www.thamesvalley.police.uk/news_info/freedom/policies_procedures/pdf/Risk%20Management.pdf (accessed 16 May 2008).

The Century Council (nda) "Cops in Shops". Available at http://www.centurycouncil.org/underage/cops.html (accessed 16 May 2008).

Titmuss, Richard (1971) *The Gift Relationship: From Human Blood to Social Policy*. New York: Pantheon Books.

Trahan, Jason (2006) "Group Seeking More Donations for Police", *Dallas Morning News*, 19 October.

Tribune Media Services (2002) "LAPD Wants License Fees from Cop Shows", 30 July. Available at http://tv.zap2it.com/tveditorial/tve_main/1,1002,271|77300|1|,00.html (accessed 16 May 2008).

Trott, Stephen. S. (1988) "The Successful Use of Informants and Criminals as Witnesses for the Prosecution in a Criminal Case". In U.S. Department of Justice (ed.), *Prosecution of Public Corruption Cases*. Washington, DC: U.S. Department of Justice, pp. 115–134.

Trumbo, John (2005) "Group Created to Fix Troubled Dispatch System", *Knight Ridder Tribune Business News*, 27 May.

Tunzi, M. (2002) "Curbside Consultation: Isn't this statutory rape?" *American Family Physician*, 1 May. Available at http://www.aafp.org/afp/20020501/curbside.html (accessed 16 May 2008).

Turnbull, Lornet and Tu, Janet. I. (2005) "Minutemen watch U.S.-Canada border", *The Seattle Times*, 4 October. Available at http://seattletimes.nwsource.com/html/localnews/2002538196_borderpatrol04m.html (accessed 16 May 2008).

Tyler, T. R. (2004) "Enhancing Police Legitimacy", *The Annals of the American Academy of Political and Social Science* 593 (May): 84–99.

Tyler, Tom and Fagan, Jeffrey (2005) "Legitimacy and cooperation: Why do people help the police fight crime in their communities?", *Columbia Public Law Research Paper* No.06–99. Available at http://

papers.ssrn.com/sol3/papers.cfm?abstract_id=887737 (accessed 16 May 2008).

U.K. Office of Government Commerce (2007) "The first eAuction in Police Procurement". Available at http://www.ogc.gov.uk/docu ments/Kent_Police.pdf (accessed 16 May 2008).

(2008) "eProcurement: Overview". Available at http://www.ogc.gov.uk/ guidance_eprocurement_guidance_4646.asp (accessed 16 May 2008).

U.S. Department of Justice (2002) "The Attorney General's Guidelines Regarding the Use of Informants", Office of Legal Policy. Available at http://www.usdoj.gov/olp/dojguidelines.pdf (accessed 16 May 2008).

(2006) *A Review of the FBI's Handling and Oversight of FBI Asset Katrina Leung*, Unclassified Executive Summary, Office of the Inspector General.

USINDO (2003) (with Welsh, B.) "Vigilante Violence in Indonesia", *USINDO Brief 2003*, Washington DC: United States – Indonesia Society. Available at http://www.usindo.org/pu2003briefs.htm (accessed 1 February 2007).

van Oorschot, Wim (2005) "A European Deservingness Culture? Public Deservingness Perceptions in European Welfare States", *CCWS Working Paper* no. 36–2005. Aalborg, Denmark: Aalborg University.

Vaznis, J. (2004) "Tax-weary New Hampshire town to close police department", *Knight-Ridder Tribune Business News* 18 July, p. 1.

Verspaadonk, Rose (2001) "Outsourcing – For and Against", *Current Issues Brief* 18. Canberra: Parliament of Australia Parliamentary Library.

VicFleet (2004) "Whole-of-Government Standard Motor Vehicle Policy". Available at http://vicfleet.vic.gov.au/CA2572270020B77B/pages/ government-vehicle-policy-whole-of-government-standard-motor-vehicle-policy (accessed 16 May 2008).

Vickers, M. and Kouzmin, A. (2001) "New Managerialism and Australian police organizations", *The International Journal of Public Sector Management* 14(1): 7–26.

Victoria Police (2003) *The Way Ahead*: Strategic Plan 2003–2008. Melbourne: Victoria Police. Available at http://www.police.vic.gov.au/ content.asp?a=internetBridgingPage&Media_ID=352 (accessed 16 May 2008).

Victoria Police (2005) "Managig the delivery of Police Services to Sporting, Entertainment & Other events: your questions answered". Melbourne: Victoria Police.

(2006) *Business Plan 2006/07*. Melbourne: Victoria Police. Available at http://www.police.vic.gov.au/content.asp?a=internetBridgingPag e&Media_ID=7990 (accessed 16 May 2008).

(2006) Personal communication to authors, April.

Victorian Auditor-General's Office (2003a), "Electronic procurement in the Victorian government", Performance Audit Report, June. Available at http://www.audit.vic.gov.au/reports_par/agp8902.html #P109_17323 (accessed 16 May 2008).

(2003b) "Outsourcing of Information Technology Services at Victoria Police", Report on Public Sector Agencies: Results of special reviews, Part 2, May. Available at http://www.audit.vic.gov.au/reports_mp_ psa/psa0402d.html (accessed 16 May 2008).

Victorian Government Purchasing Board (2007) "Regional Sourcing" Available at http://www.vgpb.vic.gov.au/CA256C450016850B/0/B13B CB6CAD6C6BF6CA256C780001E017?OpenDocument (accessed 16 May 2008).

Vincent, Michael (2002) "Police for Hire", transcript of *ABC AM* programme of 30 January, available at http://www.abc.net.au/am/stories/ s469180.htm (accessed 16 May 2008).

Vincent-Jones, Peter (2000) "Contractual Governance: Institutional and Organizational Analysis", *Oxford Journal of Legal Studies* 20(3): 317–51.

Volokh, Eugene (1999) "Duties to rescue and the anticooperative effects of law", *Georgetown Law Journal* 88: 105–14.

Walker, Jenny and Forrester, Shannon (2002) "Tangentyere Remote Area Night Patrol", paper presented at the *Crime Prevention Conference*, Sydney, 12–13 September 2002. Available at http://www.aic.gov.au/ conferences/crimpre/walker.html (accessed 16 May 2008).

Walsh, Tamara (2002) "Accounting for the Environment", *Environmental and Planning Law Journal* 19: 387–97.

Weatherburn, Don (2004) *Law and Order in Australia: Rhetoric and Reality*. Sydney: The Federation Press.

Weber, M. (1919 [1974]) "The Profession and Vocation of Politics". In P. Lassman and R. Speirs (eds.) *Weber: Political Writings*, Cambridge Texts in the History of Political Thought. Cambridge: Cambridge University Press.

Weisburd, D., Jonathan, T. and Perry, S (forthcoming) "The Israeli Model for Policing Terrorism: Goals, Strategies, and Open Questions", *Criminal Justice and Behavior*.

Weissenstein, M. (2003) "Budgets tightening, police departments turn to private money". Available at http://www.nycpolicefoundation.org/ news.asp (accessed 16 May 2008).

Westerberg, A. I. and Forssell, A. (2005) "De-regulating and Re-regulating the Swedish Police: More autonomy and more control". Paper presented at the SCANCOR/SOG workshop on *Autonomization of the State: From integrated administrative models to single purpose organizations*. Stanford University, 1–2 April 2005.

Western Australia Police (2007a) "Commercial Crime: Gold Stealing Detection Unit", available at http://www.police.wa.gov.au/AboutUs/ SupportServices/CrimeInvestigation.asp?CommercialCrime (accessed 17 May 2007).

—— (2007b) "Argyle: Argyle Police Station", available at http://www.police. wa.gov.au/LocalPolice/KimberleyDistrict.asp?Argyle (accessed 17 May 2007).

Western Australia Police Service (2000) Cannington Police Office, *Newsbeat*, 8 (Summer): 14.

Williams, Brett (1998) "Playing the Part, Understanding the Realities", *Police Journal Online*, 79(11), November. Police Association of South Australia. Available at http://www.policejournalsa.org.au/9811/12a. html (accessed 17 May 2007).

Wilson, John (2000) "Volunteering", *Annual Review of Sociology* 26: 215–240.

Wilson, Robert (2003) "Celebrity Cop Cars Chase the Crims", *The Australian*, 30 January, p. 12.

Wood, J. and Shearing, C. D. (2007) *Imagining Security*. Cullompton: Willan Publishing.

Wood, Jennifer (2000) *Reinventing Governance: A Study of Transformations in the Ontario Provincial Police*. PhD Dissertation. Centre of Criminology. Toronto: University of Toronto.

Wood, Jennifer and Kempa, Michael (2005) "Understanding Global Trends in Policing: Explanatory and Normative Dimensions". In Sheptycki, J. and Wardak, A. (eds.) *Transnational and Comparative Criminology*. London: Glasshouse Press.

Woolford, Steven (1997) "Legislation Notes: Financial Transactions Reporting Act 1996", *Auckland University Law Review* 8(2): 615–20.

Worrall, John. L. (2001) "Addicted to the drug war: The role of civil asset forfeiture as a budgetary necessity in contemporary law enforcement", *Journal of Criminal Justice* 29: 171–87.

Worton, Steve (2003) "Volunteers in Police Work: A study of the benefits to law enforcement agencies". Research project for School of Police Staff and Command, Eastern Michigan University. Available at http://www.emich.edu/cerns/downloads/papers/PoliceStaff/Police%20 Personnel%20(e.g.,%20Selection,%20%20Promotion)/Volunteers% 20in%20Po lice%20Work.pdf (accessed 29 May 2007).

Yomiuri Shimbun (2006) "Citizens Patrol Fills Policing Gap". Available at http://www.cleansafeworldwide.org/doc=471&cat=139 (accessed 10 May 2006).

Zedner, Lucia (2003) "Too much security?", *International Journal of the Sociology of Law* 31(3): 155–84.

—— (2006) "Policing Before and After the Police: The Historical Antecedents of Contemporary Crime Control", *British Journal of Criminology* 46(1): 78–96.

Zellman, G. I. and Bell, R. M. (1990) *The Role of Professional Background, Case Characteristics and Protective Agency Response in Mandated Child Abuse Reporting*. Santa Monica, CA: The RAND Corporation.

Zhong, Y. (2002) *Communities, Crime and Social Capital: Crime Prevention in Two Shenzhen Communities*. PhD Thesis, The University of Hong Kong.

Zhong Y. and Broadhurst, R. (2007) "Building Little Safe and Civilized Communities: Community Crime Prevention with Chinese Characteristics?", *International Journal of Offender Therapy and Comparative Criminology* 51(1): 52–67.

Zuboff, S. (1988) *In the Age of the Smart Machine: The Future of Work and Power*. New York: Basic Books.

Index